The publisher and the University of California Press Foundation gratefully acknowledge the generous support of the Atkinson Family Foundation Imprint in Higher Education.

Transparent and Reproducible
Social Science Research

Transparent and Reproducible Social Science Research

How to Do Open Science

Garret Christensen,
Jeremy Freese, and
Edward Miguel

UNIVERSITY OF CALIFORNIA PRESS

University of California Press, one of the most distinguished university presses in the United States, enriches
lives around the world by advancing scholarship in the
humanities, social sciences, and natural sciences. Its
activities are supported by the UC Press Foundation and
by philanthropic contributions from individuals and
institutions. For more information, visit www.ucpress.edu.

University of California Press
Oakland, California

Library of Congress Cataloging-in-Publication Data

Names: Christensen, Garret S., author. | Freese, Jeremy,
    author. | Miguel, Edward, author.
Title: Transparent and reproducible social science
    research : how to do open science / Garret Christensen,
    Jeremy Freese, and Edward Miguel.
Description: Oakland, California : University of
    California Press, [2019] | Includes bibliographical
    references and index. |
Identifiers: LCCN 2019000826 (print) | LCCN 2019004088
    (ebook) | ISBN 9780520969230 (ebook and ePDF) |
    ISBN 9780520296930 (cloth : alk. paper) |
    ISBN 9780520296954 (pbk. : alk. paper)
Subjects: LCSH: Reproducible research. | Social
    sciences—Research.
Classification: LCC Q180.55.S7 (ebook) |
    LCC Q180.55.S7 C47 2019 (print) | DDC 001.4/2—dc23
LC record available at https://lccn.loc.gov/2019000826

Manufactured in the United States of America

26 25 24 23 22 21 20
10 9 8 7 6 5 4 3

For Amy

For Beckie

And for Layla

Contents

Figures

Tables

Acknowledgments

We are grateful to the team at UC Press, including Seth Dobrin, Renee Donovan, Tim Sullivan, Benjy Malings, Kate Hoffman, and our editor Naomi Schneider for their helpful feedback and creative suggestions.

We gratefully acknowledge the useful suggestions, editing, and detailed feedback from Carson Christiano, Aleksandar Bogdanoski, Katherine Hoeberling, Kelsey Mulcahy, Don Moore, Jennifer Sturdy, Fernando Hoces de la Guardia, Justin Kitzes, Karthik Ram, Robbie van Aert, Joseph Cummins, Livia Baer-Bositis, Cristobal Young, David McKenzie, and an anonymous reviewer. Shyan Kashani did superb work to create several figures in the book, especially in Chapter 6, and Simon Zhu provided excellent research assistance as we finalized the text.

Many thanks to Uri Simonsohn for detailed and instantaneous responses to our inquiries about his research, as well as sharing his data and statistical code. Ted thanks Kate Casey and Rachel Glennerster, whose idea to write a pre-analysis plan on their Sierra Leone project was his first step down the road that led to this book. Jeremy thanks his collaborators David Peterson, Scott Long, Jamie Druckman, and Molly King, who have been important influences on his thinking about different aspects of replication and reproducibility.

Generous funding was provided by the Laura and John Arnold Foundation, though they played no role in reviewing or editing the text. Thanks go to the Berkeley Initiative for Transparency in the Social Sciences (BITSS) and the Berkeley Institute for Data Science (BIDS) for providing the time for Garret Christensen to pursue this project. We also want to thank the Center for Effective Global Action (CEGA) and especially its former executive director, Dr. Temina Madon, for guidance and support throughout the process. Participants in BITSS meetings and training courses provided invaluable feedback on beta versions of the arguments made in this book, and there are too many to name here.

Last but not least, Garret is grateful for the support of his partner, Amy Langston, whose Florida swamp fieldwork makes writing this book look easy. Jeremy thanks his spouse, the unreplicable Rebecca McDonald, for her endless encouragement, optimism, and pet photos. Ted is grateful for the love and insights of his wife, Ali Reed, without whom none of this would have been possible.

PART ONE

Introduction and Motivation

ONE

Introduction

THE NEED FOR TRANSPARENT SOCIAL SCIENCE RESEARCH

Contemporary society is complex and rapidly changing. Leaders of government, corporate, and nonprofit institutions all face a constant stream of choices. Thankfully, these leaders are increasingly investing in data acquisition and analysis to help them make good decisions. Researchers are often charged with providing this information and insight, in areas ranging from environmental science to economic policy, immigration, and health care reform. Success often depends on the quality of the underlying research. Inaccurate research can lead to ineffective or inappropriate policies, and worse outcomes for people's lives.

How reliable is the current body of evidence that feeds into decision making? Many believe it is not reliable enough. A crisis of confidence has emerged in social science research, with influential voices both within academia (Manski 2013) and beyond (Feilden 2017) asserting that policy-relevant research is often less reliable than claimed, if not outright wrong. The popular view that you can manipulate statistics to get any answer you want captures this loss of faith in the research enterprise, and the sense that too many scientific findings are mere advocacy. In this era of "fake news" and the rise of extremist political and religious movements around the world, the role of scientific research in establishing the truth as common ground for public debate is more important than ever.

Let's take, for example, the case of health care reform in the United States—the subject of endless partisan political debate. This tension can be partly explained by the simple fact that people feel strongly about health care, a sector that affects everyone at one time or another in their lives. But there are also strong ideological disagreements between the major U.S. political parties, including the role government should play in providing social services, and the closely related debate over tax rates, since higher taxes generate the revenue needed for health programs.

What role can research play in such a volatile debate? The answer is "It depends." Some people—and politicians—will hold fast to their political views regardless of evidence; research cannot always sway everyone. But data and evidence are often influential and even decisive in political battles, including the 2017 attempt by congressional Republicans to dismantle the Affordable Care Act (ACA), or Obamacare. In that instance, a handful of senators were swayed to vote "Nay" when evidence from the Congressional Budget Office estimating the likely impact of ACA repeal on insurance coverage and health outcomes was released. Media coverage of the research likely boosted the program's popularity among American voters.

The answers to highly specific or technical research questions can be incredibly important. In the U.S. case, findings about how access to health insurance affects individual life outcomes—including direct health measures, as well as broader economic impacts such as personal bankruptcy—have been key inputs into these debates. How many people will buy insurance under different levels of subsidies (i.e., what does the demand curve for health insurance look like)? How do different institutional rules in the health insurance marketplace affect competition, prices, and usage? And so on.

When the stakes are this high, the accuracy and credibility of the evidence used become extremely important. Choices made on the basis of evidence will ultimately affect millions of lives. Importantly, it is the responsibility of social science researchers to assure others that their conclusions are driven by sound methods and data, and not by some underlying political bias or agenda. In other words, researchers need to convince policymakers and the public that the statistical results they provide have evidentiary value—that you can't just pick out (or make up) any statistic you want.

This book provides a road map and tools for increasing the rigor and credibility of social science research. We are a team of three authors—one sociologist and two economists—whose goal is to demonstrate the role that greater *research transparency and reproducibility* can play in uncovering and documenting the truth. We will lay out a number of specific changes that the research community can make to advance and defend the value of scientific research in policy debates around the world. But before we get into the nitty-gritty or "how," it is worth surveying the rather disappointing state of affairs in social science research, and its implications.

HOUSTON, WE HAVE A PROBLEM: RESEARCH FRAUD AND ITS AFTERMATH

If you thought we'd have research methods all figured out after a couple centuries of empirical social science research, you would be wrong. A rash of high-profile fraud cases in multiple academic disciplines and mounting evidence that a number of important research findings cannot be replicated both point to a growing sense of unease in the social sciences. We believe the research community can do better.

Fraud cases get most of the headlines, and we discuss a few of the most egregious cases here. By mentioning these examples, we are *not* claiming that most researchers are engaging in fraud! We strongly believe that outright fraud remains the exception rather than the rule (although the illicit nature of research fraud makes it hard to quantify this claim or even assert it with much confidence). Rather, fraud cases are the proverbial canaries in the coal mine: a dramatic symptom of a much more pervasive underlying problem that manifests itself in many other ways short of fraud. We will discuss these subtler and more common problems—all of which have the ability to distort social science research—at length in this book.

The field of social psychology provides a cautionary tale about how a lack of transparency can lead to misleading results—and also how the research community can organize to fight back against the worst abuses. In recent years, we have seen multiple well-publicized cases in which prominent tenured social psychologists, in both North America and Europe, were caught fabricating their data. These scholars were forced to resign from their positions when colleagues uncovered their misdeeds. In the circles of scientific hell, this one—simply making stuff up and passing it off as science—must be the hottest (Neuroskeptic 2012).

Perhaps best known is the case of Diederik Stapel, former professor of psychology at Tilburg University in the Netherlands. Stapel was an academic superstar. He served as dean of social and behavioral sciences, was awarded multiple career prizes by age 40, and published 150 articles, including in the most prestigious journals and on socially important topics, including the psychology of racial bias (Carey 2011; Bhattacharjee

2013). Academic careers rise and fall largely on the basis of publishing (or not publishing) articles in top research journals, which is often predicated on successful fund-raising, and according to these metrics Stapel was at the very top of his field.

Unfortunately, Stapel's findings and publications were drawn mostly from fabricated data. In his autobiography, written after the fraud was discovered, Stapel describes his descent into dishonesty, and how the temptation to alter his data in order to generate exciting research results—the kind he felt would be more attractive to top journals and generate more media attention—was too much for him to resist:

> Nobody ever checked my work. They trusted me. . . . I did everything myself, and next to me was a big jar of cookies. No mother, no lock, not even a lid. . . . Every day, I would be working and there would be this big jar of cookies, filled with sweets, within reach, right next to me—with nobody even near. All I had to do was take it. (quoted in Borsboom and Wagenmakers, 2013)

As Stapel tells it, he began by subtly altering a few numbers here and there in real datasets to make the results more interesting. However, over time he began to fabricate entire datasets. While Stapel was certainly at fault, we view his ability to commit fraud undetected as an indictment of the entire social science research process. Still, there were many warning signs. Stapel never shared his data with others, not even his own graduate students, preferring to carry out analyses on his own. Over time, suspicions began to snowball about the mysterious sources of his data and Stapel's "magical" ability to generate one blockbuster article after another, each with fascinating constellations of findings.

Ultimately, a university investigation led to Stapel's admission of fraud and his downfall: he retracted at least 55 articles (including from leading research journals like *Science*), was forced to resign from his position at Tilburg, and was stripped of his Ph.D. Criminal proceedings were launched against him (they were eventually settled). The article retractions further discredited the work of his students and colleagues—collateral damage affecting dozens of other scholars, many of whom were supposedly ignorant of Stapel's lies.

Stapel's autobiography is a gripping tale of his addiction to research fraud. At times it is quite beautifully and emotionally written (by all accounts, though we have not read it in the original Dutch). It emerged after the book was published, however, that several of the most moving passages were composed of sentences that Stapel had copied (into Dutch) from the fiction writers Raymond Carver and James Joyce. Yet he presented them without quotes and only acknowledged his sources separately in an appendix! Even in his mea culpa, the dishonesty crept in (Borsboom and Wagenmakers 2013).

How many other Stapels are out there? While it is impossible to say, of course, there are enough cases of fraud to provoke concern. No academic field is immune.

Roughly a quarter of economics journal editors say they have encountered cases of plagiarism (Enders and Hoover 2004). Political science was rocked by a fraud scandal in 2015, when David Broockman, then a graduate student at the University of California, Berkeley, discovered that a *Science* paper on the impact of in-person canvassing on gay rights attitudes, written by Michael LaCour and Don Green, contained fabricated data (Broockman, Kalla, and Aranow 2015). While Green was cleared of wrongdoing—he had not collected the data and was apparently unaware of the deception—the incident effectively ended LaCour's promising academic career: at the time, he was a graduate student at the University of California, Los Angeles, and had been offered a faculty position at Princeton, which was later withdrawn.

These cases are not ancient history: they took place just a few years back. While some progress is already being made toward making research more transparent and reproducible (as we will discuss in detail throughout this book), it remains likely that other instances of data fabrication will (unfortunately) occur. Many of the problems with the research process that allowed them to occur—such as weak data-sharing norms, secrecy, limited incentives to carry out replications or prespecify statistical analyses, and the pervasive publish-or-perish culture of academia—are still in place, and affect the quality of research even among the vast majority of scholars who have never engaged in outright fraud. Even if rare, cases of scholarly fraud also garner extensive media coverage and are likely to have outsize influence on the perceptions of social scientists held by the general public, policymakers, and potential research donors.

How can we put a lid on Stapel's open cookie jar to prevent research malpractice from happening in the future? With science already under attack in many quarters, how can we improve the reliability of social science more broadly, and restore public confidence in important findings? This book aims to make progress on these issues, through several interconnected goals.

BOOK OVERVIEW

First, we aim to bring the reader up to speed on the core intellectual issues around research transparency and reproducibility, beginning with this introduction and continuing in Chapter 2 with a detailed discussion of the scientific ethos and its implications for research practices.

Next, we present existing evidence—some classic, some new—on pervasive *problems* in social science research practice. One such problem is publication bias (Chapter 3), whereby studies with more compelling results are more likely be published, rather than publication being based solely on the quality of the data, research design, and analysis. Another distinct, but closely related, problem is specification searching during statistical analysis (Chapter 4). Specification searching is characterized by the selective reporting of analyses within a particular study, generating misleading conclusions. By now, there is ample evidence that both of these problems are real and widespread, leading to biased bodies of research evidence.

The documented existence of these problems sets the stage for a series of methodological *solutions* designed to address them. Some of these solutions are well known, including approaches that enable scholars to use all possible data across studies (through study registries and meta-analysis) to reach more robust conclusions (Chapter 5). The use of prespecified hypothesis plans to discipline analysis and boost accountability harkens back to our most fundamental understanding of the scientific method (Chapter 6). We present a "how-to" guide for utilizing pre-analysis plans in practice. Meanwhile, sensitivity analyses and other antidotes to specification searching often rely on recent advances in statistics and econometrics (Chapter 7). We illustrate these tools using current examples from across the social sciences—economics, political science, psychology, and sociology.

Unfortunately, these well-intended solutions are only as effective as they are widely adopted. For outcomes to change, *practices,* norms, and institutions must also change. One change discussed in this book is the adoption of reporting standards and disclosure practices that structure the presentation of data and the design of studies (Chapter 8). Another is replication, a practice critical for enhancing accountability and discovering problems in existing work (Chapter 9). Beyond discussing the technicalities of each practice, we note how the incentives that researchers encounter often discourage replication and suggest ways to move fields toward more productive research norms.

Another critical practice for enhancing accountability is the open sharing of data and other research materials (Chapter 10). Still, there are many unresolved questions around safely sharing personal data without violating individual confidentiality. This is an area of current interest across disciplines. Thankfully, social scientists are finally beginning to adopt beneficial reproducible coding and workflow practices from computer science and data science. We discuss the adaptation of these practices to the social sciences in Chapter 11. Throughout the book, we provide technical material for readers interested in the statistical and computational details of these approaches, and for those seeking to apply them to their own research.

Finally, we discuss the evolving landscape in the areas of research transparency and reproducibility, the institutional changes that could buttress recent progress, and the importance of changing research norms in order to achieve sustainable progress (Chapter 12).

The audience for this book is intentionally broad (although we are happy to preregister our hypothesis that it is unlikely to end up a national best seller sold in airport magazine stands). Doctoral and master's-level students are perhaps its most natural users. We hope that young scholars will find the ideas presented here both inspiring and useful as they build up their technical skill set and develop their own research workflow. Given the numerous applications and examples we provide, the material should fit nicely into graduate curricula on research methods, study design, statistics, and econometrics, as well as in more specific field courses.

We believe this work will serve as a valuable bookshelf reference for more seasoned scholars who have completed their training, including faculty, postdoctoral scholars, and staff scientists in academic settings, government agencies, and the private sector, as well as for research funders, publishers, and the end consumers of social science research. Gaining a better understanding of the threats to and solutions for improving the credibility of social science is critical for anyone producing or consuming research evidence. While some of the problems we discuss are fairly well known (if not yet widely taught), many of the solutions and practices that aim to enhance research transparency and reproducibility are new to the social sciences and could be useful for scholars at all career stages.

Highly motivated undergraduates with strong training in statistics and some familiarity with social science research can also gain from reading this book. We relegate some of the more technical material to appendices and text boxes throughout, specifically to make the core text more widely accessible to undergraduates and others who are not (yet) professional researchers.

Additionally, we envision this book as a resource for graduate and undergraduate research assistants (as well as more open-minded coauthors) who are just becoming acquainted with scientific ideals and practices. Just as there is more to capturing the spirit of a great musician than learning to play the right notes, there is more to being a good scholar than simply learning how to code in R or Stata, or memorizing your field's canonical papers. The best scholars carry out research in an intellectually balanced way, with the right ethos and an open mindset. With this book, we aim to crystallize these ideals and put them into practice.

Finally, some of the material in this book has been incorporated into a massive open online course (MOOC) entitled "Transparent and Open Social Science Research" with UK-based FutureLearn, using audio from a graduate course recently taught at UC Berkeley by two of the authors. This online course contains homework exercises, videos, and discussion forums that complement this textbook. We encourage readers interested in digging deeper to check it out.

TWO

What Is Ethical Research?

If you look up "ethics in social science research" online, you will see that most discussions are dominated by issues surrounding the treatment of research participants, such as survey respondents and the people who participate in lab experiments. There are many important issues here—informed consent, confidentiality, and the rights of participants—and many past episodes demonstrate the abuse that can ensue when social scientists are cavalier about their core responsibilities to study participants (Desposato 2015).

At the same time, being an ethical social scientist goes beyond our responsibilities toward study participants. Our work as social scientists is premised on the goal of better understanding the world around us, and we do so as part of a larger community pursuing this same end. The importance of the overall enterprise and the authority granted to social scientist experts in public discourse oblige us to make our research as scientific as possible. We have to uphold our end of the bargain.

This chapter discusses the *ethos* of scientific research: the values that ought to inform the practices to which scientists aspire. We frame much of the chapter around one of the most famous and enduring discussions of the norms of science, by Robert K. Merton, a distinguished sociologist of the last century.[1] Writing in 1942, Merton was less than

---

1. Not to be confused with his son, Robert C. Merton, the Nobel Prize–winning economist.

a generation removed from the development of quantum mechanics, less than a decade away from the discovery of nuclear fission, and wrote in the very same year that the first patient was treated with antibiotics. Perhaps for this reason, Merton saw science as an extremely well-functioning system for producing knowledge, and his discussion of the ethos of science was an effort to explain why science worked so well.

Researchers have long held up the values of openness and replication as central to what they do, but as we show in the next few chapters, real-world practice has not always lived up to those ideals. Alarms have been raised about the corruption of science and the potential erosion of its credibility and effectiveness. This has led to renewed interest in Merton's writing as a guide to the core ideals of a strong scientific enterprise. As this chapter makes clear, we view the recent move toward research transparency in the social sciences as a key part of efforts to bring researchers' actions back in line with their ideals.

NORMS OF ETHICAL RESEARCH

Merton's 1942 article is arguably the most influential and most cited modern discussion of the ethos of scientific research. His treatment embeds scientists in a social system with a set of norms and describes the incentives facing individual researchers as they act within that structure. Norms have a dual character: the incentives provided by a well-functioning system support behavior that adheres to the norms, but the system also works because actors internalize the norms—they buy in. As Merton puts it, the set of scientific norms are "binding, not only because they are procedurally efficient, but because they are believed to be right and good. They are moral as well as technical prescriptions" (p. 270; here and in the rest of this chapter, we quote the reprint, Merton 1973).

Although social science training programs differ greatly across universities and fields, it is safe to say that many (if not most) graduate students never receive any formal training in the ethos of scientific research that Merton discusses. This was certainly the case for the authors of this book, who never took a course on these topics in their doctoral training programs. There has been an encouraging trend, especially in health-related fields, toward more training in the Responsible Conduct of Research, which incorporates some of the research transparency issues that we emphasize. But in most cases, students simply pick up the prevailing researcher values, expectations, and norms from their advisor, other faculty, and fellow students; the term *role model,* incidentally, also comes from Merton. Aspiring social scientists often simply absorb elements of the scientific ethos while interacting with colleagues, but there are worries that negative lessons can be passed along this way as well.

The four core values of scientific research that Merton articulates are *universalism, communality, disinterestedness,* and *organized skepticism.* We go through these in turn in the following subsections and link them back to the broader goal of research transparency.

Before diving in, you might be wondering about the origin of these norms of research practice in contemporary universities. While there are multiple influences and contributing factors, some elements of the culture of the modern research university can be traced pretty directly back to the ascetic and communal practices of medieval European monastic scholars (Clark 2006). Food for thought!

Universalism

The first core value of the scientific ethos that Merton identifies is universalism, or the principle that "the acceptance or rejection of claims . . . is not to depend on the personal or social attributes of their protagonist" (p. 270). The idea is that research findings are fundamentally "impersonal," and that the validity of a claim that's made should not rest on who's making it. In many human interactions, the rich, connected, or famous have a great degree of power and control due to their high social standing; think of how the sales of a new fashion accessory skyrocket when a Hollywood star dons it on the red carpet. But that isn't how science is supposed to work: research is supposed to lead to general truths, not fads. If I'm a powerful person and I think the world is flat, it really doesn't matter from a scientific perspective, because researchers can objectively prove that the Earth is round.[2] No one is above the law when it comes to science, and no amount of money can change the truths that emerge from physics, math, or (we hope) the social sciences.

This universalist ideal implies that anyone with the right training should be able to contribute to scientific progress, regardless of their social background, and that one's standing in the scientific community flows from intellectual contributions rather than social origins. When

2. Nor any amount of skill in the game of basketball. See the recent controversy in the United States regarding NBA star Kyrie Irving's apparently sincere belief that the Earth is, in fact, flat: http://www.rollingstone.com/culture/news/kyrie-irvings-idiotic-flat-earth-belief-is-catching-on-w494810.

Merton wrote, in the early 1940s, that "universalism finds further expression in the demand that careers be open to talents" (p. 272), his views were strongly influenced by the Nazi regime in Germany, which had begun by dismissing Jewish scientists from universities shortly after taking power, in what turned out to be the first steps toward far greater atrocities. Many of those scientists fled to the United States, and their subsequent research contributions have been credited with establishing U.S. leadership in world science, which persists up to this day.

A broader implication is that societies that promote equality of educational opportunity may experience the most rapid scientific progress: since everybody from all walks of life—regardless of gender, ethnicity, religion, sexuality, academic pedigree, or other social distinctions—can contribute to research, restricting access to scientific training would effectively shut whole groups of people out of the scientific endeavor, impoverishing learning. Of course, most human societies today, including our own, fall far short of the ideal of equality of opportunity. Social groups are often systematically excluded, or discriminated against, on the basis of their identity. Merton writes that "when the larger culture opposes universalism, the ethos of science is subjected to serious strain" (p. 271). The fact that women and members of many ethnic groups are chronically underrepresented as university faculty researchers in the United States across social science fields is an indication that our society still has a long way to go.

Communality

Merton defines the second core value, communality, as follows: "The substantive findings of science are a product of social collaboration and are assigned to the community" (p. 273). The central idea here is that open exchange, discussion, and sharing of evidence is at the heart of the scientific enterprise: "Secrecy is the antithesis of this norm; full and open communication its enactment" (p. 274).[3]

It is easy to see how keeping science open is essential to progress. If findings are not shared with the rest of the community of researchers, others are unable to build on previous work, and they may waste time and resources on less promising research directions. Sharing of data and

---

3. Originally, Merton used the term *communism* here. We follow many other scholars in modifying the term for clarity, to avoid confusion with the political ideology of the same name.

results also allows other scholars to synthesize evidence across multiple samples and settings to reach broader conclusions. Similarly, swapping ideas and working collaboratively with other scholars at early stages of a project can improve the quality of the resulting research.

In centuries past, when there were fewer scientific journals, researchers would exchange lengthy letters detailing their experiments and findings to keep others with similar interests abreast of their work, and to seek support and guidance. Technology has changed radically since then—today we can instantaneously share new research findings with a global readership via the Internet—but the value of communication within the scholarly community remains undiminished.

Merton highlights a fundamental tension between this norm of open scientific communication and the commercialization of research findings: "the [communality] of the scientific ethos is incompatible with the definition of technology as private property in a capitalistic economy" (p. 275). In other words, and in sharp contrast to many other forms of property outside of research, the scientific ethos demands that research knowledge belong to the community as a whole and not just to those who discover it.

When Merton was writing, this idea was already somewhat controversial but perhaps less so than it is today. In the 1930s and '40s, universities typically did not have campus offices attempting to spin off new technologies from their engineering departments into lucrative patents. That was not how the system operated for the most part, and many researchers adhered more closely to the ideals that Merton lays out. Things have certainly changed a lot since then, as we have seen firsthand at our Bay Area academic home institutions.

Today, developing new technologies and securing patent protection for them is seen as a normal revenue-generating activity in a research university. Some faculty spend less time doing basic research than trying to commercialize every half-decent idea they have, so they can spin out a start-up based on it. The pull of Silicon Valley investment in research, and the potential for personal riches if an idea is successful in the marketplace, has eroded attachment to the ideal of communality and open scientific communication.

As part of the same trend, a growing number of cutting-edge research activities take place outside academic institutions. The main goal of private-sector research activity is to develop something commercially viable (and proprietary). Researchers are often expressly forbidden from publishing their work and sharing it with the broader research community. This is directly antithetical to the scientific ethos as Merton

Racism in Science

There are many poignant examples of excellent scholars whose careers were hindered by prejudice—in fact, too many to count. A famous example from the San Francisco Bay Area of a researcher who overcame racial prejudice is mathematician David Blackwell (1919–2010).

Blackwell was the first African American inducted into the U.S. National Academy of Sciences (in 1965) and the first black tenured faculty member at the University of California, Berkeley (in 1955). But his research career got off to a rocky start. His attempts to attend lectures at Princeton University, and an initial effort to appoint him as a faculty member at Berkeley in the 1940s, were derailed by racist objections. While Professor Blackwell eventually overcame this bias, and made major contributions to mathematics, statistics, and game theory—many of which have found applications in the social sciences—

David Blackwell in the classroom. David Blackwell papers, BANC MSS 2001/79. Courtesy of the Bancroft Library, University of California, Berkeley.

others in the United States and in other societies have seen their research aspirations derailed by discrimination, to the detriment of scientific progress.

It seems likely that, had Blackwell been born just 10 or 15 years earlier and come of age before racist practices in the United States started to crumble, he might never have become a full-time researcher at all, and we would not even know his name. Given the potential for research advances to eventually improve human lives, society as a whole pays the price when gifted individuals like David Blackwell are shut out of scientific research.

describes it; the open-source countermovement in software and engineering is far closer to embodying the classical ideal. Later in this chapter, we present some evidence on how research norms do, in fact, often differ in academic versus corporate settings.

Disinterestedness

The ideal of disinterestedness is that researcher behavior should be consistent with a motivation for identifying the truth, and not with narrower professional self-interest or monetary motivations. The ethical researcher is supposed to report findings as they are—even if doing so is not good for your reputation, even if it goes against prevailing wisdom, even if it could make other people mad at you. The research findings themselves are more important than any person's ego or social standing, and they deserve to see the light of day. Researchers are human beings, of course, and it is natural for personal considerations or emotions to enter our minds. But we are not supposed to allow them to determine what we find as researchers.

For example, consider the case of a scholar working on topic X— let's say, the effect of immigration inflows on local wages, a prominent literature in labor economics—and imagine she has already published a body of research showing that more immigration dampens local wages. If this scholar analyzes valid new data showing something different and unexpected, even something that goes against her previous findings, she is supposed to share the new findings with the research community, just as eagerly as she would have if the earlier work had been confirmed. While researchers are often passionate about the issues they study—it is hard to make it through the rigors of graduate training without an obsession for what you are studying—ethical researchers must be dispassionate about the results of their analysis, and not put their finger on the scale to avoid being embarrassed, offending the authorities, or jeopardizing future research funding.

Social scientists often face an additional challenge of concerns about the potential social consequences of their findings. A researcher studying immigration and local wages may have strong ideological commitments, and may worry that publishing contrary results could be used by those with opposing ideologies to advocate policies that the researcher believes would be socially harmful (e.g., results showing adverse labor-market consequences of immigration could be touted by politicians who seek to deport millions of immigrants). However, for social science to be credible, researchers must be committed to making results public regardless of their perceived implications. Otherwise, those who would dismiss social science findings as ideologically biased have a point. Whatever influence empirical social science has on policy follows from trust in social scientists faithfully reporting what their evidence shows. Social scientists can make sure that their work is taken seriously by doing all they can to objectively report their results, but they cannot control all the social impacts of their work.

Writing in the 1940s, Merton was impressed by the "virtual absence of fraud in the annals of science" (p. 276), an absence he attributed, primarily, not to the integrity of scientists but to the practice of science itself. In Merton's view, the system of social control in science was exceptionally strong because "the activities of scientists are subject to rigorous policing, perhaps to a degree unparalleled in any field of activity" (p. 276). Accountability was assured—any attempted fraud would be readily exposed by other scientists.

Read today, this part of Merton's account may seem the most out-of-touch with contemporary science. As we saw in Chapter 1, Diederik Stapel compared his serial fraud to the temptation of having a cookie jar sitting on his desk, because he was so completely unmonitored that fraud was easy to get away with. The key problems we will identify in Chapters 3 and 4 are problems precisely because they erode the system that Merton saw as fostering disinterestedness. Hidden practices increase the ability of researchers to produce, consciously or unconsciously, whatever results best serve their personal interests.

The current movement to increase transparency and reproducibility in social science shares Merton's enthusiasm for accountability: at its heart, the movement connects the credibility of science to its accountability, and its accountability to openness.

Organized Skepticism

The final element of the scientific ethos is organized skepticism. A fundamental characteristic of the approach of scientific researchers is that they shouldn't take things at face value: they need to see proof. I can't just tell you I have a proof of Fermat's Last Theorem—a famous mathematical conjecture that remained unresolved for centuries—I need to prove it, and others need to verify that proof as well. Indeed, when Andrew Wiles offered his proof of the theorem in 1993, other mathematicians pored over it and did find a misstep, but after another year of work Wiles successfully fixed it and completed the proof.

A key aspect of life as a researcher is the scrutiny that our work must face. As noted, Merton regarded scientific work as subject to far more scrutiny than almost anything else, and he saw this scrutiny as key to science's success. The ability to verify data and scrutinize claims is thus critical in order for research to live up to this standard.

Skepticism extends beyond simply scrutinizing other researchers' evidence, though. Merton sees the researcher's role as questioning everything and subjecting all realms of life to rigorous scrutiny. There is nothing the scientist should accept blindly or take on faith. Merton is eloquent on this point: "The scientific investigator does not preserve the cleavage between the sacred and the profane, between that which requires uncritical respect and that which can be objectively analyzed" (p. 277–8). In other words, scientists shouldn't restrict themselves to socially acceptable topics or to what those in power say it is okay to study: the ideal is to critically examine everything. (This is obviously an area where modern researchers diverge quite radically from medieval monk-scholars; presumably the latter would not last long in the monastery if they rejected central elements of their Christian faith.)

You can immediately see the connection here between democracy, free speech, and the scientific ideal. It would be impossible to fully realize the scientific ideal of organized skepticism—not to mention those other values—in a totalitarian dictatorship. There would simply be too many topics off limits to debate, too many red lines that scientists would inevitably cross. While some scientific progress is still possible in the most repressive of regimes—think of the community of eminent nuclear physicists and mathematicians in the Soviet Union, for instance—the free exchange of ideas and the ability to reflect critically on reality give democracies a tremendous scientific advantage. For instance, Soviet social scientists were hamstrung by political demands that they place their work within the confines of Marxist political ideology, and this effectively crippled their research economists, sociologists, and political scientists.

A related critique has recently been lodged against prevailing norms in the field of macroeconomic theory. Romer (2015) argues that too much of recent theory has been based on untested (and sometimes untestable) assumptions, with too little feedback from empirical reality, leading to branches of theory that resemble exercises in ideological purity more than they resemble a truly scientific activity. In the case of modern macroeconomic theory, there is sometimes an almost religious attachment to assumptions regarding free-market efficiency, in contrast to the Marxist framework that constrained Soviet research. In any context, an unwillingness to test underlying articles of faith can slow scientific progress.

Access to the evidence that scientists produce, so that other scholars (and fellow citizens) can verify, extend, and critique it, is an important component of research openness, making replication and reanalysis of data essential. Openness, integrity, and transparency are at the very heart of Merton's influential articulation of scientific research norms: the free communication and sharing of findings, the ability of other scholars to examine and verify results, and the ability of all people to contribute to—and critique—the scientific enterprise.

We personally find it inspiring to think of ourselves as researchers who are part of this centuries-old tradition of learning and (hopefully) progress, and we are grateful for the opportunity to spend most of our waking hours struggling to better understand the world around us. Those of you reading this book who are currently receiving your academic training might feel the same. The values of openness, equality, and democracy are pretty easy to believe in.

But how closely do real-world researchers today conform to these ideal standards of conduct? In the next section, we present some data to assess the gap between the Mertonian ideal and reality in U.S. research institutions.

ACTUAL RESEARCH PRACTICES

Surveying Researcher Norms

A natural way to understand researchers' beliefs and practices is to ask about them directly. This is exactly what the article by Melissa Anderson, Brian C. Martinson, and Raymond De Vries (2007) that we focus on next set out to do. This study surveyed U.S.-based researchers to understand how strongly they identify with the Mertonian norms laid out above, how close their own behavior comes to fulfilling those values, and how close they believe other researchers are to the scientific ethos. This study's relatively large sample of 3,247 is based on a representative sample of researchers funded by the U.S. National Institutes of Health (NIH), a major research funder (to the tune of billions of dollars per year). NIH funds a wide range of researchers, from lab scientists in biomedical research to social scientists in many disciplines whose work deals with health topics. So, while this is not a fully representative sample of all scholars, it does cover a lot of ground.

The sample comprises two groups. Respondents in the first ("mid-career") group had just received their first large (R01) research grants (which enable more established researchers to sustain a lab or a research group for a considerable period, usually up to five years; thus, the individuals in this group were likely to be assistant or associate professors). Those in the second ("early-career") group had recently received post-doctoral training grants and thus were at an earlier stage (perhaps 5–10 years earlier) than the mid-career group. The survey response rate of roughly 50 percent is not ideal, but the results should at least be illustrative of broad patterns in the research community. (In what follows, we will not focus much on the possible biases caused by selective survey completion, for simplicity, but it is probably worth taking these patterns with a grain of salt.)

The survey collected information about Merton's four norms, as well as two additional values, pairing each with a "counter-norm" that scholars have identified as also existing in the research community. These six pairs of norms and counter-norms are described in Table 2.1. For example, the counter-norm of universalism is particularism, which represents a lack of openness to different types of people or researchers, and specifically a belief that scientific evidence should be judged primarily on the basis of the past research track record of the investigator rather than the quality of the evidence per se. Similarly, Merton's norm of communality is paired with the counter-norm of secrecy, disinterestedness with self-interestedness, and organized skepticism with organized dogmatism.

The two additional values, governance (vs. administration) and quality (vs. quantity) of research, have been identified by scholars in the years since Merton's work as central to the scientific ethos. The first represents the research community's self-governance, the belief that scientists themselves should influence the direction of science, based on the inherent value of the work, rather than being driven by political, administrative, or other considerations—in other words, researcher autonomy is central to the scientific ethos. The second highlights the importance of quality in relation to quantity. Of course, both are important—producing a larger quantity of valid research is certainly better than producing less—but the point here is that researchers should not be judged (for hiring and promotion, say) solely by counting the papers they've published or the amounts of grant money they've brought into their institution. Rather, the quality of the underlying research and its contributions to knowledge need to take center stage. This seems like a sensible criterion to use, given the role that a handful of the highest-quality, fundamental contributions often play in driving subsequent scientific progress.

Some observers have found that counter-norms, such as attachment to secrecy, are most prevalent in the context of "fierce, sometimes bitter competitive races for discovery" (Mitroff 1974), such as when a research group fears it is going to be "scooped" by a rival group. Indeed, people's attitudes are often somewhat contradictory, and a researcher may, for instance, express partial support for both communality and secrecy (e.g., depending on the circumstances). Anderson, Martinson, and De Vries (2007) allowed for this possibility by asking the survey respondents to rate their support of both the norms *and* the counter-norms, in terms of the respondents' own *subscription* (attitudes), their own *enactment* (practices), and their perceptions of others' typical behavior.

For subscription, the respondents were instructed: "For each item, please indicate the extent to which you personally feel it *should* represent behavior of scientists." For enactment: "Please indicate the extent to which it represents *your own* behavior." And for respondents' assessment of other scientists' behavior: "Please indicate the extent to which you feel that it *actually does* represent *the typical behavior of scientists*" (all emphases in the original). The response choices for all three sets of items were the same: 2 = to a great extent, 1 = to some extent, 0 = very little or not at all.

What Do Researchers Say and Do?

Answers were combined across the six pairs of values listed in Table 2.1, and researchers were classified by whether their responses were more in line with the norms or with the counter-norms. Those whose support for both norms and counter-norms were within one point were coded as having roughly equal support for each. The proportions of respondents in each of these categories are presented in Figure 2.1, with results presented

TABLE 2.1   SCIENTIFIC RESEARCH NORMS AND PRACTICES

Norm	Counter-norm
Communality Researchers openly share findings with colleagues.	*Secrecy* Researchers protect their newest findings for priority in publishing, patenting, or applications.
Universalism Researchers evaluate research only on its merit (i.e., by accepted standards of the field).	*Particularism* Researchers assess new knowledge and its applications by the reputation and past productivity of the individual or research group.
Disinterestedness Researchers are motivated by the desire for knowledge and discovery, and not by the possibility of personal gain.	*Self-interestedness* Researchers compete with others in the same field for funding and recognition of their achievements.
Organized skepticism Researchers consider all new evidence, hypotheses, theories, and innovations, including those that may challenge or contradict their own work.	*Organized dogmatism* Researchers spend their careers promoting their own most important findings, theories, or innovations.
Governance Researchers are responsible for the direction and control of science through governance, self-regulation, and peer review.	*Administration* Researchers rely on administrators to direct the scientific enterprise through management decisions.
Quality Researchers judge their peers' contributions to science primarily on the basis of quality.	*Quantity* Researchers assess their peers' work primarily on the basis of quantity of publications and grants.

NOTE: A similar table appears in Anderson et al. (2007).

separately for subscription, enactment, and perception of others' behavior, and also broken down by mid-career versus early-career researchers.

The first striking pattern in Figure 2.1 (top) is just how strong the stated support for the Mertonian scientific ethos is among U.S.-based researchers today. We assume that few of these scholars had actually read Merton's work on this topic or taken classes in which related material was covered—but they subscribe to the values of universal, open science just the same. Roughly 90 percent agree with the norms, and

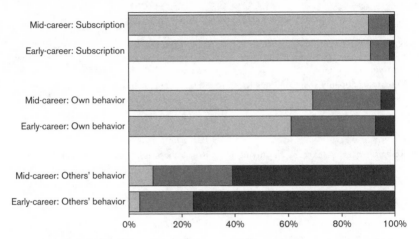

FIGURE 2.1. Attitudes, beliefs, and practices of early-career and mid-career U.S. researchers (*N* = 3,247) in regard to six pairs of scientific norms and counter-norms (see Table 2.1). Light gray indicates the proportion expressing more support for the norms, dark gray the proportion expressing roughly equal support for both the norms and the counter-norms, and black the proportion expressing more support for the counter-norms. Reprinted with permission from Anderson et al. (2007).

another 7–8 percent have some mixed views. Very few scholars say, in effect, "No, I believe in secrecy, I'm totally self-interested in my research, and totally dogmatic."

At first glance, it seems that the scientific ethos is alive and well. But what do these very same scholars actually do? Or, at least, what do they say they do when asked about the same values? As shown in Figure 2.1 (middle), 60–70 percent say, "Yes, I generally live up to these ideals." But the share of researchers in the ambiguous category is now larger than in the subscription question—basically claiming to follow the norm most of the time, but perhaps sometimes admitting to being secretive or self-interested. However, with regard to enactment, the data again suggest that the bulk of active researchers, roughly two-thirds, broadly conform to the six scientific norms and values.

The enactment data show a slightly greater adherence to the norms by mid-career scholars than by those earlier in their careers, and it is worth speculating on the difference. One possibility is that mid-career practices are actually more closely in line with Mertonian norms, perhaps because these scholars have had more time to be socialized into them. Maybe more established scholars feel more secure in their position (if they have received tenure, for instance) and thus feel less of a pressing need to pursue self-interest over higher ideals. An alternative view is that the gap is due to a difference in reporting rather than actual practices: Perhaps more experienced scholars have simply learned to be dishonest and lie with a straight face? It is impossible to say from these data alone.

In our view, the most interesting data in Figure 2.1 are those at the bottom, which capture researchers' beliefs about other researchers' behavior. There is a strikingly bleak pattern: only about 5–10 percent believe that other researchers tend to mainly follow the norms, while 60 to 75 percent believe that the counter-norms are generally practiced more than the norms. The "punch line" of this figure, as the study's authors interpret it, is that there is pervasive normative dissonance among researchers—what Anderson, Martinson, and De Vries (2007) call the "disillusionment gap." The vast majority of scholars subscribe to the Mertonian norms of science but believe that few in their fields are actually living up to them. Anderson, Martinson, and De Vries (2007, p. 4) summarize their view on this gap between researchers' values and practices:

> Persistent mismatches between beliefs and actions can contribute to work strain, disillusionment and alienation. Confusion or ambiguity about right action can prompt people to try to reduce dissonance by aligning their behavior with their peers', especially if they think that not doing so would put them at a competitive disadvantage.

Which part of Figure 2.1 should we believe—the middle (mixed but broadly supportive of the norms) or the bottom (with its pessimistic view of the research field as a whole)? It remains possible that the latter is too pessimistic. Perhaps everyone hears about a few "bad apples," like the fraud cases discussed in Chapter 1, and thereafter (unfairly) condemns the state of ethics of their whole field.

There is also a potentially important temporal element here, which may lead to some ambiguity in interpretation. Many social science researchers are quite secretive about their work while they are doing it, for fear of being scooped (i.e., that others will copy them), but are then happy to discuss it widely, and share their data and materials, once it is published. As a result, they may view their own practices as being in line with Mertonian norms (in the long run, at least), while simultaneously being critical of other researchers' lack of openness with work-in-progress and viewing that behavior as partially inconsistent with the norms.

However, in our view, this would be too easy a way out. If there is one thing that two of the authors of this book have learned in development economics over the past two decades, as original survey data collection has become ubiquitous, it is that when you want to get a reliable answer to a sensitive question, you might be better off asking people not about what they do but about what "other people like them" do. There is a whole subliterature on the study of corruption patterns in economics and political science that takes this approach, asking firm owners not about the bribes that they themselves pay (since admitting so might be illegal) but instead asking them about the likely behavior of other firms that are similar to theirs. If the same sorts of reporting issues apply when asking researchers about whether or not they break with a widely held norm, then the bottom part of Figure 2.1 is most reliable.

The data also reveal some other patterns among particular subgroups of researchers. One of the most interesting has to do with the breakdown of academic versus private-sector researchers mentioned above. Anderson, Martinson, and De Vries (2007) report significantly more norm following and stated norm following among the academic researchers in the sample than among researchers at private for-profit firms. This is perhaps not too surprising, since for-profit firms are in the business of developing new technologies that they want to patent and profit from, and their focus on generating proprietary data runs directly counter to the Mertonian norm of communality.

Anderson, Martinson, and De Vries (2007) also asked scholars about how competitive they felt their research field was, and they found that researchers in fields that were described as more competitive showed far less attachment to scientific norms. It is not exactly clear why this is the case, but one possibility is that the pressure to publish—and publish fast—in such fields sometimes tilts the balance toward self-interest and away from disinterested behavior.

A peaceful "ivory tower" life is apparently more conducive to following the high ideals laid out by Merton than high-pressure academic or private-sector research settings. That said, could it be the case that fierce competition has an upside, in more rapidly driving research progress forward? That is certainly what incentive theory in economics might suggest, and it's part of the rationale underlying contemporary technology patents. Self-interest could play a role in generating more research effort and dedication. This is not an issue that features in Merton's work, but it cannot be ignored out of hand when we consider how to design a research system that generates the most useful science. We return to this issue in our discussion of open sharing of data and research materials in Chapter 10.

LOOKING FORWARD

We have discussed some evidence that researcher practices often do not live up to the highest scientific ideals. In Chapters 3 and 4, we continue this discussion and provide further evidence on the pervasive issues of publication bias and specification searching, and elaborate on how they can lead to misleading bodies of social science. In the subsequent chapters, we then provide a road map for ways forward, possible solutions to these concerns, and approaches that can help bring researcher practices back in line with our fundamental values, addressing the normative dissonance described by Anderson, Martinson, and De Vries (2007).

PART TWO

Problems

THREE

Publication Bias

The webcomic *xkcd* once depicted a scientist reporting, "We found no link between purple jellybeans and acne (p > .05)." In the next panel the scientist says, "We found no link between brown jellybeans and acne (p > .05)." There are 20 such panels and 20 jellybean colors. The only difference is somewhere in the middle, where the scientist says, "We found a link between green jellybeans and acne (p < .05)." The comic ends with a newspaper headline announcing, "Green jellybeans linked to acne! Only a 5% chance of coincidence."

Of course, the joke is that, having seen all 20 studies, we know that one result with a 1 in 20 chance of being a coincidence is in fact perfectly consistent with it being a coincidence. But if that were the only result published, we would not know about the other 19 results, and we might be easily fooled into taking that "(p < .05)" at face value.

"Green jellybeans linked to acne" is a playful example of a *false positive:* a finding that provides support for a conclusion that is not true. This is also known as a type I error.[1] A big worry is that false positives

1. Type I errors are false positives (rejecting a null hypothesis when it is in fact true), whereas type II errors are false negatives (failing to reject a hypothesis when it is in fact false). More recently, there has been discussion of type S (sign) and type M (magnitude) errors (see Gelman and Carlin 2014; Gelman and Tuerlinckx 2000). Type S error is described as the probability that the replicated estimate has the incorrect sign, if it is statistically significantly different from zero, and type M error is a measure of exaggeration: the expectation of the estimate absolute value divided by the effect size, if statistically significantly different from zero. While we consider this a useful reframing of the issue,

may be far more common in science than previously thought, perhaps even to the point of sometimes being rampant. In genetic epidemiology, for example, researchers refer to there being a whole era in which many hundreds of positive results were published using methods now recognized as so underpowered that nearly all the results were false positives.[2] Because of false positives, whole scientific literatures can grossly exaggerate the evidentiary support for particular ideas.

This chapter and the next introduce the two primary villains at the root of problems of false positives. *Publication bias* occurs when some studies are more likely to be published than others on the basis of their results. *Specification searching* occurs when some analyses within a particular study are more likely to be reported by the researchers. The green jellybean example is publication bias if we think of it as involving 20 separate studies, and specification searching if we think of a researcher churning through 20 different ways of divvying up the sample in order to find something to write up. The two are closely related: researcher anticipation of publication bias provides a strong incentive for specification searching.

Both problems also relate to the issues of research ethics discussed in Chapter 2. In broad terms, we generally attribute bias across a collection of multiple studies to publication bias, which we discuss in this chapter, and bias in the results of a single study to specification searching, which we discuss in Chapter 4.

A CONCEPTUAL MODEL FOR APPROACHING THE PROBLEM

A helpful model to frame both the key issues introduced above was developed in the provocatively titled "Why Most Published Research Findings Are False" by John Ioannidis (2005), which is among the most highly cited research articles from recent years in any field. Ioannidis develops a simple model that demonstrates how greater flexibility in data analysis and publication may lead to an increased rate of false positives and, thus, incorrect inference.

Specifically, the Ioannidis model estimates the positive predictive value (PPV) of research, or the likelihood that a claimed empirical

---

which can highlight just how likely small-sample studies are to lead people to incorrect conclusions, we have chosen to focus on standard type I and type II terminology.

2. Briefly, power, defined as $1 - \beta$, where β is the type II error rate, is the likelihood that an experiment will detect a statistically significant effect, based on the sample size and assumptions about the true magnitude and variation of the effect in the population. For more, see the Appendix.

relationship is actually true, under various assumptions. In literatures for which studies typically have high PPV, claimed findings are likely to be reliable; a low PPV means that the body of evidence may be riddled with false positives. The model is similar to that of Wacholder et al. (2004), which estimates the closely related false positive report probability (FPRP).[3]

For simplicity, consider the case in which a relationship or hypothesis can be classified in a binary fashion as either a "true relationship" or "no relationship." Define R_i as the ratio of true relationships to no relationships commonly tested in a research field i (e.g., development economics). Prior to a study being undertaken, the probability that a true relationship exists for a given claim is thus $R_i/(R_i + 1)$. Using the usual notation for statistical power of the test $(1 - \beta)$ and the desired statistical significance level (α), the PPV in research field i is given by

$$PPV_i = (1 - \beta)R_i/((1 - \beta)R_i + \alpha). \qquad \text{Eqn. 3.1}$$

The interested reader can find the derivation of this formula in Example 3.1.

From the equation, it is hopefully clear that the better powered the study (higher $1 - \beta$), and the stricter the statistical significance level (lower α), the closer the PPV is to 1, in which case false positives are largely eliminated. At the usual significance level of $\alpha = .05$ and in the case of a well-powered study $(1 - \beta = 0.80)$ in a literature in which one third of all hypotheses are thought to be true *ex ante* $(R_i = 0.5)$, the PPV is relatively high at 89 percent, a level that would not seem likely to threaten the validity of research in a particular research subfield.

However, reality is considerably messier than this best-case scenario and, as Ioannidis describes, could lead to much higher rates of false positives in practice due to the presence of underpowered studies, specification searching, researcher bias, and the possibility that only a subset of the analysis in a research literature is published. We discuss these extensions in turn.

We start with the issue of statistical power. In empirical economics, Doucouliagos and Stanley (2013), Doucouliagos, Ioannidis, and Stanley

---

3. We should note that there is also a relatively small amount of theoretical economic research modeling the researcher-and-publication process. For example, Henry (2009) predicts that, under certain conditions, more research effort is undertaken when not all research is observable, if such costs can be made to demonstrate investigator honesty (see also Henry and Ottaviani 2014; Libgober 2015).

Example 3.1 Deriving the Positive Predictive Value

Here we show how to derive Ioannidis' formula using Bayes' law. We are interested in the positive predictive value (PPV), or the probability that a finding is true, given that a significant statistical association is found. We define R as the ratio of true to false relationships, and the (pre-study) probability that any given relationship is real is $\frac{R}{R+1}$. T is the observed test statistic and t_α is the relevant threshold. So, we are looking for

$$\text{PPV} = \Pr(\text{True}|T > t_\alpha). \qquad 3.1$$

Prior to the study, the quantities involved are as follows:

- Probability of a relationship being true: $\frac{R}{R+1}$

- Probability of a relationship being false: $1 - \frac{R}{R+1} = \frac{1}{R+1}$

- Probability of finding a positive statistical association given that the relationship is false: α
- Probability of finding a positive statistical association given that the relationship is true (i.e., power): $1 - \beta$

Bayes' law says that $\Pr(A|B) = \frac{\Pr(B|A)\Pr(A)}{\Pr(B)}$, though it is almost always the case that the denominator is more useful when written out with the law of total probability, as follows:

$$\Pr(A|B) = \frac{\Pr(B|A)\Pr(A)}{\Pr(B|A)\Pr(A) + \Pr(B|\neg A)\Pr(\neg A)}. \qquad 3.2$$

By using Bayes' law, we know that

$$\Pr(\text{True}|T > t_\alpha) = \frac{\Pr(T > t_\alpha|\text{True})\cdot\Pr(\text{True})}{\Pr(T > t_\alpha|\text{True})\cdot\Pr(\text{True}) + \Pr(T > t_\alpha|\text{False})\cdot\Pr(\text{False})} \qquad 3.3$$

Substituting, we find:

$$\Pr(\text{True}|T > t_\alpha) = \frac{(1-\beta)\,\frac{R}{R+1}}{(1-\beta)\,\frac{R}{R+1} + \alpha\cdot\frac{1}{R+1}} \quad\text{and} \qquad 3.4$$

$$\Pr(\text{True}|T > t_\alpha) = \frac{\dfrac{(1-\beta)R}{R+1}}{\dfrac{(1-\beta)R+\alpha}{R+1}} . \qquad\qquad 3.5$$

Simplifying:

$$\Pr(\text{True}|T > t_\alpha) = \frac{(1-\beta)R}{(1-\beta)R+\alpha} = \frac{(1-\beta)R}{R-\beta R+\alpha} . \qquad 3.6$$

This is the same as the formula in Ioannidis (2005) and Eqn. 3.1.

(2017), and others have documented that studies are in practice quite underpowered. With a more realistic level of statistical power for many studies (say, .50), but maintaining the other assumptions above, the PPV falls to 83 percent, which is beginning to look like more of a potential concern. For power = .20, fully 33 percent of statistically significant findings are false positives (PPV = 67 percent). If low-powered studies are routinely used to test hypotheses more likely than not to be false, the false positive rate can exceed 50 percent (e.g., power = 0.20 and R_i = 0.2 yields PPV = 0.44).

This concern, and those discussed next, are all exacerbated by bias in the publication process. If all estimates in a literature were available to the scientific community, researchers could begin to undo the concerns over a low PPV by combining data across studies, effectively achieving greater statistical power and more reliable inference, for instance, using meta-analysis methods. However, as we discuss below, there is growing evidence of a pervasive bias in favor of significant results in the publication process across research fields. If only significant findings are ever seen by the researcher community, then the PPV is the relevant quantity for assessing how credible an individual result is likely to be.

Ioannidis extends the basic model to account for the possibility of what he calls *bias,* defined as "the combination of various design, data, analysis, and presentation factors that tend to produce research findings when they should not be produced" and denoted by *u.* We call this *researcher bias,* which could take many forms, including any combination of data manipulation, specification searching (running numerous variations of statistical tests and reporting only those with desired outcomes), selective reporting (testing a number of different outcomes or samples and reporting only those with desired outcomes), and even outright fraud; below, we attempt to quantify the prevalence of these behaviors among researchers.[4] There are many checks in place that seek to limit this bias, and through the lens of empirical social science research, we might hope that the robustness checks typically demanded of scholars in seminar and conference presentations and during journal peer review manage to keep the most extreme forms of bias in check. Yet most social scientists would agree, we believe, that there remains considerable wiggle room in the presentation of results in practice, in most cases due to behaviors that fall far short of outright fraud.

Extending the above framework to incorporate the researcher bias term u_i in field i leads to the following expression:

$$\text{PPV}_i = ((1 - \beta)R_i + u_i\beta R_i)/((1 - \beta)R_i + \alpha + u_i\beta R_i + u_i(1 - \alpha)) \quad \text{Eqn. } 3.2$$

Here the actual number of true relationships (the numerator) is almost unchanged, though there is an additional term that captures the true effects that are correctly reported as significant only due to researcher bias. The total number of reported significant effects could be much larger due to both sampling variation and researcher bias. If we go back to the case of 50 percent power, $R_i = 0.5$, and the usual 5 percent significance level, but now assume that author bias is relatively low at 10 percent, the PPV falls from 83 percent to 65 percent. If 30 percent of authors are biased in their presentation of results, the PPV drops dramatically to 49 percent, meaning that half of reported significant effects are actually false positives.

In a further extension, Ioannidis examines the case where there are n_i different research teams in a field i generating estimates to test a research hypothesis. Once again, if only the statistically significant findings are published, there is no ability to pool all estimates, and so the likelihood that any published estimate is truly statistically significant can again fall dramatically.

Table 3.1 presents a range of parameter values and the resulting PPV. The R_i term may vary across research fields, where literatures that are in an earlier stage and thus more exploratory presumably have lower likelihoods of true relationships.

This simple framework brings a number of the issues we deal with in this book into sharper relief and contains a number of lessons. Ioannidis

---

4. For more on the terms and types of specification searching, see Chapter 4.

TABLE 3.1 POSITIVE PREDICTIVE VALUE (PPV) OF RESEARCH FINDINGS FOR VARIOUS COMBINATIONS OF POWER $(1 - \beta)$, RATIO OF TRUE TO NOT-TRUE RELATIONSHIPS (R_i), AND RESEARCHER BIAS (u)

$1 - \beta$	R_i	u	Practical example	PPV
0.80	1:1	0.10	Adequately powered RCT with little bias and 1:1 pre-study odds	0.85
0.95	2:1	0.30	Confirmatory meta-analysis of good-quality RCTs	0.85
0.80	1:3	0.40	Meta-analysis of small inconclusive studies	0.41
0.20	1:5	0.20	Underpowered, but well-performed phase I/II RCT	0.23
0.20	1:5	0.80	Underpowered, poorly performed phase I/II RCT	0.17
0.80	1:10	0.30	Adequately powered exploratory epidemiological study	0.12
0.20	1:1,000	0.80	Discovery-oriented exploratory research with massive testing	0.0010
0.20	1:1,000	0.20	As in previous example, but with more limited bias (more standardized)	0.0015

NOTES: Reproduced from Ioannidis (2005: table 4; DOI: 10.1371/journal.pmed.0020124.t004). The estimated PPVs are derived assuming $\alpha = .05$ for a single study. RCT = randomized controlled trial.

(2005) himself concludes that the majority of published findings in medicine are likely to be false, and while we are not prepared to make a similar claim for empirical social science research—in part because it is difficult to quantify some of the key parameters in the model—we do feel that this exercise raises important concerns about the reliability of findings in many literatures.

First off, literatures characterized by statistically underpowered studies are likely to have many false positives. The familiar worry with low-powered studies is that individual results are less likely to be statistically significant even when they are true, but the corresponding problem is that, when significant findings in low-powered studies are reported, they are more likely to be the result of noise or researcher bias. A study may be underpowered because of small sample sizes and/or because the underlying effect sizes are relatively small.[5] A possible approach to address this concern is to employ larger datasets or tests that are more powerful.

Second, the hotter a research field, with more teams (n_i) actively running tests and higher stakes around the findings, the more likely it is that

---

5. *Effect size* refers to the strength, or magnitude, of an effect, and not just its statistical significance. If a medical treatment decreases mortality rates, does it do so by a lot or a little?

findings are false positives. This is because multiple testing generates a larger number of false positives and also because researcher bias (u_i) may be greater when the stakes are higher. Researcher bias is also a concern when there are widespread prejudices in a research field—for instance, against publishing findings that contradict core theoretical concepts or assumptions. This must be weighed against the valuable scientific practice of building on previous knowledge—"standing on the shoulders of giants."

Third, the greater the flexibility in research design, definitions, outcome measures, and analytical approaches in a field, the less likely the research findings are to be true, again due to a combination of multiple testing concerns and researcher bias. One possible approach to address this concern is to mandate greater data sharing so that other scholars can assess the robustness of results to alternative models. Another is through approaches such as pre-analysis plans that effectively force scholars to present a certain core set of analytical specifications, regardless of the end result. These potential solutions are discussed in later chapters.

With this framework in mind, we next present empirical evidence from multiple social science fields regarding the extent of publication bias and other problems discussed by Ioannidis, and in later chapters we turn to several potential ways to address them.

ORIGIN OF THE PROBLEM

The concepts of statistical significance and associated p-values were popularized in large part by R. A. Fisher in the early twentieth century. In discussing error rates in experiments and a specific cutoff point for significance, he wrote:

> If one in twenty does not seem high enough odds, we may, if we prefer it, draw the line at one in fifty (the 2 per cent. point), or one in a hundred (the 1 per cent. point). Personally, the writer prefers to set a low standard of significance at the 5 per cent. point, and ignore entirely all results which fail to reach this level. (Fisher 1992)

It is not entirely clear why Fisher's exact suggestion was 5 percent (although multiples of five do generally feel like nice round numbers—probably because humans have five fingers), but it has become the norm across a wide variety of disciplines. Fisher was clearly aware of the concept of false positives and error rates, but it seems very unlikely that he would have approved of what researchers started to do with this specific cutoff: publish only the results on one side.

TABLE 3.2   TESTS OF SIGNIFICANCE IN FOUR PSYCHOLOGY JOURNALS

Journal and year	Articles reporting tests of significance	Articles that reject H_0 with $p < .05$	Articles that fail to reject H_0	Articles that are replications of previous studies
Experimental Psychology (1955)	106	105	1	0
Comparative and Physiological Psychology (1956)	94	91	3	0
Clinical Psychology (1955)	62	59	3	0
Social Psychology (1955)	32	31	1	0

NOTES: Data are from Sterling (1959). H_0 is the null hypothesis of no effect.

Publication bias arises if the outcome of a study systematically influences its likelihood of being published. Usually the bias is expected to work against studies that fail to reject the null hypothesis, as these typically generate less support for publication among referees and journal editors. Yet if the research community is unable to track the complete body of statistical tests that have been run, including those that fail to reject the null (and thus are less likely to be published), then we cannot determine the true proportion of tests in a literature that reject the null. Thus, it is critically important to understand how many tests and analyses have been run across the entire scholarly community.

The term "file drawer problem" was coined decades ago by the psychologist Robert Rosenthal to describe this problem of results that are missing from a body of research evidence (Rosenthal 1979), but the basic issue was a concern even earlier. In 1959, Theodore Sterling published a short article that is generally considered to be the first distillation of the problem. He warned that "when a fixed level of significance is used as a critical criterion for selecting reports for dissemination in professional journals it may result in embarrassing and unanticipated results." He then provided a small tabulation of recent articles from a handful of psychology journals, which we summarize in Table 3.2.

Sterling (1959) states the unfortunate question that this forces the reader to ask as follows:

> What risk does he take in making a Type I error by rejecting H_0 with the author? The author intended to indicate the probability of such a risk by stating a level of significance. On the other hand, the reader has to consider the selection that may have taken place among a set of similar experiments for which the one that obtained large differences by chance had the better opportunity to come under his scrutiny. The problem simply is that a Type I

error (rejecting the null hypothesis when it is true) has a fair opportunity to end up in print when the correct decision is the acceptance of H_0 for a particular set of experimental variables. Before the reader can make an intelligent decision he must have some information concerning the distribution of outcomes of similar experiments or at least the assurance that a similar experiment has never been performed. Since the latter information is unobtainable he is in a dilemma. One thing is clear however. The risk stated by the author cannot be accepted at its face value once the author's conclusions appear in print.

That was about 60 years ago already. Thirty years after his original work, Sterling conducted a similar exercise and found that little had changed in this field (Sterling, Rosenbaum, and Weinkam 1995). Eight psychology journals from 1986 or 1987 covering the same fields as in the earlier article were examined, and over 95 percent of articles using hypothesis testing rejected the null hypothesis. One potential solution suggested by the authors is what they call "blind-to-outcome peer review," in which reviewers are blind to the results of the analysis and instead base their review on the importance of the study and the relevance of the proposed methods. We discuss this exact idea in more detail in Chapter 6.

EVIDENCE OF THE PROBLEM

Important recent research by Franco, Malhotra, and Simonovits (2014) affirms the continued importance of the issue of publication bias in practice in contemporary social science research. They document that a large share of empirical analyses in the social sciences are never published or even written up, and that the likelihood of a finding being shared with the broader research community falls sharply for "null" findings (i.e., findings that are not statistically significant). They were able to look inside the file drawer in a clever way, through their access to the universe of studies that passed peer review and were included in a nationally representative social science survey—namely, the Time-sharing Experiments for the Social Sciences, or TESS, supported by the National Science Foundation.[6]

TESS funded studies across social science fields, including in economics (e.g., informational influences on adoption of energy-efficient lightbulbs; Allcott and Taubinsky 2015), political science (e.g., perception of electoral fraud; Beaulieu 2016), and sociology (e.g., gender equality in the workplace; Pedulla and Thébaud 2015). Franco, Malhotra, and

6. See http://tessexperiments.org for more information.

Most null results are never written up
The fate of 221 social science experiments

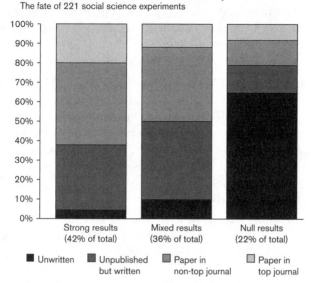

FIGURE 3.1. Publication rates and rates of writing-up of results from experiments with strong, mixed, and null results. These 221 experiments represent nearly the complete universe of studies conducted by the Time-sharing Experiments for the Social Sciences. The figure is from Mervis (2014), based on data from Franco, Malhotra, and Simonovits (2014). Reprinted with permission from AAAS.

Simonovits (2014) successfully tracked nearly all of the original studies over time, keeping track of the nature of the empirical results as well as the ultimate publication of the study, across the dozens of studies that participated in the original project.

They found a striking empirical pattern: studies where the main hypothesis test yielded null results are 40 percentage points less likely to be published in a journal than a strongly statistically significant result, and 60 percentage points less likely to be written up in any form. This finding has potentially severe implications for our understanding of findings in whole bodies of social science research, if zeros are never seen by other scholars, even in working-paper form. This implies that the PPV of research is likely to be lower than it would be otherwise, and also has negative implications for the validity of meta-analyses, if null results are not known to scholars attempting to draw broader conclusions about a body of evidence. Figure 3.1 reproduces some of the main patterns from Franco, Malhotra, and Simonovits (2014), as described by Mervis (2014).

Not to deliberately be even more depressing about this, but there is some evidence that the problem may be getting worse over time. Fanelli (2012) gathered a random sample of papers from all disciplines published during 1990–2007 and found that the rate of positive results (the fraction of papers that conducted hypothesis tests and report support for the hypothesis) increased from 70 percent in 1990 to 86 percent in 2007.

Aside from the evidence above from psychology journals (Masicampo and Lalande 2012) and the sciences generally (Head et al. 2015), scholars working in several other specific areas of the social sciences have shown evidence of the presence of considerable publication bias, including labor economics literatures on minimum wage impacts and on the value of a statistical life, as well as several other bodies of evidence in economics (see Table 3.3). We discuss both briefly in Examples 3.2 and 3.3 and give examples in political science and sociology later in this chapter.

Example 3.2 The Minimum Wage and Unemployment

Every student of Economics 101 can tell you that economic theory predicts that setting an artificial floor on price leads to oversupply relative to demand. A minimum wage is a price floor on the cost of labor, and so economic theory predicts that setting a high minimum wage will result in a higher quantity of labor supplied by workers than demanded by employers, leading to higher levels of unemployment. However, empirical tests of whether raising the minimum wage results in additional unemployment do not produce such an unambiguous picture.

Card and Krueger (1995) conducted an early meta-analysis of literature on the minimum wage and unemployment. If there is a true effect and no publication bias, then, for a given research design, effect size estimates will get more precise as sample size increases, but they should not get systematically bigger or smaller. Because the standard error decreases as sample size increases, a constant effect size implies that t-statistics—the ratio of an effect size to its standard error—would tend to be positively correlated with sample size if there is a true effect and no publication bias. As Card and Krueger explain:

A doubling of the sample size should lower the standard error of the estimated employment effect and raise the absolute t ratio by about 40 percent if the additional data are independent and the statistical model is stable. More generally, the absolute value of the t ratio should vary proportionally with the square root of the number of degrees of freedom, and a regression of the log of the t ratio on the log of the square root of the degrees of freedom should yield a coefficient of 1.

In a similar test in political science, Gerber, Green, and Nickerson (2001) document likely publication bias in the voter mobilization campaign literature, showing that studies with larger sample sizes tend to produce smaller effect size estimates.

Card and Krueger (1995) find that t-statistics from the 15 studies using quarterly data available at the time of writing are actually *negatively* correlated with sample sizes. A possible explanation is that a structural change in the effect of the minimum wage (a decline over time) had taken place, coinciding with later studies more often using larger sample sizes, but the authors consider publication bias and specification searching a more likely explanation. Neumark and Wascher (1998) construct an alternative test for publication bias, which attempts to account for this structural change in effects by instead conducting meta-analysis using a benchmark specification across all samples. They conclude there is more evidence for the structural change explanation (i.e., actual effects declined over time) and discount the possibility of publication bias.

Another explanation has been proposed for Card and Krueger's (1995) findings: the simple lack of a true effect of the minimum wage on unemployment. If the null hypothesis of no effect is true, the t-statistic would have no relationship with sample size. Studies that advance this alternative explanation (Stanley 2005; Doucouliagos and Stanley 2009) argue that the minimum wage literature likely does suffer from some publication bias, since many studies' t-statistics hover around 2 (near the standard 5 percent significance level) and other tests, described in this chapter and in Chapter 5, indicate as much. Doucouliagos, Ioannidis, and Stanley (2017) show that estimates among the subset of statistically well-powered studies (that are most reliable) have extremely small effect sizes, at less than one-tenth the magnitude of the body of literature as a whole. This is further indication that publication bias can lead to misleading inference on an issue of intense public policy interest.

TABLE 3.3 EXAMPLES OF RECENT META-ANALYSES IN ECONOMICS

Paper	Topic	Publication bias?	Number of papers (and estimates) used	Notes
Brodeur et al. (2016)	Wide collection of top publications	+	641 (50,078)	Finds that 10–20% of significant results are misplaced and should not be considered statistically significant.
Vivalt (2015)	Developing country impact evaluation	+	589 (26,170)	Finds that publication bias/specification search is more prevalent in nonexperimental work.
Viscusi (2015)	Value of a statistical life (VSL)	+	17 (550)	Use of better and more recent fatality data indicates that publication bias exists, but that accepted VSL is correct.
Doucouliagos, Stanley, and Viscusi (2014)	VSL and income elasticity	+	14 (101)	Previous evidence was mixed, but controlling for publication bias shows that the income elasticity of VSL is clearly inelastic.
Doucouliagos and Stanley (2013)	Meta-meta-analysis	+	87/3,599 (19,528)	87 meta-analyses with 3,599 original articles and 19,528 estimates show that 60% of research areas feature substantial or severe publication bias.
Havranek and Irsova (2012)	Foreign direct investment spillovers	~	57 (3,626)	Finds publication bias only in published papers and only in the estimates authors consider most important.
Mookerjee (2006)	Exports and economic growth	+	76 (95)	Relationship between exports and growth remains significant but is significantly smaller when corrected for publication bias.
Nijkamp and Poot (2005)	Wage curve literature	+	17 (208)	Finds evidence of publication bias in the wage curve literature (the relationship between wages and local unemployment); adjusting for it gives an elasticity estimate of –0.07 instead of the previous consensus of –0.1.

Study	Topic	Publication bias	N (studies)	Findings
Abreu, De Groot, and Florax (2005)	Growth rate convergence	–	48 (619)	Adjusting for publication bias in the growth literature on convergence does not change estimates significantly.
Doucouliagos (2005)	Economic freedom and economic growth	+	52 (148)	Literature is tainted, but relationship persists despite publication bias.
Rose and Stanley (2005)	Trade and currency unions	+	34 (754)	Relationship persists despite publication bias. Currency union increases trade 30–90%.
Longhi, Nijkamp, and Poot (2005)	Immigration and wages	–	18 (348)	Publication bias is not found to be a major factor. The negative effect of immigration is quite small (0.1%) and varies by country.
Knell and Stix (2005)	Income elasticity of money demand	–	50 (381)	Publication bias does not significantly affect the literature. Income elasticities for narrow money range from 0.4 to 0.5 for the United States and from 1.0 to 1.3 for other countries.
Doucouliagos and Laroche (2003)	Union productivity effects	+	73 (73)	Publication bias is not considered a major issue. Negative productivity associations are found in the United Kingdom, with positive associations in the United States.
Gorg and Strobl (2001)	Multinational corporations and productivity spillovers	+	21 (25)	Study design affects results, with cross-sectional studies reporting higher coefficients than panel data studies. There is also some evidence of publication bias.
Ashenfelter, Harmon, and Oosterbeek (1999)	Returns to education	+	27 (96)	Publication bias is found, and controlling for it significantly reduces the differences between types of estimates of returns to education.

NOTES: Table shows a sample of recent papers conducting meta-analyses and testing for publication bias in certain literatures in economics. Positive evidence for publication bias indicated by +, evidence for no publication bias by –, and mixed evidence by ~.

Example 3.3 The Value of a Statistical Life and Other Economic Topics

Life may be precious, but economists don't believe it's infinitely valuable. (If it were, you'd never drive anywhere, cross a street, or leave your house, and no one would work in the logging or fishing industries, as all these activities carry some increased risk of injury and death.) Estimates for what economists call the value of a statistical life (VSL, defined as the additional cost that individuals would be willing to pay to reduce risks that in sum are expected to save one additional life) typically run in the $5–10 million range in the United States. Given that government regulations in health, environment, and transportation are frequently based on this value, accurate estimation is of great public importance, but also a source of potential publication bias, since higher values might be more likely to be noticed or affect policy.

There is growing consensus that there is substantial publication bias in this literature, leading to a strong upward bias in reported estimates (Ashenfelter and Greenstone 2004). Using the collection of 37 VSL studies in Bellavance, Dionne, and Lebeau (2009), Doucouliagos, Stanley, and Giles (2012) find that correcting for publication bias reduces the estimates of VSL by 70–80 percent from that produced by a standard meta-analysis regression, and Doucouliagos, Ioannidis, and Stanley (2017) similarly argue that estimates from statistically well-powered studies yield estimated VSLs in the range of just $1–2 million (but see Viscusi [2015] for an alternative perspective). Correcting for publication bias, the VSL also appears largely inelastic (i.e., relatively nonresponsive) to individual income, meaning that an individual's VSL increases less than proportionally with income (Doucouliagos, Stanley, and Viscusi 2014), an important finding in its own right.

Evidence for publication bias has been documented in many other economics research literatures, although not in all; for notable examples, see Longhi, Nijkamp, and Poot (2005), Knell and Stix (2005), and Roberts (2005). Table 3.3 describes a number of related publication bias studies that might be of interest to readers, but for reasons of space they are not discussed in detail here. In the most systematic approach to date (to our knowledge), Doucouliagos and Stanley (2013) carried out a meta-meta-analysis of 87 meta-analysis papers (many of which are reported in Table 3.3), finding that over half of the literatures suffer from "substantial" or "severe" publication bias, with particularly large degrees of bias in empirical macroeconomics and in empirical research based on demand theory, and somewhat less publication bias in subfields with multiple contested economic theories.

Publication Bias and Effect Size

Another important issue related to publication bias and null hypothesis testing is the reporting of the magnitude of effect sizes. Some social science literatures historically have had many articles that failed to report the magnitude of effect sizes at all, instead reporting only test statistics. (This may be changing, as some now advocate reporting effect sizes, such as Cohen's *d*, and confidence intervals; see, for example, Cumming [2014, 2017].) Even when effect size estimates are reported, interpretation may still focus only on the issue of statistical significance, and not on whether effect sizes are large or of practical importance. Even in economics, the social science with the strongest tradition of close attention to effect sizes, McCloskey and Ziliak (1996) found that 70 percent of full-length *American Economic Review* articles did not distinguish between statistical and practical significance, and follow-up reviews in 2004 and 2008 concluded that the situation had not meaningfully improved (Ziliak and McCloskey 2004, 2008).

DeLong and Lang (1992) made an early contribution addressing the issue of publication of null findings and effect sizes in economics. They show that only 78 of 276 null hypotheses tested in empirical papers published in leading economics journals at the time were not rejected—not quite as extreme as Sterling's early evidence but still a concern. However, using the uniform distribution of *p*-values under a true null hypothesis, and the startling lack of published *p*-values close to 1, they conclude it is likely that practically all economic hypotheses are indeed false. They also conclude that the null results that actually do get published in journals may also result from publication bias: a null result is arguably more interesting if it contradicts previous statistically significant results. DeLong and Lang go on to suggest that since almost all economic hypotheses are false, empirical evidence should pay more attention to practical significance and effect size rather than statistical significance alone, as is too often the case.

METHODS OF DETECTION

Consistent with the findings described above, other recent analyses have documented how widespread publication bias appears to be in social science research. Brodeur et al. (2016) collected a large sample of test statistics from papers published between 2005 and 2011, from three top journals that publish largely empirical results *(American Economic Review, Quarterly Journal of Economics,* and *Journal of Political Economy).* They propose a method to differentiate between a journal's selection of papers with statistically stronger results and inflation of significance levels by the authors themselves. First, they point out that a distribution of Z-statistics under the null hypothesis would have a monotonically decreasing probability density. (With random data and no true effect, you should expect many Z-statistics below 1 or 2, and fewer and fewer the further you go from zero.) Next, if journals prefer results with stronger significance levels, this selection could explain an increasing density. (If journals like publishing strong results, then the larger the Z-statistic, the more likely you are to be published.) However, Brodeur et al. imagined three types of tests: clearly rejected tests (yes, published), unclear tests (maybe published), and non-rejected tests (not published). If it is easier and more rewarding to push a maybe into the yes territory than to push a no into a maybe, this wouldn't match the journals' selection for uniformly higher test statistics (there would be more in the yes category than in the maybe, but also more in the no category than in the maybe). This would result in a local minimum, which is consistent with the additional presence of inflation of significance levels by authors.

Brodeur et al. (2016) document a rather disturbing two-humped density function of test statistics, with a relative dearth of reported p-values just above the standard .05-level (i.e., below a t-statistic of 1.96) cutoff for statistical significance, and greater density just below .05 (i.e., above 1.96 for t-statistics with high degrees of freedom). This is a strong indication that some combination of researcher bias and publication bias is fairly common. Using a variety of possible underlying distributions of test statistics, and estimating how selection would affect these distributions, they estimate the residual ("the valley and the echoing bump") and conclude that 10–20 percent of marginally significant empirical results in these journals are likely to be unreliable. They also document that the proportion of misreporting appears to be lower in articles without "eye-catchers" (such as asterisks in tables that denote statistical significance), as well as in papers written by more senior authors, including tenured authors.[7]

7. There is an interesting note about certain subfields having less publication bias: Brodeur et al. (2016) examined the distribution of test statistics from papers describing randomized trials. To the naked eye, the distribution appears smoother, without the two-humped pattern associated with publication bias. Unfortunately, for statistical reasons (trials cost money and are designed to be just powerful enough to reliably detect an effect, eliminating very large test statistics) they could not statistically test whether RCTs have more or less test statistic inflation. However, as practitioners of randomized trials ourselves, we believe that we are more likely to write up the results of large and expensive field trials, which often take years and hundreds of thousands of dollars to design, implement, and analyze, regardless of a statistical null finding, compared to a relatively easy-to-implement analysis of observational data.

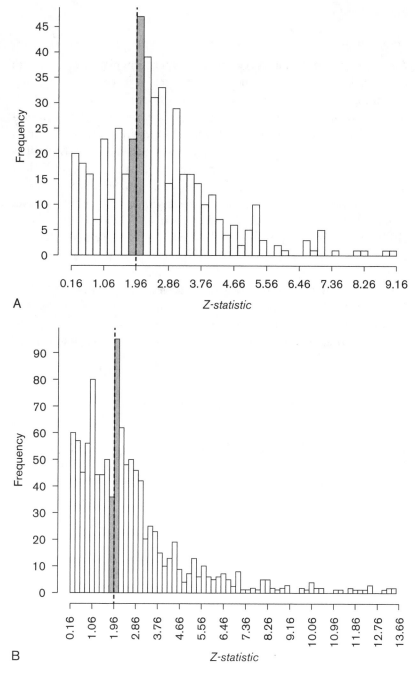

FIGURE 3.2. Collection of Z-statistics from top sociology and political science journals: histograms from (**A**) *American Sociological Review, American Journal of Sociology,* and *Sociological Quarterly* (two-tailed) and (**B**) *American Political Science Review* and *American Journal of Political Science* (two-tailed). Width of bars (0.20) approximately represents 10 percent caliper. Dotted line represents critical Z-statistic (1.96) associated with p = .05 significance level for one-tailed tests. Reprinted with permission from Gerber and Malhotra (2008a, 2008b).

Caliper Tests

A similar pattern strongly suggestive of publication bias also appears in other social science fields, including political science, sociology, and psychology, as well as in clinical medical research. Gerber and Malhotra (2008a, 2008b) used the caliper test to examine reported empirical results in several leading sociology and political science journals (Figure 3.2). The caliper test compares the frequency of test statistics just above and below the key statistical significance cutoff, which is similar in spirit to a regression discontinuity design. Specifically, Gerber and Malhotra compared the number of z-scores lying in the interval $[1.96 - X\%, 1.96]$ to the number in $(1.96, 1.96 + X\%]$, where X is the size of the caliper; they examined these differences at 5 percent, 10 percent, 15 percent, and 20 percent critical values.[8] Data from *American Sociological Review, American Journal of Sociology,* and *Sociological Quarterly* reject the hypothesis of no publication bias at the 1 in 10 million level (Gerber and Malhotra 2008a). Data from *American Political Science Review* and *American Journal of Political Science* reject the hypothesis of no publication bias at the 1 in 32 billion level (Gerber and Malhotra 2008b).

MODELS TO MEASURE OR ADDRESS PUBLICATION BIAS

Rosenthal's Fail-Safe N

In addition to caliper tests, another method to measure publication bias is to estimate the number of studies that would have to be unpublished to cast serious doubt on the results of published studies. (Note that we present this method because we find it simple and helpful for understanding. Researchers have developed tests with far better statistical properties in the intervening 40 years, so we are mentioning it only as a relatively simple thought experiment.) As noted above, Rosenthal coined the term "file drawer problem" in his 1979 paper: "The extreme view of this problem, the 'file drawer problem,' is that the journals are filled with the 5% of the studies that shows Type I errors, while the file

---

8. Note that when constructing z-scores from regression coefficients and standard errors, rounding may lead to an artificially large number of round or even integer z-scores. Brodeur et al. (2016) reconstruct original estimates by randomly redrawing numbers from a uniform interval; that is, a standard error of 0.02 could actually be anything in the interval [0.015, 0.025). This does not alter results significantly. (For those rusty on their interval notation, a parenthesis means that the interval excludes the value listed as the bound, and a square bracket means that the interval includes it.)

drawers back at the lab are filled with the 95% of the studies that show nonsignificant (e.g. $p > .05$) results." Rosenthal goes on to quantify a study's "tolerance for future null results," a method that later became known as "fail-safe N." Simply put, the idea is "to calculate the number of studies averaging null results that must be in the file drawers before the overall probability of a Type I error is brought to any desired level of significance, say, $p = .05$" (Rosenthal 1979). To calculate the number of missing studies, first sum the Z-statistics from the published studies:

$$Z_c = \frac{k\bar{Z}_k}{\sqrt{k}} = \sqrt{k}\,\bar{Z}_k \;,$$ Eqn. 3.3

where Z_c is the new combined Z, k is the number of published studies combined, and $\bar{Z}_k$ is the mean Z from the k studies. To calculate the number of missing studies averaging null results that would have to be in the file drawer to make the entire collection nonsignificant, just solve

$$1.645 = \frac{k\bar{Z}_k}{\sqrt{k + X}}$$ Eqn. 3.4

for X (for a one-tailed tailed test at $p = .05$). This can be rearranged to solve for X:

$$X = \left(\frac{k}{2.706}\right)[k(\bar{Z}_k)^2 - 2.706].$$ Eqn. 3.5

Or, if you sum the Z-statistics instead of taking the average,

$$X = \frac{(\Sigma Z)^2}{2.706} - k,$$ Eqn. 3.6

which helps make it clear that the larger the sum of observed studies and the fewer studies it takes to get that large a sum of Z-statistics, the more file-drawered studies it would take to question a body of evidence.

While this method is helpful, and quite useful in its simplicity, it is not entirely clear how any particular value of fail-safe N should make you feel about the reliability of a finding.[9] Rosenthal admitted as much, saying that in certain areas 100 to 500 unpublished studies might be reasonable, while 10 to 20 might be completely implausible in other

---

9. There are more pointed critiques of the fail-safe N test. For example, there is no test to evaluate the resulting N (Becker 2005), and the assumption that studies in the file drawer are unbiased is unlikely to be true (Scargle 2000). For a summary of these and other critiques, see Heene (2010).

fields, for instance, depending on the number of active research groups, the availability of different datasets, and the like. Rosenthal himself suggested a benchmark of $5k + 10$ studies as a conservative rule for considering a body of research safe from being a spurious result solely due to publication bias. Even then, an important assumption is that published studies are free from researcher bias, as any findings that are significant only due to researcher bias markedly increase the fail-safe N.

Hsiang, Burke, and Miguel (2014) developed a similar method in a discussion of a meta-analysis on climate change and human conflict across many different measures. In response to a claim that missing studies (due to some combination of the file drawer problem and publication bias) could derail their main estimate, the authors conducted a "stress test," finding that four out of five studies would have to be missing in order for the main effect to be rendered statistically insignificant at the traditional 5 percent level. In other words, for each published study in their case, there would need to be four others with point estimates and standard errors equal to the most negative finding in the published literature, in order to lead an analyst to reach a qualitatively different conclusion about the sign of the effect. The number of missing studies needed is similar to Rosenthal's informal benchmark above. Hsiang, Burke, and Miguel (2014) argue that the existence of so many hidden studies seems unlikely.

A Satisficing Model

Imagine a world where researchers only ever published results that were significant at the $\alpha = .05$ significance level. What could you do as a reader to restore a 5 percent rate of false positives, given that you are only able to read supposedly significant results? A model of publication bias described by McCrary, Christensen, and Fanelli (2015) suggests that you can skim the cream of the *cream* (the cream of the crop has already been skimmed by our strong publication bias). That is, if you reject the null in the top 5 percent *of* the top 5 percent of tests, then you're back where you wanted to be, with only 5 percent false positives.

This requires strong assumptions regarding the rate of non-publication of statistically nonsignificant results (i.e., a rate of zero) as well as a constant rate of publication for significant results. With these assumptions, however, readers of research studies could potentially adjust their significance threshold to "undo" the distortion caused by publication bias. For instance, instead of using $\alpha = .05$ significance level and requiring a test statistic of 1.65 or higher for rejection for a one-tailed t-test with a large sample size, a reader could take only the top 5 percent of the 5 percent ($\alpha * \alpha = .05 * .05 = .0025$) and use a more stringent t-test statistic of 2.81 ($t_{1-.0025} = t_{.9975} = 2.81$) to infer statistical significance with true 95 percent confidence.

The math behind this generalizes. The proof is complicated but goes as follows: Suppose authors calculate a test statistic, T, and plan to reject at the $1 - \alpha$ percent level a given null hypothesis if $T > c_{1-\alpha}$, for a known critical value $c_{1-\alpha}$. Let the distribution function of T under the null hypothesis be denoted $F(\cdot)$ and let $F^{-1}(\cdot)$ denote the corresponding quantile function. (They also assume that the quantile function is uniquely defined; that is, $F(\cdot)$ is strictly monotonic.) The critical value $c_{1-\alpha}$ is given by $F^{-1}(1 - \alpha)$, because then the probability of false rejection is $P(T > c_{1-\alpha}) = 1 - F(F^{-1}(1 - \alpha)) = \alpha$.

The major assumption is that authors submit statistically insignificant results with probability π_0, but submit statistically significant results with probability π_1. (In fact, to get a solution, you have to assume the worst, that $\pi_0 = 0$.) Formally, we assume that

$$P(D = 1|T) = \pi_0 1(T \leq c_{1-\alpha}) + \pi_1 1(T > c_{1-\alpha}), \quad \text{Eqn. 3.7}$$

where $D = 1$ if a study is submitted and $D = 0$ otherwise. Thus, the conditional probability of submission is a step function, with step occurring at $c_{1-\alpha}$ and with step height $\pi_1 - \pi_0$. The assumption would be unreasonable if different individuals had differing views regarding the significance level at which tests should be conducted. However, to the extent that there is a clear default of $\alpha = .05$, the assumption is reasonable.

What is important about this assumption is the constant submission rate to the right of $c_{1-\alpha}$, which is essentially why this model is "satisficing": there is a test statistic beyond which authors are likely to submit an article, and it doesn't matter how much further beyond the cutoff the result is. Clearly, in reality a researcher is probably more likely to submit a paper with test statistics in tens or hundreds than 1.97, but it may still be useful to see what happens when you model the world dichotomously.

From this, one can use Bayes' law and Eqn. 3.7 to determine the distribution function of submitted test statistics:

$$G(t) = \begin{cases} \dfrac{\pi_0}{\pi} F(t) & \text{if } t \leq c_{1-\alpha} \\ 1 - \dfrac{\pi_1}{\pi} (1 - F(t)) & \text{if } t > c_{1-\alpha} \end{cases}, \quad \text{Eqn. 3.8}$$

where π is the unconditional probability of submission: $\pi = \alpha\pi_1 + (1 - \alpha)\pi_0$. Then, by inverting $G(\cdot)$, you can derive a formula for critical values that undo size distortions induced by file drawer bias:

$$G^{-1}(1 - \alpha) = F^{-1}(1 - \alpha\pi/\pi_1) = c_{1-\alpha\pi/\pi_1}. \qquad \text{Eqn. 3.9}$$

This means that to undo the selection effect created by authors' selective submission, an editor should calculate the critical value for the relevant testing procedure, using any standard table for the test, but pretending that the desired type I error rate was $\alpha\pi/\pi_1$. Under the null hypothesis and the main assumption above, such a procedure will guarantee a testing procedure with type I error rate α (the originally intended error rate).

This conclusion would seem to be of little practical consequence, since neither π_1 nor π_0 is known. However, you can derive bounds under a worst-case scenario where $\pi_0 = 0$ (nobody submits anything statistically insignificant) and in this case, under the null hypothesis and the assumption, a test with type I error rate no more than α is obtained by utilizing a critical value of $F^{-1}(1 - \alpha^2)$.[10] This is where the test statistic of 2.81 comes in, since a t distribution with large degrees of freedom is greater than 2.81 with probability $.05^*.05 = .0025$.

Simply put, if you think that everyone is only publishing research above a certain significance threshold, square that threshold to restore the original intended error rate. If you think people only publish beyond the 5 percent significance threshold, then you should believe only the research that appears significant at the .25 percent significance threshold (t-statistic of 2.81 or greater for high degrees of freedom and one-tailed test) if you only want to make false positive errors 5 percent of the time.

But how much of published research would you be ignoring if you followed this rule? Somewhere between 20 percent and 50 percent, depending on your discipline. McCrary, Christensen, and Fanelli (2015) show a collection of meta-analyses from different disciplines and the often larger fraction of results that lie in between the standard t-statistic with high degrees of freedom cutoff and the adjusted cutoff.

Sadly, this game works only if you're the only one playing it. As soon as others adopt it, the method will break down and result in a "t-statistics arms race," so it is mostly intended for illustrative purposes.

10. Proof is as follows: since $G(\cdot)$ is increasing in π_0, an upper bound on the critical value is obtained by setting $\pi_0 = 0$. Since $G^{-1}(1 - \alpha) > F^{-1}(1 - \alpha)$, we have $1 - \alpha = G(d^*_{1-\alpha}) = 1 - \frac{1}{\alpha}(1 - F(d^*_{1-\alpha})) \leftrightarrow F(d^*_{1-\alpha}) = 1 - \alpha^2$ where $d^*_{1-\alpha} \equiv \sup_{\pi_0, \pi_1} G^{-1}(1 - \alpha)$.

As an aside, it is also possible that publication bias could work *against* rejection of the null hypothesis in some cases. For instance, within economics, in cases where there is a strong theoretical presumption among some scholars that the null hypothesis of no effect is likely to hold (e.g., in certain tests of market efficiency), the publication process could be biased by a preference among editors and referees for non-rejection of the null hypothesis of no effect. This complicates efforts to neatly characterize the nature of publication bias, and it may be an example where the assumption necessary for the method in McCrary, Christensen, and Fanelli (2015) does not hold.

CONCLUSION

Taken together, a growing body of evidence indicates that publication bias is widespread in many—if not all—fields of social science. As discussed above, there are relatively simple ways to measure publication bias that consistently show that publication bias remains a pervasive problem. There are a few relatively simple ways for readers to deal with the problem of publication bias as is, in a sort of solo effort (e.g., calculating the number of "hidden" null results that would have to exist to make existing published evidence nonsignificant). But as useful as these efforts may be, they often require strong assumptions, and they do not solve the underlying cause of the problem. We address some potential solutions that aim to do so in Chapter 5.

Stepping back, these patterns do not appear to occur by chance, but are likely to indicate some combination of selective editor (and referee) decision making, the file drawer problem alluded to above, and/or widespread specification searching, which is closely related to what Ioannidis (2005) calls bias. We examine this latter issue at length in the next chapter.

FOUR

Specification Searching

Social psychologists Brian Nosek and Matt Motyl recount an experiment in which they showed participants words printed in gray, and then provided a grayscale spectrum and asked them to identify the shade of gray that had been used (Nosek, Spies, and Motyl 2012). The study had a large sample size for experimental psychology ($N = 1,979$) and a striking finding: participants who were politically moderate more accurately identified the shade of gray than did participants with more extreme views on the political left or right. The tentative conclusion: "Political extremists perceive the world in black and white figuratively and literally."

Only the story does not end there. Instead of writing and submitting the result to a journal, the authors first directly replicated their own work. It was an easy experiment to implement. They drew a new sample of $N = 1,300$, enough to detect the original effect with a high level of statistical power (.995 at statistical significance $\alpha = .05$). Unfortunately for their publication prospects, but perhaps fortunately for science and the good name of political extremists, the statistical significance disappeared ($p = .59$) and the results became much more difficult, if not impossible, to publish.

If the authors had conducted only their first experiment, they likely could have published the result in a leading academic journal. But what if the situation were a little less (ahem) black and white, and they had conducted the replication, but in a slightly different format? What if they had looked at multiple ways to define who is politically extreme, and found that some held up while others did not? What if some statistical tests were significant and others were not? They might have been able to convince themselves that there was a good reason for the discrepancy (e.g., it was only true for Americans, or only true for younger people, or a certain definition of political extremism was the best) and still publish the result.

This type of flexibility in research—flexibility in sample size or statistical test, among many other dimensions of research degrees of freedom—and the manipulation or repeated searching through statistical or regression models unknowingly (or deliberately) until significance is obtained is often called "p-hacking," "specification searching," "data mining," "data dredging," or "fishing." (The plethora of names to describe the problem may be indicative of the widespread nature of the problem itself.)

In describing this problem, political scientists Andrew Gelman and Erik Loken (2013) say that a

> dataset can be analyzed in so many different ways (with the choices being not just what statistical test to perform but also decisions on what data to [include] or exclude, what measures to study, what interactions to consider, etc.), that very little information is provided by the statement that a study came up with a $p < .05$ result.

As mentioned in Chapter 3, while publication bias implies a distortion of a body of multiple research studies, bias is also possible within any given study. In the 1980s and '90s, expanded access to computing power and new datasets led to rising concerns that some researchers were carrying out growing numbers of analyses and selectively reporting analysis that supported preconceived notions—or that were seen as particularly interesting within the research community—and ignoring, whether consciously or not, other specifications that did not. Concerns about specification searching have only become more prominent in the decades since.

FLEXIBILITY IN COVARIATES, OR "THE CON IN ECONOMETRICS"

One of the most widely cited articles from the 1980s and '90s is Leamer's (1983) "Let's Take the Con Out of Econometrics." The paper's title already gives you a good sense of where its author stands on the credibility of most quantitative research findings in economics. Leamer discusses the promise of improved research design (namely, randomized trials) and argues that in observational research (i.e., research based on measurement conducted without a deliberately associated experiment or randomized trial), researchers ought to transparently report the entire range of estimates that result from alternative analytical decisions. Leamer's illustrative application employs data from a student's research project—namely, U.S. data from 44 states—to test for the existence of a deterrent effect of the death penalty on the murder rate. Leamer classifies variables in the data as either "important" or "doubtful" determinants of the murder rate and then runs regressions with all possible combinations of the doubtful variables. Depending on which set of control variables, or covariates, were included (choosing from among state median income, unemployment, percent population nonwhite, percent population 15–24 years old, percent male, percent urban, percent of two-parent households, and several others), the main coefficient of interest—the number of murders estimated to be prevented by each execution—ranges widely on both sides of zero, from 29 lives saved to 12 lives lost.

Leamer's recommendation that observational studies employ greater sensitivity checks, or extreme bounds analysis (EBA), was not limited to testing the effect of including different combinations of covariates. The recommendations that flowed from Leamer's EBA were controversial, at least partly because they exposed widespread weaknesses in the practice of applied economics research at the time, and perhaps partly due to Leamer's often salty (or humorous, we think) writing style. Few seemed eager to defend the state of applied economics, but many economists remained unconvinced that sensitivity analysis, as implemented with EBA, was the right solution. In "What Will Take the Con out of Econometrics," authors McAleer, Pagan, and Volker (1985), critics of EBA, sensibly considered the choice of which variables to deem important and which doubtful to be potentially just as open to abuse by researchers as the original issue of covariate inclusion.

Echoing some of Leamer's (1983) recommendations, a parallel approach to bolstering applied econometric inference focused on improved research design instead of sensitivity analysis. LaLonde (1986) applied widely used techniques from observational research to data from a randomized trial and showed that none of the methods reproduced the experimentally identified, and thus presumably closer to true, estimate.

Since the 1980s, empirical research practices in economics have changed significantly, especially with regard to improvements in research design. Angrist and Pischke (2010) make the point that improved experimental and quasi-experimental research designs have made much econometric inference more credible. However, Leamer (2010) argues that researchers retain a significant degree of flexibility in how they choose to analyze data, and that this leeway could introduce bias into their results.

This flexibility was highlighted by Lovell (1983), who shows that with a few assumptions regarding the variance of the error terms, searching for and including only the best k of c explanatory variables (k variables are included from the choice set c) means that a coefficient that appears to be significant at the level $\hat{\alpha}$ is actually only significant at the level $1 - (1 - \hat{\alpha})^{(c/k)}$. In the case of $k = 2$ included and $c = 5$ candidate variables, this risks greatly overstating significance levels, and the risk is massive if there are, say, 100 candidate variables. Lovell (1983) goes on to argue for the same sort of transparency in analysis as Leamer (1983). Denton (1985) expands on Lovell's work and shows that data mining can occur as a collective phenomenon even if each individual researcher tests only one prestated hypothesis, if there is selective reporting of statistically significant results (an argument closely related to the "file drawer" problem discussed in detail in Chapter 3).

FLEXIBILITY IN SAMPLE SIZE AND OUTCOMES

Researchers in psychology have recently conducted work similar to Leamer's. Simmons, Nelson, and Simonsohn (2011) "prove" statistically that listening to the Beatles song "When I'm Sixty-Four" made listeners a year and a half younger. How, you may wonder, did these scholars accomplish a feat that has eluded seekers of the fountain of youth since time immemorial? They conducted two experiments to investigate the possibility that listening to certain songs could change the age of the listeners. The first dealt with subjective age, by randomly assigning 30 subjects to listen to either a control song (an instrumental track) or a children's song.[1] Listeners were then asked to rank how old they felt on a scale of very young to very old. Those who listened to the children's song felt significantly older than those who listened to the control song ($p = .03$). So, according to the first experiment, people who listen to a children's song feel older. Do people who listen to a song about old age *actually become* younger? (Spoiler: No! But statistics . . .) The researchers had

---

1. We recommend you *not* listen to either song if you appreciate good music. However, if you insist, "Kalimba" by Mr. Scruff can be heard at https://www.youtube.com/watch?v=7uyF_RoXAQg, and "Hot Potato" by the Wiggles at https://www.youtube.com/watch?v=78scU6O1jYk.

10 students listen to "When I'm Sixty-Four" by the Beatles[2] and had a different 10 students listen to the control song from the first experiment. Statistical analysis showed that subjects who heard the Beatles were almost a year-and-a-half younger than the control group ($p = .04$). What the researchers don't tell you until later in the paper is that the statistical significance appears only if you include a control variable (participant's father's age), which was only one of several measures collected in the study, and that the sample size for the second experiment was not predetermined: the authors peeked at the data approximately every 10 participants until they obtained the desired result.

Perhaps it's not too surprising that researchers can manipulate a single, small experiment to show statistical significance. After all, we should expect that they would only have to run the experiment 20 times if they wanted to report a single 5 percent significant sample. Were they just (un)lucky to be able to do it with just the one sample, or does this happen all the time? The authors ran simulations to get a sense of this, creating 15,000 samples of 20 observations per treatment condition (arm) from a normal distribution with zero population difference between treatment conditions, and four possible adjustments to the data, as follows:

1. Multiple Outcomes—two correlated dependent (outcome) variables ($r = 0.5$)

2. Collecting Additional Data—increasing the sample size from 20 to 30 per treatment condition

3. Controls and Subgroup Analysis—controlling for gender or interacting gender with treatment

4. Dropping Conditions—flexibility to drop or not drop one of three treatment conditions

As shown in Table 4.1, the rate of false positives (remember, the simulations all had true zero effects) is definitely higher than the 5 percent rate you'd expect if you were interpreting p-values at face value. Combining all four approaches listed above implies that flexibility can result in false positives over 60 percent of the time. This is a staggering number, especially when you consider that the four approaches listed above have been standard practice in many social science fields.

---

2. We do recommend you listen to the Beatles, but most YouTube links to Beatles songs get taken down for copyright violation, so you'll have to find a copy yourself.

TABLE 4.1   LIKELIHOOD OF OBTAINING A FALSE POSITIVE

Researcher degrees of freedom	Samples $p < .05$
(1) Two correlated dependent variables	9.5%
(2) Adding 10 more observations per cell	7.7%
(3) Controlling for or interacting with gender	11.7%
(4) Dropping (or not) one of three treatments	12.6%
Combine 1 and 2	14.4%
Combine 1, 2, and 3	30.9%
Combine 1, 2, 3, and 4	60.7%

NOTES: Table shows the likelihood of obtaining a p-value <.05 with simulated data with no true effect. Given no true effect, we should expect 5 percent of the samples to have p-values <.05, but taking advantage of researcher degrees of freedom gives us many more low p-values.

In an abstract sense, and in the obviously false case of the effect of listening to the Beatles song, these flexible choices may feel more like *manipulations* or possibly even fraud. Certainly, for demonstration purposes, Simmons, Nelson, and Simonsohn (2011) deliberately manipulated their statistical data collection and analysis in the two experiments described above, but the point is that it seems within the realm of possibility that people subjectively feel a little older after listening to a children's song. It might also be within the realm of possibility for gender to make a difference in that effect. And exploiting some research degrees of freedom in research isn't something that only evil people do. Reasonable people often disagree about which statistical test is appropriate, and then after you've seen the results, humans are excellent at motivated reasoning: "*Of course* this model (with the significant results) is correct! That's what I thought all along." Psychologists have shown (without any data manipulation!) the prevalence of motivated reasoning in complex or ambiguous situations (Nosek, Spies, and Motyl 2012), and statistics is certainly complex and often ambiguous.

The extent and ease of this "data fishing" in analysis is also described in political science research by Humphreys, Sanchez de la Sierra, and van der Windt (2013), who use simulations to show how a multiplicity of outcome measures and of heterogeneous treatment effects (similar to subgroup analyses; see Example 4.1) can be used to generate a false positive, even with large sample sizes. The specific avenues of flexibility that they simulate are similar to those in the Simmons, Nelson, and Simonsohn (2011) exercise: multiple outcomes, adding covariates, splitting the sample to search for heterogeneous treatment effects, dichotomizing a continuous outcome variable, and selecting among the linear probability model, logit, and probit regressions. The results of their calculations and simulations are shown in Figure 4.1. For multiple outcomes, a researcher can calculate a simple probability: with k independent measures, the probability of finding a significant relation (even though there are no true relationships) at the 95 percent level is $1 - 0.95^k$. This is true regardless of sample size, so testing across 30 outcomes gives a greater than 78 percent chance of finding at least one significant relationship.

Also largely unrelated to sample size is testing for multiple heterogeneous treatment effects. If you test 100 heterogeneous treatment effects (not out of the question for individual surveys that can last a few hours and ask several hundred questions) you have more than a 90 percent chance of finding something statistically significant. Less extreme, testing only 10 heterogeneous treatments results in a more than 40 percent chance of finding something significant. Results are only slightly less alarming if the researcher is constrained to dividing the sample in half instead of any arbitrary division along the lines of the heterogeneous outcome. (That is, if the sample is half women and half men, we're almost, though not quite, as likely to find a significant heterogeneous treatment effect by gender as we are when we can arbitrarily split the sample into "old" and "young" groups, defined how we wish.) For more information on subgroup analysis, see Example 4.1.

As Leamer (1983) established, adding covariates can also increase a researcher's odds of finding a significant relationship. This ability is much easier with smaller ($N < 50$) samples, where researchers can have 50 percent or higher likelihoods of finding a significant effect. The general pattern is similar whether researchers are adding a single covariate or multiple covariates (up to $N - 3$, nearly exhausting the degrees of freedom in the analysis) but adding multiple covariates produces even higher odds of finding a false positive. As one might expect, having more potential cut points where a researcher can choose to dichotomize an outcome variable increases the odds of finding a false positive. The one bright spot in the simulations by Humphreys, Sanchez de la Sierra, and van der Windt (2013) is that choosing between the linear probability model, logistic, and probit regressions provides relatively little opportunity to game the system.[3]

---

3. In the authors' experience, many economists seem to prefer reporting estimates from linear probability models for binary outcomes despite their obvious statistical issues, perhaps because of their ease of interpretation. So, at least that potential problem of selectively choosing logistic or probit models instead is not, apparently, a major issue.

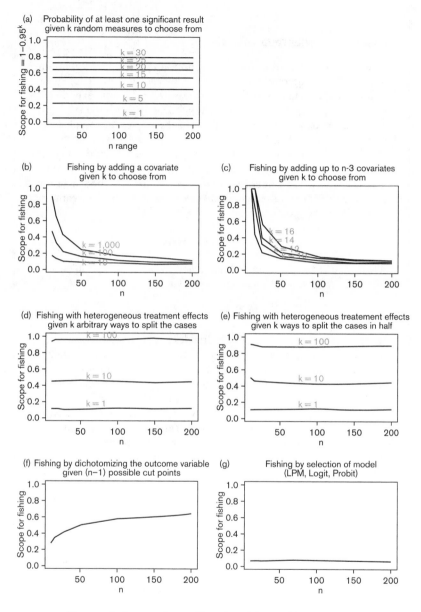

FIGURE 4.1. Chances that researchers will produce false positives given different ways of altering analysis plans *ex post*. Each point in panels **b, d, e, f,** and **g** is based on 4,000 simulations. Points in panel **c** are based on 1,450 simulations for $k = 10, 12$, and 14, and 514 simulations for $k = 16$. Data for panel **a** are calculated, not simulated. Reprinted with permission from Humphreys, Sanchez de la Sierra, and van der Windt (2013).

Example 4.1 Subgroup Analysis

One area of analytical flexibility that appears particularly important in practice is subgroup analysis. This is the practice of dividing the sample by some characteristic that is measured before the experiment or study (e.g., age, gender, height, weight, or socioeconomic status) and then testing for an effect in only one subgroup of the sample (e.g., only the women). This is very similar to what is referred to as "treatment effect heterogeneity," which is testing for a difference in effect size between subgroups. In practice, heterogeneity tests are often conducted by adding an interaction term to a regression model. In the situation of a randomized controlled experiment with one treatment and one control group, instead of

$$y_i = \alpha + \beta_1 T_i + \epsilon_i, \qquad\qquad 4.1$$

where T_i is a binary treatment status indicator, y_i is the outcome of interest, and ϵ_i is the idiosyncratic error, we run

$$y_i = \alpha + \beta_1 T_i + \beta_2 X_i + \beta_3 X_i T_i + \epsilon_i, \qquad\qquad 4.2$$

where X_i is one of any number of variables measured before the experiment. Often researchers will transform the X_i to measures of standard deviations from the mean, which makes the coefficient on treatment (β_1) stable across the two different equations, and comparison simpler.

In many cases, there are multiple distinct interaction effects that could plausibly be justified by theory, and current datasets have a growing richness of potential covariates. Yet it is rare for applied studies to mention how many different interaction effects were tested, increasing the risk that only statistically significant false positives are reported. Researchers can also easily test for double or triple interactions, compounding the problem. Perhaps the effect is significant for low-income white men, or wealthy black women, or whatever combination you can imagine.

While, to our knowledge, there are few systematic treatments of this issue in the social sciences, there has been extensive discussion of this issue within medical research, where the use of non-prespecified subgroup analysis is strongly frowned upon. The FDA does not use subgroup analysis in its drug approval decisions (Maggioni et al. 2007). An oft-repeated, and humorous, case comes from a trial of aspirin and streptokinase use after heart attacks (myocardial infarction) conducted in a large number of patients ($N = 17,187$; Isis-2 Collaborative Group 1988). Aspirin and streptokinase were found to be quite beneficial, with strong statistical results ($p < .00001$)—except for patients born under Libra and Gemini, for whom there was a harmful (but not statistically significant) effect! The authors included the zodiac subgroup analysis because journal editors had suggested that 40 subgroups be analyzed, and the authors relented under the condition that they could include a few subgroups of their own choosing to demonstrate the unreliability of such analysis (Schulz and Grimes 2005).

Simmons, Nelson, and Simonsohn (2011) propose a few requirements for authors to help reduce the flexibility:

1. Authors must decide the rule for terminating data collection before data collection begins and report this rule in the article.

2. Authors must list all variables collected in a study.

3. Authors must report all experimental conditions, including failed manipulations.

4. If observations are eliminated, authors must also report what the statistical results are if those observations are included.

5. If an analysis includes a covariate, authors must report the statistical results of the analysis without the covariate.

These suggestions are a good start, and they make a lot of sense for typical psychology or behavioral economics lab experiments in which study participants engage in a short randomized activity, with one or two randomized treatment conditions.[4] However, for longer surveys, or for observational work, a more thorough statement may be necessary. Imagine, for example, a study using extremely detailed surveys, such as the U.S. General Social Survey, the international Demographic and Health Surveys, or the American Community Survey. Sharing the survey documentation (it's already available to the public online in all of these cases) would obey the letter of the law in regard to recommendation 3

---

4. Simmons and colleagues originally suggested six rules, the additional one being a minimum-sample-size rule, but they now clearly acknowledge that the minimum sample size they suggested (20 per cell) was too low, noting that "an obvious effect like, 'Smokers think that smoking is less likely to result in death than do non-smokers' is not consistently detectable with fewer than 150 per cell (Simmons et al., 2013). Second, we would not advocate for a strict sample size cutoff, but rather emphasize that samples smaller than these are usually diagnostic of insufficient power. Thus, we would suggest that you should assume that a study with fewer than 50 per cell is underpowered unless there is evidence to the contrary" (Simmons, Nelson, and Simonsohn 2018).

above, but to be useful, a reader would need to know more than just the fact that the survey contains hundreds of questions and variables. Which of these variables did the authors look at? Which were tested, with which statistical models and functional forms?

To address these concerns, Humphreys, Sanchez de la Sierra, and van der Windt (2013) describe what they call a "mock report approach." For a project where they evaluated a large, randomized development-aid project in the Democratic Republic of Congo, the authors simulated data before they had any real data, and attempted to exactly define their entire analysis, writing code to define variables and conduct analysis with a masked version of their treatment variable. This code and analysis were shared with implementation and academic partners before unmasking the treatment variable and conducting the real analysis. In this case there is no ambiguity about what the authors' intentions were, what analyses they ran, and ultimately (once the data comes in) what the key findings are. This proposal leads us directly to our next two chapters. Study registrations have been adopted and are rapidly growing in the social sciences, and these registrations encourage researchers to submit mock reports that reduce researcher flexibility. We call these "pre-analysis plans," the subject of Chapter 6.

The greater use of extra robustness checks in applied research is designed to limit the extent of specification searching and represents a shift in the direction proposed by Leamer (1983), but it is unclear how effective these changes will be in reducing bias in practice. This remains a critical open question. As noted in Chapter 3, Brodeur et al.'s (2016) analysis of 641 recent articles from three top economics journals shows a disturbing two-humped distribution of p-values, with relatively few p-values between .10 and .25 and far more just below .05, despite the adoption of practices at least partially in line with Leamer's recommendations. Brodeur et al.'s analysis also explores the correlates behind this pattern, finding that this apparent misallocation of p-values just below the accepted statistical significance level was less pronounced for articles written by tenured authors, and tentatively less pronounced among studies based on randomized controlled trials, suggesting that improved research design itself may partially constrain data mining. However, Brodeur et al. did not detect any discernible differences in the pattern based on whether the authors had publicly posted the study's replication data in the journal's public archive, another tool that could conceivably constrain data mining.

THE *P*-CURVE

Psychologists have recently developed a useful tool called the "*p*-curve" that helps observers characterize the extent of likely bias in a research literature. The *p*-curve does something simple: it describes the density of reported *p*-values in a literature, taking advantage of the fact that if the null hypothesis were true (i.e., no effect), *p*-values should be uniformly distributed between 0 and 1 (Simonsohn, Nelson, and Simmons 2014a). Intuitively, under the null of no effect, a *p*-value <.08 should occur 8 percent of the time, a *p*-value <.07 should occur 7 percent of the time, and so on; therefore, a *p*-value between .07 and .08, or within any other .01-wide interval, should occur roughly 1 percent of the time. In the case of true nonzero effects, the distribution of *p*-values should be right skewed (with a decreasing density), with more low values (.01) than higher values (.04) (Hung et al. 1997). By contrast, in bodies of empirical literature that suffer from specification searching (or "*p*-hacking," in the authors' terminology), in which researchers evaluate significance as they collect data and only report results with statistically significant effects, the distribution of *p*-values would be left skewed (assuming that researchers stop searching across specifications or collecting data once the desired level of significance is achieved). Figure 4.2 shows three simulations: (A) a null effect that was hacked by adding observations if the results were not significant, (B) a null effect honestly reported with essentially a flat curve, and (C) a true strong effect.

A researcher can conduct multiple tests of whether a *p*-curve is right or left skewed. Tests of right or left skew are analogous, but we describe everything as a test for right skew, which is evidence of evidential (i.e., real) value. A low *p*-value on these tests indicates evidence of evidential value. Perhaps the simplest test is to divide *p*-values into high ($p > .025$) and low ($p < .025$) bins and test the observed fraction of high *p*-values using a binomial test (under the null, one would expect half the *p*-values to be in the high bin). A more efficient test is to first construct a "*pp*-value," or *p*-value of the *p*-value—the probability of observing a significant *p*-value at least as extreme if the null were true. (Using normal test statistics that haven't been binned as above, this conditional probability is just $p/.05$.) Then aggregate the *pp*-values in a literature with Stouffer's method and test for skew with a Z-test. Large test statistics indicate a right skew and significant evidential value.

Stouffer's method is a way to aggregate test statistics, similar to Fisher's method, but less sensitive to a few extreme tests statistics. With individual

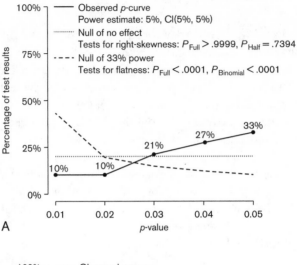

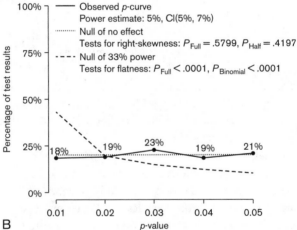

FIGURE 4.2. Examples of *p*-curves, showing the density of significant (α<.05) *p*-values (solid lines) from three simulations. **(A)** A true zero effect that is hacked and has a left skew: more observations are added 10 at a time if there are nonsignificant results. The observed *p*-curve includes 92 statistically significant (*p* < .05) results, of which 25 are *p* < .025. There were no nonsignificant results entered. **(B)** A true zero effect honestly reported, with essentially a flat, or uniform, density. The observed *p*-curve includes 272 statistically significant (*p* < .05) results, of which 130 are *p* < .025. There were no nonsignificant results entered.

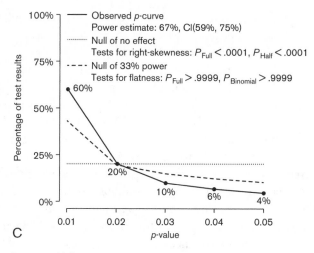

FIGURE 4.2. *(continued)* **(C)** A right skew, the result of the *p*-values from a true effect. The observed *p*-curve includes 124 statistically significant (*p* < .05) results, of which 107 are *p* < .025. There were no nonsignificant results entered.

test statistics from the normal distribution Z_i, the sum divided by the square root of the number of tests is standard normally distributed:

$$Z \sim \frac{\sum_{i=1}^{k} Z_i}{\sqrt{k}}.$$ Eqn. 4.1

Fisher's method uses *p*-values instead of *Z*-statistics. The sum of the natural log of a set of *k* *p*-values is distributed χ^2:

$$\chi_{2k}^2 = -2\sum_{i=1}^{k} \ln(p_i).$$ Eqn. 4.2

The *p*-curve originally used Fisher's method of combining tests instead of Stouffer's method. This change was described in Simonsohn, Simmons, and Nelson (2015a). Readers curious about the statistics should also see Whitlock (2005).

The authors also suggest a test of comparing whether a *p*-curve is flatter than the curve that would result if studies were (under)powered at 33 percent, and interpret a *p*-curve that is significantly flatter or left skewed than this as largely lacking in evidential value (i.e., is unlikely to contain reliable information on the true underlying relationship).

The *p*-curve can also be used to correct effect size estimates in literatures suffering from publication bias; corrected estimates of the "choice overload" literature exhibit a change in direction from standard published estimates (Simonsohn, Nelson, and Simmons 2014b).[5]

One application of the *p*-curve has been to analyze the collection of research articles on the "power pose," an influential idea famously associated with a Harvard Business School psychologist, Professor Amy Cuddy. It has spread widely through one of the most-watched TED talks ever—between the TED website and YouTube, the video has been watched 50 million times as of February 2017.[6] Cuddy also has a best-selling book on the subject (Cuddy 2015) and apparently presents on her research at lucrative corporate speaking engagements as well.[7]

The idea behind the power pose is simple: humans (and animals) tend to adopt expansive, open postures to express power. Think of a sprinter with arms raised wide in victory, a confident person with hands on hips commanding an audience, or a peacock fanning his tail feathers. But we adopt closed or contracting positions when powerless (a human with arms or legs crossed, or a turtle retracting inside its shell). But is this correlation or causation? And can adopting a power pose actually improve one's performance or status in some way? Research published in 2010 said yes: randomly assign study participants to adopt high-power nonverbal displays for two minutes, and you see higher testosterone (which is associated with physical strength), less cortisol (a sign of stress), more risk tolerance, and higher self-reported feelings of power than in the participants assigned to low-power nonverbal displays (Carney, Cuddy, and Yap 2010).

The results are irresistible and were picked up widely in popular media. Cuddy specifically encourages those with a lack of resources or low hierarchical rank to adopt the practice as a way to move up the ladder. For those with no power, just "their bodies, privacy, and two minutes . . . can significantly change the outcomes of their life" (Cuddy 2012, at 20:30). Or with slightly less bombast: "Thus, a simple 2-min power-pose manipulation was enough to significantly alter the physiological, mental, and feeling states of our participants. The implications of these results for everyday life are substantial" (Carney, Cuddy, and Yap 2010, p. 1366).

---

5. For an online implementation of the *p*-curve, see http://p-curve.com. Also see a discussion of the robustness of the test in Ulrich and Miller (2015) and Simonsohn, Simmons, and Nelson (2015a).

6. See https://www.youtube.com/watch?v=Ks-_Mh1QhMc.

7. The *New York Times Magazine* published a long article (Dominus 2017) about the sometimes personal nature and repercussions of the statistical back-and-forth that we describe.

But is the effect real? The original paper used just 42 participants, which is very much in the false-positive danger zone if the true effect size is small. Another experiment that attempted to repeat a similar, but not identical, experiment with 200 participants confirmed the self-reported feelings of power but not the hormonal changes (Ranehill et al. 2015). Critical blog posts by respected academics started to appear (Simmons and Simonsohn 2015; Gelman and Fung 2016), but perhaps the most attention was gained when one of the authors of the original paper, Professor Dana Carney of UC Berkeley, posted a two-page statement on her website. The statement reads, in part: "As evidence has come in over these past 2+ years, my views have updated to reflect the evidence. As such, *I do not believe that 'power pose' effects are real*" (emphasis in original).

First of all, we enthusiastically applaud Carney for updating her beliefs on the basis of new evidence! Second, what is this new evidence? Some of it is provided by Simmons and Simonsohn in a p-curve analysis of the power pose (Simmons and Simonsohn 2017). They make the data from 33 power pose studies on the p-curve available publicly, and run them through the p-curve analysis described above.[8] Each of the 33 studies appears to back up the idea of power posing—indeed, the list of studies comes from Carney, Cuddy, and Yap (2015), a response by the original authors to the failure to replicate in Ranehill et al. (2015)—but after using the p-curve, the authors conclude that the distribution of p-values from the studies is indistinguishable from what one would expect if the true effect of power poses were zero and selective reporting were the main driving force in study publication.

Not all of the 33 studies reported the necessary statistical tests, and the p-curve can only use significant ($p < .05$) tests, so the final sample is 24 p-values from 24 studies. The resulting p-curve is shown in Figure 4.3. The solid line indicates the density of the p-values from the 24 included tests of power pose effects. The major takeaway is that the p-curve is basically flat. If there were a true effect, over several studies we would be more likely to observe additional p-values in the 0.01 to 0.02 range, compared to higher (.04 to .05) p-values, so the distribution would be right skewed. This is evidently not the case.

Eyeballing lines is not enough, but there are also formal statistical approaches to assess this. The results, from the p-curve online app, are shown in Table 4.2. In the left column is a simple binomial test that compares the fraction of p-values less than .025 to the fraction you would

8. See https://osf.io/ujpyn/.

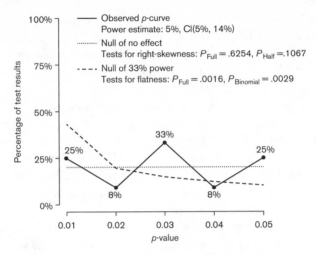

FIGURE 4.3. The *p*-curve of "power pose" studies. Figure generated by the authors using p-curve.com, app version 4.051. Original sample is 33 studies mentioned in Carney, Cuddy, and Yap (2015), with data from Simmons and Simonsohn (2017), available at https://osf.io/ujpyn/. The flat nature of the *p*-values is consistent with a lack of evidential value in the relevant studies.

expect if there is no effect. Forty-two percent of the *p*-values are less than .025; with no effect you would always expect 50 percent (since we're considering only *p*-values between 0 and .05, and they would be uniformly distributed under the null, as described above). The results indicate that the body of power pose studies largely lacks evidential value.

The right column reports *pp*-values for each test (the probability of at least as extreme a *p*-value, given that the *p*-value is <.05, standard normalized). These 24 values are summed and divided by the square root of the number of tests, per Stouffer's method, which produces a Z-statistic and corresponding *p*-value. Again, a look at the entire distribution of the *p*-curve indicates that the power pose studies largely lack evidential value. Lastly, the authors test what value of statistical power (in the individual studies) between 5 percent and 99 percent most closely reproduces that observed *p*-curve; the answer comes back as close to the minimum as possible: 5 percent power. In other words, the studies that make up this research literature are woefully underpowered, which greatly increases the risk of reported false positives.

The debate continues, however. A more recent paper (Cuddy, Schultz, and Fosse 2018) applies the *p*-curve to 21 additional (55 total) papers and

TABLE 4.2 STATISTICAL TESTS OF *p*-CURVE OF "POWER POSE" STUDIES

	Binomial test (share of results *p < .025*)	Continuous test (*pp* value)	
		Full p-curve (p < .05)	*Half p-curve (p < .025)*
(1) Studies contain evidential value (right skew)	*p* = .8463	Z = 0.32, *p* = .6254	Z = –1.24, *p* = .1067
(2) Studies' evidential value, if any, is inadequate (flatter than 33% power)	*p* = .0029	Z = –2.95, *p* = .0016	Test not needed
Power of tests included in *p*-curve (correcting for selective reporting)	Statistical power Estimate: 5% 90% confidence interval: [5%, 14%]		

NOTES: A simple binomial test is shown that compares the fraction of *p*-values <.025 to the fraction expected if there is no effect; the results indicate that the body of "power pose" studies largely lack evidential value. Also shown are aggregate *pp* values for each test (the probability of at least as extreme a *p*-value, given that the *p*-value is <.05, standard normalized); the 24 *pp* values were summed and divided by the square root of the number of tests, using Stouffer's method, which produces the Z-statistics and corresponding *p*-values shown.

finds evidential value in support of power posing. Simmons, Nelson, and Simonsohn (2017) take issue with the selection of the additional papers, stating that (1) *p*-curves need a clear, reproducible, prespecified paper selection rule; (2) authors should follow guidelines from their original paper (Simonsohn, Nelson, and Simmons 2014a) regarding which test from each paper to include; and (3) outliers need to be carefully scrutinized, since they exert heavy influence on the *p*-curve. Simmons, Nelson, and Simonsohn (2017) examine four outliers in detail, find serious issues (e.g., a paper with an implausibly large 24-point average effect on a 24-point scale), and conclude that the expanded 55-paper *p*-curve is not valid evidence in support of power posing. As with any meta-analysis (see Chapter 5), authors need to be transparent (and ideally prespecified) with regard to which studies will be included in their *p*-curve analysis.

CONCLUSION

In simulations of data with zero true effects, researchers across social science disciplines have shown that you can easily get a much higher rate of false positives than the 5 percent you should expect under ideal conditions. Ideal conditions are rarely met, since researchers have significant flexibility in which covariates to include, how large a sample to collect, and how to define variables. The problem is not just a theoretical one from simulations: new tools like the p-curve are allowing scholars to reassess the reliability of existing bodies of findings, and the results don't look very good for the power pose. We can't be sure exactly which avenues of flexibility the power pose researchers used to publish so many studies with relatively flimsy evidence, but it seems that they did so, and it is likely that there are many other such subliteratures across fields that suffer from similar problems. We should note that we are absolutely *not* casting aspersions regarding the intentions of the individual researchers involved in the power pose debate, and we're sorry if we seem to be singling them out. We give them the benefit of the doubt and assume only that they are human and subject to the same motivated reasoning as most other *homo sapiens,* scholars included (not all of us are emotionless Vulcans).

Where does that leave us? We know researchers have a lot of flexibility in their research, and this can lead to bias in individual studies, and in entire research literatures. The p-curve is one way to detect whether researchers have taken advantage of this flexibility after the fact. In the next several chapters, we begin to discuss ways to avoid, detect, and control for abuse of this flexibility beforehand, starting with approaches to using all available research evidence.

PART THREE

Solutions

FIVE

Using All Evidence

Registration and Meta-analysis

This chapter describes how the research community can systematically collect, organize, and analyze a body of research work. Employing all research on a topic is an important way to limit selective reporting, such as the cherry-picking of favorable findings, which could lead to biased conclusions (as detailed in Chapter 3 on publication bias).

The traditional alternative to meta-analysis is the narrative literature review, but it has important limitations. For one, literature reviews are often quite subjective in practice, allowing different scholars to reach starkly divergent conclusions even when focusing on the same research evidence base, heightening concerns about researcher bias. Succinctly characterizing an entire literature in narrative form also becomes difficult (if not impossible) as the number of underlying studies grows, making objective statistical analysis particularly valuable.

But how can we know that we are capturing all relevant research when carrying out a meta-analysis? Study registries are one important way for scholars to discover existing research on a topic, even if the work doesn't end up being published in a journal.

The first part of this chapter lays out the origins of these registries in medical research, as well as their recent expansion in the social sciences. The second part lays out how we can systematically combine the information contained in registries and published research in a statistical sense through the use of meta-analysis methods.

This chapter marks a transition from the first half of this book—which is mainly devoted to documenting and understanding problems in social science research—to the second half, where the focus is on solutions and improved practices. Using all available evidence and combining it in the right way can be an important first step forward.

THE ORIGINS OF STUDY REGISTRATION

A basic definition of registration is to publicly declare research that one plans on conducting. This would ideally be done in a public registry designed to accept registrations in the given research discipline, and would take place before the analysis begins, although (as we discuss below) study registration can be useful even if it's done after a study has been completed.

The purpose of a study registry is to make public key details of planned, current, and completed research studies to the broader community of scholars, policymakers, and the population at large. These key study details include the central research hypotheses to be examined, the nature of the research design and the data used to test the hypotheses, the intervention (if applicable), and other study characteristics that are important for the interpretation of results, such as information on the study population or setting, and ethics approvals for the protection of human subjects. Registries typically also allow researchers to later update information about summary results and journal publications that have resulted from the research. That said, a potentially big upside of registries is the dissemination of information about studies that are not published (or not *yet* published) in journals.

Taken together, study registries aim to be one-stop shops for information on research projects. Requiring scholars to register their hypotheses and carefully describe their research could have a range of potential benefits, including making the full body of work more visible (and searchable) to the scholarly community and comprehensible to non-researchers, and perhaps even improving the quality of the underlying research.

Registration of randomized trials has achieved widespread adoption in medicine but is still relatively new to the social sciences. After the U.S. Congress passed a law requiring the creation of a registry for FDA-regulated trials in 1997 (namely, the Food and Drug Administration Modernization Act of 1997), the National Institutes of Health created the ClinicalTrials.gov site in 2000. Building on this momentum, the International Committee of Medical Journal Editors (ICMJE), a collection of editors at top medical journals, instituted a common policy of publishing only registered trials starting in 2005 (De Angelis et al. 2004). The policy has spread to other journals, and clinical trial registration was rapidly adopted by researchers (Laine et al. 2007). Several other countries and organizations have their own national trial registries (including the European Union Clinical Trial Register, the Pan-African Clinical Trials Registry, etc.), and the World Health Organization created the International Clinical Trials Registry Platform (ICTRP) in 2007 to automatically gather all this information in a single place.

A profoundly important example of the potential benefits of trial registries is presented in Turner et al. (2008), which details the publication rates of studies related to the phase 2 and phase 3 clinical trials for 12 FDA-approved antidepressants (see also Kirsch et al. 2008; Ioannidis 2008). The FDA makes an internal decision about whether the trial results provide evidence of a positive impact of the drug. The authors collected information on the FDA decision for each trial—some of which was available on the FDA website, while some required Freedom of Information Act requests—as well as information on eventual article publication from a variety of sources, including PubMed, the Cochrane Central Register of Controlled Trials, and via certified mail to trial sponsors. The outcome is perhaps what only the most hardened cynic would expect: essentially all the trials with positive results were published in journals, about 50 percent of studies with questionable results were published, and a majority of the studies with negative results (i.e., no positive impact of the drug) were unpublished at least four years after the study was completed. Worse, many of the negative results that were published were presented in a way that, according to Turner et al. (2008), conveyed a positive outcome. Figure 5.1 shows the drastically different rates of publication, and the correspondingly large degree of publication bias. Simply put, the published literature alone provides a highly misleading perspective on the effectiveness of these drugs.

A similar test was conducted by Easterbrook et al. (1991), who reviewed the universe of protocols submitted to the Central Oxford Research Ethics Committee (akin to an institutional review board in the United States), including both experimental and nonexperimental studies, and found significantly higher publication rates for tests that yield statistically significant results. This finding is a precursor to the results of Franco, Malhotra, and Simonovits (2014) on publication bias in the social sciences (see Chapter 3). Of course, for the sort of exercise described in Turner et al. (2008), Easterbrook et al. (1991), and Franco, Malhotra, and Simonovits (2014) to be possible, researchers either need

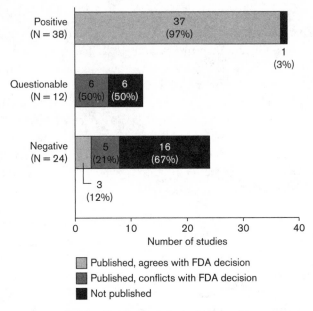

FIGURE 5.1. Publication bias in clinical trials of antidepressants (*N* = 74 studies). Reprinted with permission from Turner et al. (2008).

unique access to unpublished results through an institutional database, and/or must go to great lengths to contact many individual researchers, something that is often impractical, especially for relatively large bodies of research.

ClinicalTrials.gov requires full reporting of results even for unpublished trials for certain classes of FDA trials, but it appears that these guidelines are often not followed—probably due, in part, to a lack of enforcement.[1] Hartung et al. (2014) raised concerns about these discrepancies between reporting of outcomes in published papers and in the ClinicalTrials.gov database: up to 20 percent of studies had discrepancies in primary outcomes, and up to 33 percent had some discrepancies

---

1. Prayle, Hurley, and Smyth (2012) found that compliance with results reporting, even among those required to do so, was fairly low (22 percent). The U.S. Department of Health and Human Services and the National Institutes of Health took steps in November 2014 to seek public comment and expand the amount of results reporting required (for more information, see http://www.nih.gov/news/health/nov2014/od-19.htm). The new rules took effect on January 18, 2017 (see https://clinicaltrials.gov/ct2/manage-recs/fdaaa).

in the reporting of adverse events (such as participant side effects), so there is definitely room for improvement even in the largest and longest-standing study registries.

There remain other concerns with medical trial registration. For one, not all relevant journals have adopted the ICMJE policy mentioned above, so while registration is widespread, complete enforcement of the norm is elusive. For instance, Mathieu et al. (2009) examined trials related to three medical conditions and found that only 46 percent of studies were registered before the end of the trial with primary outcomes clearly specified. Even among those trials adequately registered, 31 percent showed some discrepancies between registered and published outcomes, with bias in favor of statistically significant variable definitions, suggesting some degree of selective reporting by researchers.

To date, most study registration efforts have been limited to randomized control trials, as opposed to observational data. While we believe that registering all types of analysis in the social sciences should be accepted and even encouraged, there are some obvious concerns to registering observational and nonprospective work, not least of which is the inability of other scholars to verify that study registration preceded the analysis. We discuss this central issue around the ideal scope for study registration in greater detail in Chapter 6, and there is a helpful discussion of the pros and cons of observational study registration in Dal-Ré et al. (2014).

The discussion above suggests that clinical trial registration has not eliminated all underreporting of null results, or other forms of publication bias and specification searching. Even so, registration has been a major step forward for research transparency in medical research. The existence of trial registries has allowed the medical research community to quantify the extent of publication bias and specification searching, and over time this may help to constrain inappropriate practices. The adoption of an almost universal standard by journals in favor of clinical trial registration has eliminated the most extreme forms of self-serving publication decisions by pharmaceutical companies and associated researchers. Major registries like ClinicalTrials.gov have helped thousands of scholars locate studies that are delayed in publication or that were never published, helping to fill in gaps in the literature and thus resolve some of the problems discussed in Chapter 3.

The success of study registration in medical research, even if partial, has more recently inspired similar changes in the organization of social science research, and we next discuss this progress.

SOCIAL SCIENCE STUDY REGISTRIES

Registries in the social sciences are newer but are growing ever more popular (for a brief overview of major medical and social science registries, see Table 5.1). To our knowledge, the move toward social science study registration began when the Abdul Latif Jameel Poverty Action Lab at MIT began hosting a hypothesis registry for randomized control trials in 2009. This pioneering effort was superseded in 2013 by the American Economic Association (AEA) trial registry (www.socials-cienceregistry.org). While it is too soon to fully comprehend its impact on research practices, the AEA registry is already being used by many empirical researchers: since 2013, over 2,100 studies conducted in more than 100 countries have been registered, and the pace of registrations continues to rise rapidly (Figure 5.2). A review of the projects currently included in the registry suggests that there are a particularly large number of development economics studies, which is perhaps not surprising given the widespread use of field experimental methods in that subfield.

Several other social science registries have recently been created in addition to the AEA registry, including the Registry for International Development Impact Evaluations (RIDIE, http://ridie.3ieimpact.org), launched in September 2013 by the International Initiative for Impact Evaluation (3ie) (Dahl Rasmussen, Malchow-Møller, and Barnebeck Andersen 2011), and the Evidence in Governance and Politics (EGAP) registry, also created in 2013. These are currently smaller in terms of the volume of registered studies, but they are growing. The EGAP registry is open to research other than randomized trials and is described as "an unsupervised stopgap function to store designs until the creation of a general registry for social science research. The EGAP registry focuses on designs for experiments and observational studies in governance and politics." Meanwhile, the site AsPredicted.org provides a mechanism for preregistration that emphasizes simplicity: researchers only need to fill out nine questions and the result is a single page.

The Center for Open Science's Open Science Framework (OSF, https://osf.io) accommodates the registration of essentially any study or research document by allowing users to create a frozen time-stamped web URL with associated digital object identifier (DOI) for any uploaded materials (we discuss it as a way of archiving data in Chapter 10). Several popular data and code storage options (including Dropbox, Dataverse, and GitHub) can also be synced with the OSF and its storage,

TABLE 5.1 MAJOR MEDICAL AND SOCIAL SCIENCE REGISTRIES

Registry	Sponsor	Year started	Study design	Field	Studies registered as of December 2018	Notes
ClinicalTrials.gov	National Institutes of Health	2000	Randomized controlled trial	Medicine	292,000+	Major U.S. medical registry
International Clinical Trials Registry Platform	World Health Organization	2007	Randomized controlled trial	Medicine	462,000+	Not a registry per se; collects data from registries worldwide, including ClinicalTrials.gov
EGAP Design Registry	Experiments in Governance and Politics	2012	Any	Political science	1,000+	
AEA RCT Registry (SocialScienceReg- istry.org)	American Economic Association	2013	Randomized controlled trial	Economics	2,100+	
Open Science Framework	Center for Open Science	2013	Any	Any	25,000+	

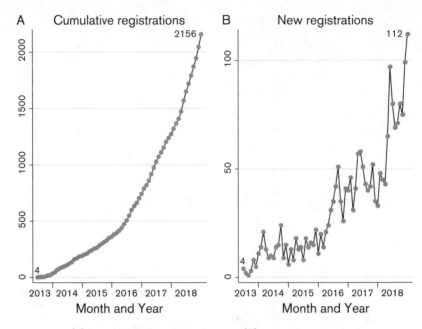

FIGURE 5.2. (**A**) Cumulative trial registrations and (**B**) new registrations in the American Economic Association Trial Registry, May 2013 to November 2018 (http://socialscienceregistry.org). Figure available in public domain: http://dx.doi.org/10.7910/DVN/FUO7FC.

creating a flexible way for researchers to register or share their research and materials with the research community, as well as to collaborate with coauthors. As of December 2018, over 25,000 public registrations had been created on OSF since the service launched in 2013.

To sum up, study registration was unknown less than a decade ago but has rapidly become part of the fabric of social science research practice. But what do we do with research study estimates once we have successfully retrieved them from published articles, a study registry, or other sources? That is the focus of the next section.

META-ANALYSIS

Meta-analysis is the systematic combination of data or estimates across studies. There are many ways to do this, with varying degrees of sophistication. Even basic approaches can constitute a large improvement over just "eye-balling" dozens of estimates in a research literature in an attempt to discern patterns, or trying to roughly summarize a set of findings in a literature review.

We lay out the basic concepts of meta-analysis here; for more detailed discussion of the large statistical literature on this topic, refer to Borenstein et al. (2009) and Cooper, Hedges, and Valentine (2009). We first consider the process of assembling estimates from different studies. Then we discuss procedures for combining them and formally considering heterogeneity across estimates.

Selecting Studies

The first step in a meta-analysis is to include all relevant studies for consideration (Stanley 2001). This can be done by searching journal publications for certain keywords, of course, as well as sometimes combing through existing survey articles or annual reviews on the topic. But this is also where study registries come in: to the extent that most relevant studies are registered—as has quickly become the case for clinical trials, for instance, and may soon be routine in development economics and other social science subfields—an appropriate search of the study registry could augment the set of studies being considered.

In some cases, deciding what constitutes a body of studies may be straightforward. Imagine a coordinated body of 10 clinical trials with the exact same treatment—say, injection with the same Ebola vaccine—and a single common outcome (perhaps individual survival one year later). In many settings, however, this process of extracting relevant estimates is one of the most difficult and time-consuming parts of conducting a meta-analysis. Different studies may use slightly divergent measures of a common concept, allowing for some scholarly discretion regarding which measures are "close enough" to be included.

This discretion has led to some examples of contemporaneous meta-analyses on the same topic finding opposite conclusions. "The meta-analyses were supposed to provide the meta-solution," writes James Tabery (2014, p. 87) about one such example from psychiatric genetics, "but instead they only elevated it to a meta-problem." The worry, of course, is that decisions about what studies to include may be biased toward what analysts expect or want to find. As a result, it is often best practice in meta-analysis work to assess the robustness of meta-analysis results to different inclusion conditions; Doucouliagos, Ioannidis, and

Stanley (2017) discuss different study inclusion options, with an application to economics meta-analysis.

Assembling Estimates

The second step in the process is to choose the statistic that will be included in the meta-analysis. We will call the included set of studies J and index particular studies by $j \in J$, where there are N_J total studies in the set. The relevant estimate of the statistic from study j is denoted $\hat{\beta}_j$, and the associated standard error (SE) is $\hat{\sigma}_j$. These are the estimates that are to be combined in the meta-analysis with a goal of characterizing the set of estimates in the literature as a whole.

As with selecting studies in the first place, extracting the relevant estimate $\hat{\beta}_j$ may or may not be straightforward. At times the underlying research articles present several regression specifications with slightly different results, often in the form of robustness checks, and here, too, choosing which estimate is the single "best" estimate is fraught, especially in cases where the original author's preferred approach differs from that of other scholars in a literature. The question of which individual study estimates to use can generate some of the most heated debates in meta-analysis work. Debates over variable definition can also translate into disagreements over which studies the meta-analysis includes (in the set J), as studies with measures that are deemed sufficiently different from the ideal may be excluded from consideration.

The discussion so far has been rather abstract, and a specific example may help make things more concrete. Hsiang, Burke, and Miguel (2013) provide a useful illustration of the use of meta-analysis in contemporary social science research. Their study attempts to synthesize the growing quantitative empirical literature on links between extreme climate and human violence. This is a daunting but surmountable challenge. There are dozens of potentially relevant studies using distinct datasets, different approaches to statistical analysis, and outcomes ranging from personal crime (e.g., murder and assault) to land invasions, religious riots, and civil war. Some studies examine effects of different sources of climatic variation, including both temperature and precipitation.

The authors' first key decision was how to classify outcomes in a coherent way. They chose to group interpersonal violence into one category, and forms of intergroup violence (e.g., civil war) into a second group. While there remain some differences in outcomes grouped together in this way—the dynamics around land invasions differ from those in civil war—this absorbs a major dimension of differences across studies. The authors also normalized all violence outcomes as percent changes with respect to the mean of the outcome (in that dataset).

A second key choice was how to standardize climatic variation across studies, given that different studies consider various measures. Here they chose to normalize climate measures in terms of deviations from the local area mean, in standard deviation units (SD; based on the local distribution of the measure). This is important because a rise in monthly temperature of 2 °C may be less of a climate "shock" for a region that has considerable variation in temperature across months than for a region that experiences little variation in temperature over time.

These two normalizations allow the authors to create comparable statistics across studies, in units of the percent change in a conflict outcome as a function of a 1 SD shock to local climate. Each study contributes an estimate $\hat{\beta}_j$ (with $\hat{\sigma}_j$) to the resulting meta-analysis. With this example in mind, we next turn to the mechanics of creating a meta-analysis estimate.

Combining Estimates

The most basic goal of meta-analysis is to provide a reliable estimate of the average effect across multiple studies and to characterize the uncertainty around this estimate. A typical assumption in the simplest forms of meta-analysis is that there is a single true effect to be uncovered, β, and that it is common across all studies. This is called the "fixed-effect meta-analysis approach." This is unlikely to be strictly true in practice, due to differences in measures, aggregation across units, fundamental differences across populations, use of different statistical specifications and covariates, and so on, but it is a useful starting point.

The simplest approach to fixed-effect meta-analysis is one where each study on a topic receives equal weight (EW):

$$\hat{\beta}_{EW} = \Sigma_j \omega_j \hat{\beta}_j = \Sigma_j \hat{\beta}_j / N_J \qquad \text{Eqn. 5.1}$$

Here the weight ω_j applied to each study is just $1/N_J$, to construct the simple average.

A more attractive and more widely used approach applies different weights to individual study estimates, placing more weight on estimates that are more precise. This has the advantage of emphasizing findings from studies that are more reliable—for instance, studies that have larger sample sizes, all else equal. Statistical precision is the reciprocal of the variance, namely, $1/\hat{\sigma}_j^2$. The precision-weighted (PW) meta-analysis estimate is

$$\hat{\beta}_{PW} = \frac{\Sigma_j \left(\frac{1}{\hat{\sigma}_j^2}\right)\hat{\beta}_j}{\Sigma_j \left(\frac{1}{\hat{\sigma}_j^2}\right)} \, . \qquad \text{Eqn. 5.2}$$

The weight ω_j placed on each study in this approach is proportional to the precision of the estimate in that study:

$$\omega_j = \frac{\frac{1}{\hat{\sigma}_j^2}}{\Sigma_j \left(\frac{1}{\hat{\sigma}_j^2}\right)} \, .$$

If the underlying data-generating process is exactly the same for all studies (including in the variability in the measured outcome), then this approach implies that weight is placed on estimate j in proportion to its sample size. In the limit, a study with almost no data, whose estimates have extremely large SEs, gets close to zero weight in this fixed-effect meta-analysis.

The precision-weighting approach also has the important advantage of minimizing the variance in the resulting meta-analysis estimate:

$$\text{Var}(\hat{\beta}_{PW}) = \Sigma_j \omega_j^2 \hat{\sigma}_j^2 = \frac{1}{\Sigma_j \left(\frac{1}{\hat{\sigma}_j^2}\right)} \qquad \text{Eqn. 5.3}$$

The SE of the estimate, $\hat{\sigma}_{PW}$, is the square root of this variance. All else being equal, the inclusion of additional estimates in a meta-analysis always reduces the SE of the resulting estimate $\hat{\beta}_{PW}$. Even a body of individual studies each of which has relatively imprecise estimates can, when combined in meta-analysis, generate considerable certainty about the magnitude of an effect.

Let's work through a simple example with made-up data. Imagine that the literature on climate-conflict links consists of three studies. The first study finds an increase in violence of 5 percent for each 1 SD unit increase in temperature ($\hat{\beta}_1 = 0.05$, and associated SE, $\hat{\sigma}_1 = 0.03$), the second study estimates a 10 percent effect ($\hat{\beta}_2 = 0.10$, $\hat{\sigma}_2 = 0.03$), and the third a 15 percent effect, although this last estimate is quite imprecise ($\hat{\beta}_3 = 0.15$, $\hat{\sigma}_3 = 0.09$).

The simple equal-weighted average approach (Eqn. 5.1) would imply a meta-analysis estimate of 10 percent, $\hat{\beta}_{EW} = \frac{0.05+0.10+0.15}{3} = 0.10$. Applying Eqn. 5.3 to the case of equal weight on each estimate ($\omega_j = 1/3$), the SE is $\hat{\sigma}_{EW} = 0.033$.

The precision-weighted meta-analysis estimate is slightly different, due to the fact that less weight is placed on the "noisier" estimate 3. Using the formula above, the weight placed on both estimate 1 (ω_1) and estimate 2 (ω_2) is

$$\omega_1 = \omega_2 = \frac{\frac{1}{\hat{\sigma}_i^2}}{\Sigma_j\left(\frac{1}{\hat{\sigma}_i^2}\right)} = \frac{\frac{1}{(0.03)^2}}{\frac{1}{(0.03)^2}+\frac{1}{(0.03)^2}+\frac{1}{(0.09)^2}} = 0.474.$$

Far less weight is placed on estimate 3, $\omega_3 = 0.053$. Taken together, this implies a precision-weighted estimate of $\hat{\beta}_{PW} = 0.474 \times 0.05 + 0.474 \times 0.10 + 0.053 \times 0.15 = 0.079$, or a 7.9 percent increase in violence for each 1 SD increase in local temperature, with associated SE, $\hat{\sigma}_{PW} = 0.021$. Note that the SE is considerably smaller in this case than in the EW approach, since less weight is placed on the noisy estimate.

While only one of the three underlying estimates is statistically significant at the traditional $p < .05$ level (namely, estimate 2), the precision-weighted meta-analysis estimate is significant at the $p < .01$ level.

Heterogeneous Estimates in Meta-analysis

The fixed-effect meta-analysis approach is computationally simple and usually a good starting point for researchers assessing whether there is an overall effect in a body of studies. An important limitation is that there may be different true effects across studies. These differences are themselves of great interest to the scholarly community. Moreover, when there may not even be a common underlying effect to speak of, it may call into question the entire approach of combining studies into a single meta-analysis.

One approach to relaxing the assumption of a common effect is the weighted least squares (WLS) meta-analysis estimate. This generates the same estimated combined effect as $\hat{\beta}_{PW}$, but (under slightly different assumptions than the fixed-effect model) the effect is best interpreted as the average of potentially heterogeneous underlying effects rather than as the estimate of the single common effect. WLS meta-analysis estimates are also typically less precise than precision-weighted estimates. This useful approach is described in Stanley and Doucouliagos (2015).

A more common approach to relaxing the assumption of a common effect and allowing for heterogeneous treatment effects is random-effects meta-analysis. There are various ways to model this heterogeneity, including the hierarchical Bayesian approach we discuss below (Gelman and Hill 2006; Gelman et al. 2013). We lay out the general approach, illustrating throughout with the climate-conflict example we began to develop above, following Hsiang, Burke, and Miguel (2013) and Burke, Hsiang, and Miguel (2015).

The random-effects meta-analysis approach is able to systematically characterize the extent to which there is a general effect across studies (in our specific example, to characterize the link between climate and conflict that is general across societies) while simultaneously allowing for effect heterogeneity (here, the possibility that different types of conflict in distinct contexts may respond to climate shocks heterogeneously). The magnitude and precision of the common component represents the generalizable conclusions we might draw from a literature.

We adopt the same notation as above, where each study j contributes an estimated (standardized) effect $\hat{\beta}_j$ and an SE for that estimate, $\hat{\sigma}_j$. Following Hsiang, Burke, and Miguel (2013) and Burke, Hsiang, and Miguel (2015), we assume that there is some common component to these results, called μ, but that there might also be heterogeneity in how different populations are affected by the climate. That is, we allow for the fact that the cross-study differences we observe might not be driven solely by sampling variability; in other words, even if each study were executed with infinite data, they would not converge to the exact same estimated effect.

This situation is well suited for a random-effects framework. Assume that the true effect β_j that generates the data in each study j can be thought of as being drawn from a normal distribution of all possible samples and studies, where

$$\beta_j \sim N(\mu, \tau^2).$$ Eqn. 5.4

The terms μ and τ are unobserved "hyperparameters" that, respectively, determine the central tendency and the dispersion of findings in the literature. μ is the generalizable component describing the mean response to changes in climate. τ describes the extent of heterogeneity across contexts in these responses.

The relationship between these two terms sheds light on the degree of heterogeneity in estimated effects in a literature. If the dispersion term τ is much larger than μ, then differences between results are much greater than their commonalities. That said, it is worth pointing out that if μ is large, this may be of theoretical or policy interest, regardless of whether or not τ is large. Separately, if τ is large, it suggests there are important differences between studies that may be worth modeling explicitly, perhaps by splitting the sample of studies into distinct subsets with particular characteristics. For instance, in the climate and violence case above, it is possible that rainfall has quite distinct effects on conflict in agrarian societies (where economic production is heavily dependent on rainfall) versus non-agrarian societies.

The objective of the random-effects meta-analysis approach is to estimate both the common effect μ and dispersion parameter τ, which we illustrate here using the Bayesian approach in Gelman and Hill (2006). (The frequentist approach to random-effects meta-analysis is also very common and can be implemented using standardized routines in statistical software packages.) Under a uniform prior, the conditional posterior distribution for μ is as follows (where y denotes the outcome of interest):

$$\mu \mid \tau, y \sim N(\hat{\mu}, V_\mu). \qquad \text{Eqn. 5.5}$$

In this case, the estimated common effect is

$$\hat{\mu} = \frac{\Sigma_j\left(\frac{1}{\hat{\sigma}_j^2 + \hat{\tau}^2}\right)\hat{\beta}_j}{\Sigma_j\left(\frac{1}{\hat{\sigma}_j^2 + \hat{\tau}^2}\right)} \qquad \text{Eqn. 5.6}$$

and its estimated variance (V_μ) becomes

$$\text{Var}(\hat{\mu}) = \frac{1}{\Sigma_j\left(\frac{1}{\hat{\sigma}_j^2 + \hat{\tau}^2}\right)}. \qquad \text{Eqn. 5.7}$$

Note the similarity to the precision-weighted estimates above, with the main change being the role of the estimated dispersion, $\hat{\tau}$ in the expressions. In this setup, $\hat{\tau}$ is estimated to have larger values if the between-study differences in $\hat{\beta}_j$ are large in relation to the within-study SE estimates, $\hat{\sigma}_j$ (i.e., SEs reported for individual estimation results). Intuitively, if estimated treatment effects in all studies are near one another and have relatively wide and overlapping confidence intervals, then most of the difference in estimates is likely the result of sampling variation, and the true value of τ (the degree of treatment effect heterogeneity across studies) is likely to be close to zero.[2] Alternatively, if there is extensive variation in the estimated average treatment effects, but each effect is estimated quite precisely, random sampling variation alone is unlikely to be able to explain the pattern of results. In this case $\hat{\tau}$ will be large in relation to $\hat{\sigma}_j$, indicating that there is likely to be considerable heterogeneity in treatment effects across studies.

Statisticians quantify the proportion of total variation that can be attributed to variation across study effects using the I^2 statistic, which takes on values between zero and one (Higgins and Thompson 2002; Higgins et al. 2003). In the simplest setting where the within-study variance $\hat{\sigma}_j$ is the same for all studies ($\hat{\sigma}_j = \hat{\sigma}$ for all j), this statistic takes on the simple form $I^2 = \hat{\tau}^2/(\hat{\tau}^2 + \hat{\sigma}^2)$. When there is little heterogeneity in true effects across studies and so $\hat{\tau}$ is small, this statistic immediately takes on values close to zero.

It is also instructive to work through comparing results from Eqn. 5.6 and Eqn. 5.7 for different values of $\hat{\tau}$ and $\hat{\sigma}_j$. The first thing to note is that the weight placed on individual study estimates differs from the precision-weighted estimate. In particular, greater cross-study effect dispersion (higher $\hat{\tau}$) leads to a partial convergence in the weights placed on different studies, and it is immediately clear that the estimated common effect $\hat{\mu}$ falls between $\hat{\beta}_{EW}$ and $\hat{\beta}_{PW}$. The intuition here is that the extra weight given to a more precise estimate is diminished to whatever extent it is estimating a fundamentally different effect than other studies.

To fix thoughts, consider the two extreme cases of $\hat{\tau} \to \infty$ and $\hat{\tau} \to 0$. When differences in estimates across studies are large in relation to uncertainty in parameter estimates within studies ($\hat{\tau} \to \infty$), then all studies are weighted uniformly when estimating the average effect, and $\hat{\mu}$ converges to $\hat{\beta}_{EW}$. Yet if $\hat{\tau}$ is close to zero, then it is far more likely that the true β_j values are drawn from a narrow distribution, and that sampling variability drives most of the variation in the estimated $\hat{\beta}_j$ values. In this case, the relative weight placed on each study approaches its precision, estimates with large uncertainty are down weighted, and $\hat{\mu}$ approaches $\hat{\beta}_{PW}$. As $\hat{\tau}$ grows, the variance of $\hat{\mu}$ also increases unambiguously.

Returning to the literature on links between climate and conflict helps to illustrate. A glance at Figure 5.3 (reproduced from Burke, Hsiang, and Miguel 2015) suggests a climate-conflict literature somewhere in between: there is substantial overlap in confidence intervals,

2. One must also estimate $\hat{\tau}$. A common method is that of DerSimonian and Laird (1986), but more recent research indicates that other methods have better statistical properties (see Veroniki et al. 2016; Langan, Higgins, and Simmonds 2017).

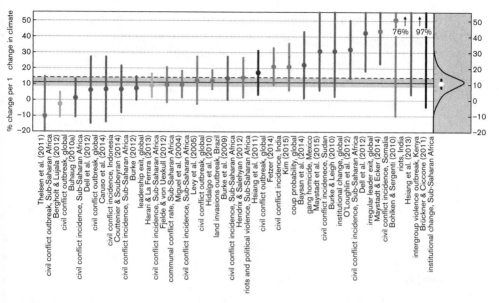

FIGURE 5.3. Estimated effects of climatic events on the risk of intergroup conflict, using respective study authors' preferred specifications. Each marker represents the estimated effect of a 1 SD increase in a climate variable, expressed as a percentage change in the conflict variable in relation to its mean; whiskers represent 95 percent confidence intervals. The dashed line is the median estimate, and the solid dark gray line is the precision-weighted mean with its 95 percent confidence interval shown in lighter gray. The shaded panel on the right shows the precision-weighted mean effect (circle) and the distribution of study results (gray ticks); probability distributions are the posterior for the expected distribution of an additional study (solid black line). Reproduced from Burke, Hsiang, and Miguel (2015).

but also meaningful variation in the estimated effects across these 26 studies, with some confidence intervals that do not overlap.

The estimated values are also informative and largely confirm the perspective one gets from visually examining study effects. Using a neutral uniform prior, they apply Bayes' rule to update estimates of μ, τ, and the β_j values from the studies on intergroup violence. They then use 10,000 simulations to characterize the posterior distributions of each of these variables. The estimated average common effect is $\hat{\mu} = 11.0$ percent, with SE (the square root of Var $\hat{\mu}$) of 1.2 percent. Thus, the overall average effect of a 1 SD increase in a climate variable is quite large and statistically significant at high levels of confidence ($p < .01$). The estimated cross-study SD $\hat{\tau}$ is also large, though (at 8.5 percent), which suggests that results differ substantially by context.

Whether these effects are all substantially capturing the same phenomenon, or rather grouping together multiple distinct concepts, is a question of interpretation and is difficult to answer definitively. In light of these issues, Burke, Hsiang, and Miguel (2015) go on to examine meta-analysis estimates for different subgroups of studies—for instance, those that focus on temperature effects versus those that emphasize precipitation. The variation in $\hat{\tau}$ across study estimates thus also serves as a useful measure of what the research community still needs to learn in a literature, in terms of the sources of this heterogeneity and the underlying mechanisms.

There is a more general question around just how representative existing study findings (summarized in a meta-analysis) are in comparison to those that would obtain in a global population, and how well these estimates might travel to other settings. There is growing awareness of the possibility that the samples chosen for early research studies might differ systematically from others.

For instance, Allcott (2015) examines a range of estimated effects of an experimental energy efficiency intervention conducted among different subpopulations of U.S. consumers, finding that effects in early pilot areas are systematically larger than those in a more representative sample. The authors of the intervention study appear to have chosen, or received more community cooperation in, areas where consumers were more receptive to conservation themes at baseline. This raises important questions of external validity, and the possibility that many of the studies that we combine in a meta-analysis may still be quite different from what might obtain in a more global program, even if the underlying studies are all high-quality and well-powered randomized controlled trials.

One recent effort to build greater external validity into a research program from the start is the "metaketa" initiative in political science, in which a group of authors deliberately coordinated multiple experiments—in their case, on the effects of voter information treatments—in distinct settings in an attempt to draw valid broader inference at the conclusion of the study.[3] We believe that other efforts of this kind—namely, to build up a body of literature that is designed to be more representative of the population as a whole, rather than simply relying on the decentralized decisions of individual researchers about which samples to focus on—are likely to be fruitful in many instances.

---

3. For more information, see http://egap.org/metaketa and https://www.washingtonpost.com/news/monkey-cage/wp/2017/06/08/this-new-initiative-is-trying-to-make-scientific-research-more-reliable.

META-REGRESSION ANALYSIS AND PUBLICATION BIAS

In Chapter 3, we discussed some tests for publication bias, some of which have overlap with meta-analysis methods. These include Rosenthal's (1979) method (the "fail-safe N") and that of Card and Krueger (1995), who tested for statistical relationships between study sample sizes and t-statistics in the minimum wage and unemployment literature.

Meta-regression analysis, which is somewhat different from meta-analysis, and the related funnel plot visualization approach, can also be used to test and correct for publication bias. The idea underlying these methods is that, all else being equal, studies with larger sample sizes should tend to produce more precise estimates (i.e., smaller $\hat{\sigma}_j$) than studies with fewer data. A violation of this basic idea across studies indicates that perhaps publication bias is at play, so that, for example, only studies with sufficiently large test statistics get published. Alternatively, there may be other differences, either in the nature of the research design or in the measures used across studies, that are correlated in some way with sample size, and this means that interpretation of these patterns should always be done with caution.

Researchers can get a handle on these issues using the funnel plot, which is a scatter plot of some measure of statistical precision (typically the inverse of the SE, $1/\hat{\sigma}_j$) versus the estimated effect size $\hat{\beta}_j$. In the absence of publication bias or any design effects, estimates generated from smaller samples should form the wider "base" (i.e., noisier estimates) of an inverted funnel, whereas estimates from studies with more data would be more tightly clustered around the same true average effect.

The method is illustrated with several economics examples in Stanley and Doucouliagos (2010), and two of these are reproduced in Figure 5.4. Panel A presents data from estimates of the correlation between worker unionization and labor productivity. Visually, the plot is generally symmetric around zero, suggesting an average effect near zero and a relative absence of publication bias. Panel B plots estimates from studies on the relationship between increases in the minimum wage and employment. Once again, the most precise estimates are close to zero, but the plot is strikingly asymmetric, with most of the underpowered (small $1/\hat{\sigma}_j$) studies showing negative employment effects. This is suggestive of publication bias in the minimum wage literature, as earlier claimed by Card and Krueger (1995).

Beyond eyeballing visual plots, which is hard for human beings to do reliably (Terrin, Schmid, and Lau 2005), formal tests can be conducted

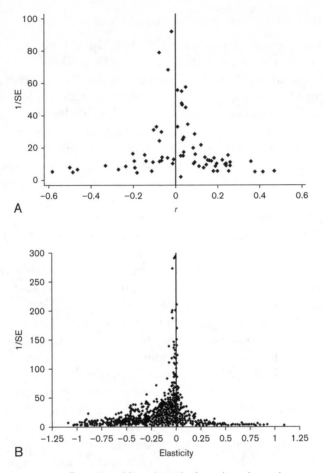

FIGURE 5.4. Examples of funnel graphs from the union and minimum wage literatures in labor economics. The more symmetric graph (**A**) is from the union productivity literature, while the more skewed graph (**B**) shows estimates from the minimum wage literature. On each graph, the estimate is on the horizontal axis and precision on the vertical axis, with each dot representing an estimate from a study or paper. Panel A was constructed by the authors using data from Doucouliagos and Laroche (2003). Panel B is from Doucouliagos and Stanley (2009) and is used by permission (© Blackwell Publishing Ltd/ London School of Economics 2009).

using data from across multiple studies by regressing the relevant effect size on the inverse of the SE. This meta-regression approach is described in Eqn. 5.8, which is based on the intuitive WLS model mentioned above:

$$\hat{\beta}_j = b_0 + b_1 \left(\frac{1}{\hat{\sigma}_j}\right) + e_j .$$ Eqn. 5.8

There are two key terms in this regression. The b_1 term captures the correlation between estimated effect size and statistical precision, and thus tests for publication bias. In the absence of publication bias, there is no clear reason why the magnitude of the effect would correlate with the precision of the estimate; publication bias could lead these to be systematically related, for instance, if only results with t-statistics larger than 2 can readily be accepted for publication. The test of statistical significance on the b_1 term is closely related to the funnel asymmetry test (FAT) proposed in Stanley (2008). This is a useful test under the assumption that study sample size is uncorrelated with other research design features, an assumption that is debatable (Simonsohn 2017). Using the FAT, Doucouliagos and Stanley (2009) find strong evidence of publication bias in Card and Krueger's (1995) sample of minimum wage studies ($b_1 \neq 0$), consistent with their own interpretation of the published literature at that time.

The other term, b_0, can here also be interpreted as the true effect free of publication bias and is closely related to the precision effect test (PET). One way of thinking about this term is as the effect size that one would obtain in a study with nearly infinite precision. Using an approach similar to Eqn. 5.8, Doucouliagos and Stanley (2009) similarly find no evidence of a true effect of the minimum wage on unemployment. The authors also conduct the FAT-PET tests with 49 additional, more recent studies in this literature and find the same results: evidence of significant publication bias and no evidence of an effect of the minimum wage on unemployment. The interested reader can find more details on additional meta-analysis methods, including this "FAT-PET" approach, in Stanley and Doucouliagos (2012) and Doucouliagos, Ioannidis, and Stanley (2017).

CONCLUSION

The meta-analytic approach helps to synthesize a body of scientific evidence and characterize its central tendency, the uncertainty around this average, and the dispersion of estimates. At its best, meta-analysis does so in a way that is more objective—and credible—than any literature review or traditional survey article could hope to be. The existence of a study registry can greatly facilitate the process by providing a comprehensive accounting of existing estimates for use in the analysis.

There are several important concerns with meta-analysis, however, that are worth keeping in mind when you do this kind of research. The first is that some meta-analyses combine interventions, outcomes, or settings that are not truly comparable. For instance, a meta-analysis of the impact of a particular educational intervention might pool results collected in the short run (say, after six months) with those collected in the longer term (six years) into a single estimate. While this is arguably valid as the research community's best estimate of overall program effects, there are often strong conceptual reasons to expect distinct impacts over different time horizons. Similar concerns arise regarding differences in intervention design and implementation, as well as the nature of outcome measures and study populations. The power of meta-analysis lies in its ability to synthesize many statistical findings into a single estimate, but researchers must be careful not to push it to the point where the underlying inputs no longer measure the same thing. This is an issue that some of the authors of this book have grappled with in their own work. While we find the approach in Hsiang, Burke, and Miguel (2013) sensible, other scholars have critiqued those authors' decision to pool several different forms of organized intergroup violence in a single meta-analysis (Buhaug et al. 2014).

Second, and just as importantly, a meta-analysis result is only as credible as the underlying studies that are included in the analysis. A meta-analysis estimate composed of biased study estimates will itself be of little utility. As mentioned above, a meta-analysis estimate composed of unbiased but unrepresentative study estimates may also be of limited value.

The next two chapters—Chapter 6 on pre-analysis plans and Chapter 7 on sensitivity analysis—provide a detailed discussion of approaches that yield more reliable study estimates. These are of value on their own, in improving the value of individual estimates, and are also critical tools for generating useful meta-analyses.

SIX

Pre-analysis Plans

BACKGROUND

Study registration serves as a useful way to search for research findings on a particular topic and to potentially deal with publication bias across a body of literature. Most supporters of study registration also promote the preregistration of studies, including pre-analysis plans (PAPs) that can be posted and time-stamped even before analysis data are collected or otherwise available (Miguel et al. 2014). All the registries discussed in Chapter 5 allow for inclusion of a PAP during registration.

Registration is now the norm in medical research for randomized trials, and registrations often include (or link to) prospective statistical analysis plans as part of the project protocol.[1] Official guidance from the U.S. Food and Drug Administration's Center for Drug Evaluation and Research describes eight broad categories of items that should be included in a statistical analysis plan: prespecification of the analysis; analysis sets; missing values and outliers; data transformation; estimation, confidence intervals, and hypothesis testing; adjustment of significance and confidence levels; subgroups, interactions, and covariates; and integrity of data and computer software validity (Food and Drug Administration 1998).

---

1. In medicine, these protocols are even sometimes published as stand-alone articles (see, e.g., Arnold et al. 2013).

While there are scattered early cases of PAPs being used in the social sciences (most notably by Neumark [2001], which we discuss below), the quantity of published papers employing prespecified analysis has grown rapidly in the past few years, mirroring the rise of studies posted on the AEA registry discussed in Chapter 5.

WHAT TO INCLUDE IN A PAP

Detailed discussions of the ongoing debate about what should be included in a PAP can be found in Glennerster and Takavarasha (2013), David McKenzie's World Bank Research Group blog post,[2] and Alejandro Ganimian's template for PAPs.[3] Ganimian's template may be particularly useful to researchers when developing their own PAPs, and instructors may find it a useful tool to present in their courses.

Building on the Food and Drug Administration's 1998 checklist, along with insights from these recent treatments, in our view there appears to be a growing consensus that social science PAPs should consider discussing the following 10 issues.

1. Study Design. State how many arms are in the trial, whether multiple treatments are mutually exclusive or overlapping, and how exactly randomization is conducted or stratified. If the study is not a randomized trial, specify the design method to be used (e.g., controlling for observables, regression discontinuity, instrumental variables, panel data with fixed effects, difference in differences).

2. Study Sample. Who is going to be included in, and excluded from, the study? Researchers should describe how any variations from the intended sample (e.g., attrition, noncompliance with assigned treatment, missing data) are to be dealt with. Details should be provided on any use of multiple surveys or data sources (e.g., repeated follow-ups) or multiple years of administrative data (e.g., several rounds of the U.S. General Social Survey).

3. Outcome Measures. Define the outcome measures of the study and state which are of primary and secondary importance, based on the study's research aims and hypotheses. Carefully define these by referring

2. See http://blogs.worldbank.org/impactevaluations/a-pre-analysis-plan-checklist.
3. See https://osf.io/exyb8/.

to specific variables from the survey. If more than one survey question is used to construct an outcome, state exactly how these variables will be combined. For example, if a continuous variable is to be turned into a dichotomous variable, state the cutoff. Outcomes should also be defined throughout the causal chain when possible. That is, if there are mechanisms or moderators that drive the final outcome, these should also be stated. For example, if researchers are testing whether a government program increased household income by boosting the amount of time spent on self-employment, they should state this and refer to the exact survey questions that provide these data.

4. Families of Mean Effects. A scholar who plans on testing numerous outcome measures should consider grouping the outcomes into families and presenting a smaller number of index outcomes (we discuss the details of this in Chapter 7). The PAP should list the exact sets of outcomes that comprise the families as well as the survey questions or other data sources that make up the variables and outcomes.

5. Multiple Hypothesis Testing Adjustment. The very nature of null hypothesis statistical testing means that a certain fraction of tests will appear statistically significant even if there is no underlying truth to the relationship. Simply put, if you run more tests, you get more false positives. This should be explicitly accounted for by adjusting p-values, specifically by controlling the family-wise error rate (FWER) or false discovery rate (FDR) (see Chapter 7). The PAP should include a description of how this will be done, including exactly which hypotheses will be considered in the adjustment.

6. Subgroups. Outcomes are often interacted with baseline characteristics to test for heterogeneous treatment effects. Since essentially *every* baseline characteristic that a dataset contains could be used to assess these heterogeneous treatment effects, regardless of whether or not there is a reasonable theory behind a differential effect, subgroups are especially important to prespecify in a PAP. List every subgroup to be tested, linking them to specific survey questions or variables. The multiplicity-of-subgroups problem can also be addressed using FWER and FDR methods, and if this is the researcher's plan, the PAP should explicitly state it.

7. Direction of Effect. One advantage conferred by writing a PAP is the greater power of one-sided statistical tests. As long as the direction—

ideally with some explanation of the mechanism or theory of change—is prespecified, a one-directional test is statistically valid.

8. Exact Statistical Specification. What is the exact statistical specification that will be used in a hypothesis test? For example, if regression is to be conducted, the PAP should state whether the regression is linear, generalized linear (Poisson, negative binomial, etc.), or some other form; what control variables, fixed effects, and so on will be included; and how standard errors will be calculated (robust to heteroskedasticity, clustered, bootstrapped, delta method, or other). In other words, a statistical equation should be presented with explicit description of the relevant distributional assumptions. This isn't as easy as it sounds! (OK, maybe it doesn't even sound easy.) But given the flexibility that exists in choosing a regression specification *ex post,* this aspect of the PAP is essential.

9. Structural Model. If you are testing a structural model—that is, building a formal mathematical model from first principles of utility maximization and estimating structural model parameters, as economists sometimes do—you should be sure to include a detailed discussion of your approach. The functional form of a utility function or profit maximization equation is subject to at least as much post hoc flexibility as is standard regression.

10. Time-Stamp It! Look, you're a good person—you wouldn't conduct your analysis first, write your PAP second, and lie about the order, right? We believe you, but that person next to you might be shady. So you need to *verifiably* write your analysis plan ahead of time. To do this, post your PAP in a trusted registry so it has a time stamp. Your own website isn't good enough, not only because it's not verifiable, but also because that wouldn't make it easy for other researchers to find or cite your work.

Pre-analysis plans are still new to the social sciences, and this list is likely to evolve in the coming years as researchers explore the potential, and possible limitations, of this new tool. But this list is a very good starting point.

For those concerned about the possibility of the scooping of new research designs and questions from publicly posted PAPs or project descriptions, several of the social science registries currently allow the temporary embargoing of project details. For instance, the AEA registry allows a user to hide certain details of the study until the end of the trial, as submitted by the researcher registering the study. The Open Science Framework allows a four-year embargo until the information is made public. What you plan to do will eventually be made public, but hopefully after you have had the chance to follow through on your idea and publish your research.

EXAMPLES OF PAPS

Two well-known recent examples of social science papers based on experiments with PAPs include Casey, Glennerster, and Miguel (2012) and Finkelstein et al. (2012), and we discuss them here.

Casey, Glennerster, and Miguel (2012) discuss evidence from a large-scale field experiment on community-driven development projects in Sierra Leone. The project, called GoBifo, was intended to make local institutions in war-torn Sierra Leone more democratic and egalitarian. GoBifo funds were spent on a variety of local public goods infrastructure (e.g., community centers, schools, latrines, and roads), agriculture, and business training projects, and were closely monitored to limit leakage.

The analysis finds significant short-run benefits in terms of the "hardware" aspects of infrastructure and economic well-being: the latrines were indeed built. However, the larger goals of the project—reshaping local institutions, making them more egalitarian, increasing trust, improving local collective action, and strengthening community groups, which the researchers call the program's "software effects" —largely failed. There are a large number of plausible outcome measures along these dimensions, hundreds in total, which the authors analyze using a mean effects index approach for nine different families of outcomes (with multiple testing adjustments). The null hypothesis of no impact cannot be rejected at 95 percent confidence for any of the nine families of software outcomes, including social capital, trust, political engagement, and participation by socially marginalized groups, including women and youth. Table 6.1A shows the null effect across all hypotheses of whether the program was linked to social or institutional change, showing that the effect is small in magnitude and not statistically significant.

Yet Casey et al. (2012) go on to show that, given the large numbers of outcomes in their dataset, and the multiplicity of ways to define the software outcome measures, finding some statistically significant results would have been relatively easy for researchers. In fact, the paper

TABLE 6.1 ERRONEOUS INTERPRETATIONS UNDER "CHERRY-PICKING"

Outcome variable	Treatment effect	Standard error	Mean in control group
A. Main institutional and social change or "software" effects			
Mean effect for family B (hypotheses 4–12; 155 unique outcomes)	0.028	0.020	0.00
B. GoBifo "weakened institutions"			
Attended meeting to decide what to do with the tarpaulin (tarp)	–0.04+	0.02	0.81
Everybody had equal say in deciding how to use the tarp	–0.11+	0.06	0.51
Community used the tarp (verified by physical assessment)	–0.08+	0.04	0.90
Community can show research team the tarp	–0.12*	0.05	0.84
Respondent would like to be a member of the Village Development Committee	–0.04*	0.02	0.36
Respondent voted in the local government election (2008)	–0.04*	0.02	0.85
C. GoBifo "strengthened institutions"			
Community teachers have been trained	0.12+	0.07	0.47
Respondent is a member of a women's group	0.06**	0.02	0.24
Someone took minutes at the most recent community meeting	0.14*	0.06	0.30
Building materials stored in a public place when not in use	0.25*	0.10	0.13
Chiefdom official did not have the most influence over tarp use	0.06*	0.03	0.54
Respondent agrees with "Responsible young people can be good leaders"	0.04*	0.02	0.76
Correctly able to name the year of the next general elections	0.04*	0.02	0.19

SOURCE: Adapted from Casey, Glennerster, and Miguel (2012: tables II and VI).
NOTES: Significance levels (per comparison p-value): $+ p < .10$, $* p < .05$, $** p < .01$, with robust standard errors.

includes an example of how the authors could have reported either a number of statistically significant positive effects or significantly negative effects, depending on the nature of the cherry-picking in the absence of a PAP. Table 6.1B presents the statistically significant negative impacts identified in the GoBifo data, and Table 6.1C highlights positive effects. In the absence of full disclosure of the full set of outcomes that were collected in the study, or open access to the replication data, other scholars viewing just Table 6.1B or 6.1C might come away with a highly misleading perspective on the impacts of the program.

These findings raise an important question: How many empirical social science papers with statistically significant results are, unbeknownst to us, really just some version of either Table 6.1B or 6.1C? In other words, how many present cherry-picked results chosen to give the appearance of an impact, when the truth is a null effect (Table 6.1A)?

In another noteworthy article that employs a PAP, Finkelstein et al. (2012) studied the politically charged question of the impacts of health insurance expansion, using the case of Oregon's Medicaid program, called the Oregon Health Plan. In 2008, Oregon determined it could afford to enroll 10,000 additional adults, and it opted to do so by random lottery, making a randomized controlled trial possible. Most of the analyses in the article were laid out in a detailed PAP, which was publicly posted on the National Bureau of Economic Research's website in 2010, before the researchers had access to the data.

To Finkelstein et al.'s credit, all analyses that were not prespecified are clearly labeled as such in the text; in fact, the exact phrase "This analysis was not prespecified" appears in the paper six times. Tables in the main text and appendix that report analyses that were not prespecified are clearly labeled with a "^" character to set them apart. This is important because, as in Casey et al. (2012), the researchers examined a large number of outcomes: hospital admissions through the emergency room and not through the emergency room; hospital days; procedures; financial strain (bankruptcy, judgments, liens, delinquency, medical debt, and nonmedical debt, measured by credit report data); self-reported health from survey data; and so on. When running such a large number of tests, the researchers again could have discovered some "significant" effects simply by chance. The PAP, in conjunction with multiple hypothesis testing adjustments, gives us more confidence in the main results of the study: namely, that recipients did not improve significantly in terms of objective physical health measurements, but were more likely to have health insurance (as one would hope, given the program's original aims), had better self-reported health outcomes, utilized emergency rooms more, and had better detection and management of diabetes.

Additional studies that have resulted from the Oregon experiment have also employed PAPs, and they show that health insurance increased emergency department use (Taubman et al. 2014), had no effect on measured physical health outcomes after two years, but did increase health care use and diabetes management, as well as leading to lower rates of depression and financial strain (Baicker et al. 2013). The health care expansion had no detectable effect on employment or earnings (Baicker et al. 2014).

Other examples of recent papers in the social sciences that employ PAPs include poverty-targeting programs in Indonesia, an evaluation of the Toms shoe company's donation program, a job training program in Turkey, and the effect of authoritarian iconography on political attitudes, among many others (Olken, Onishi, and Wong 2012; Alatas et al. 2012; Wydick, Katz, and Janet 2014; Hirshleifer et al. 2015; Huff and Kruszewska 2016; Bush et al. 2016). In psychology, a prespecified replication of an earlier paper that had found a link between female conception risk (related to timing within the menstrual cycle) and racial prejudice failed to find a similar effect (see Example 6.1).

Example 6.1 Conception Risk and Prejudice: PAP in Psychology

An example of a PAP from psychology is the preregistered replication of an implicit association test (IAT) in Hawkins, Fitzgerald, and Nosek (2015). For readers unfamiliar with this test, the IAT is a computer-implemented test that shows words such as *good* or *nice,* as well as their opposites, *bad* or *mean,* and pairs these adjectives with a member of a group: a typically male name, a typically female name, an African American face, or a white face, to name a few. The test records how long it takes the participant to make a simple keystroke associating a member of a group with a certain characteristic. To exaggerate the findings: a white American might be racist if it takes her longer to click "friendly" when she sees an African American face on the screen. (We encourage you to take a minute and try it for yourself at http://projectimplicit.com. You've been warned, though! You might discover biases you'd prefer to believe you didn't have.)

Existing IAT research showed evidence of stronger implicit racial preferences among white American women in the fertile phase of their menstrual cycle, especially among women who had high self-perceived vulnerability to sexual assault ($N = 77$; Navarrete et al. 2009). Another study using both black and white women found the effect especially strong among women who associated the racial outgroup with physical formidability ($N = 252$; McDonald et al. 2011). However, other researchers, wishing to test whether this outgroup bias was limited to race or whether it also applied to age, weight, religion, or other characteristics, replicated the original test as closely as possible with a high-powered design ($N = 2,226$) and a prespecified analysis plan

(Hawkins, Fitzgerald, and Nosek 2015), which is available online on the Open Science Framework at https://osf.io/dr42m/.

As shown in the table below, the replicating researchers failed to reproduce the original result. In particular, the 95 percent confidence intervals for the coefficient estimate on conception risk and for conception risk interacted with physicality stereotypes contain zero for both of the study samples presented in the table. This suggests that there is no true relationship between conception risk and racial bias. This paper was the first preregistered study published in the journal *Psychological Science*.

MULTIPLE REGRESSION RESULTS: PREDICTING IMPLICIT INTERGROUP BIAS FROM CONCEPTION RISK AND IMPLICIT PHYSICALITY STEREOTYPES, CONTROLLING FOR PARTICIPANT'S RACE

Predictor	Study 3 (*n* = 92)			Study 4 (*n* = 154)		
	b	*95% CI*	*β*	*b*	*95% CI*	*β*
Race	−0.01	[−0.17, 0.14]	−0.02	−0.01	[−0.10, 0.08]	−0.01
Conception risk	1.09	[−1.47, 3.64]	0.08	−0.14	[−2.10, 1.83]	−0.01
Implicit physicality stereotypes	0.54	[0.31, 0.77]	0.46	0.32	[0.17, 0.47]	0.36
Interaction: conception risk * implicit physicality stereotypes	0.2	[−6.73, 7.14]	0.01	−2.53	[−7.54, 2.48]	−0.08

SOURCE: Data from Hawkins, Fitzgerald, and Nosek (2015: table 1).

NOTES: Sample size restricted to black women and white women. Race coded as black (−1) or white (+1). Conception risk and implicit physicality stereotypes centered around their means.

STRENGTHS, LIMITATIONS, AND OTHER ISSUES AROUND PAPS

There remain many open questions about whether, when, and how PAPs could and should be used in social science research. There are open debates about how useful they are in different fields, and in subfields of the social science disciplines. Olken (2015), for example, highlights both their "promises and perils." On the positive side, PAPs greatly limit specification searching and allow researchers to take full advantage of the power of their statistical tests (even making one-sided tests reasonable). On the negative side, PAPs are often complex and take valuable time to write. Scientific breakthroughs often come at unexpected times and places, often as a result of exploratory analysis, and the time spent writing PAPs may lead researchers to spend less time on valuable but less structured data exploration.

Coffman and Niederle (2015) argue that there is limited upside from PAPs when replication (in conjunction with hypothesis registries) is possible. In experimental and behavioral economics, where lab experiments utilize samples of locally recruited students, and the costs of replicating an experiment are relatively low, they argue that replication could be a viable substitute for PAPs. There does appear to be a growing consensus, endorsed by Coffman and Niederle, that PAPs can significantly increase the credibility of reporting and analysis in large-scale randomized trials that are expensive or difficult to repeat, or when a study that relies on a particular contextual factor makes it impossible to replicate. For instance, Berge et al. (2015) carried out a series of lab experiments timed to take place just before the 2013 elections in Kenya. Replication of this lab research is clearly impossible due to the context—there is simply no way another scholar could replicate this specific election setting—and thus their use of a PAP is particularly valuable.

A further advantage of the use of PAPs is that they are likely to help shield researchers from pressures to affirm the policy agenda of donors and policymakers, in cases where these actors have a vested interest in the outcome. This is especially the case if researchers and their institutional partners can agree on the PAP, as a sort of *ex ante* evaluation contract. This was the approach that Casey et al. (2012) took in their interactions with government and donor partners for their Sierra Leone project.

One issue that has arisen for studies that registered a PAP is characterizing the extent to which the analysis conforms to the original plan, or whether it deviates in meaningful ways. To appreciate these differences, scholars will need to compare the actual analysis to the plan, a step that could be seen as adding to the burden placed on journal editors and referees. Even if the analysis does conform exactly to the PAP, there is still the possibility that authors are consciously or unconsciously emphasizing a subset of the prespecified analyses in the final study. Berge et al. (2015) develop an approach to comparing the distribution of p-values in the paper's main tables versus those in the PAP in order to quantify the extent of selective reporting between the plan and the paper, as a way to assess these concerns, and this approach could be usefully applied by authors of other studies.

A complementary approach is to subscribe to a set of research "standard operating procedures," such as those described by Lin and Green (2016). These link to a set of default practices that will be used if unforeseen circumstances arise in the study (e.g., regarding outliers, attrition, and noncompliance) and are not mentioned in the PAP. This can lower the cost of preregistration by eliminating the need to specify repetitive statistical details in every PAP; of course, the flipside is the time cost of developing these general procedures upfront.

There is also the question of *when* one should write the PAP. "Before you begin to analyze your data" seems like the obvious answer, but this could be more precisely defined. In terms of options, one could write the PAP before any baseline survey data have been collected; after any experimental intervention has occurred but before endline data collection; or after endline collection but before data analysis has begun. All of these seem defensible to us, and norms have not yet evolved sufficiently in the social sciences to know which approach will become the standard. Each approach has its benefits and potential drawbacks.

Registering the PAP before baseline data collection is the purest approach and the one most immune from any possibility of *p*-hacking. This makes it attractive, but registering so early in the process may lead the researcher to miss out on valuable information and learning in the field and thus could weaken the research. For example, suppose that the baseline data indicate that the intended primary outcome question is poorly phrased in the survey and elicits high rates of nonresponse, or that there is much less variation in responses than expected. If the PAP was instead written after baseline data collection, one could have potentially addressed those concerns. Moreover, the researcher would also be free to learn from those initial data and potentially refine the scope of the analysis. For example, if the baseline survey of a field experiment designed to increase individual labor wages revealed that few of the subjects even worked outside the home, the researcher could change the focus of the analysis to another outcome, or shift the research to a different study setting where the hypothesis is more relevant.

PAPs could alternatively be written and registered after endline data have been collected but before the investigators have begun to analyze the data. Some have suggested that one could even examine endline data from the control group only before writing up the PAP, and this in fact was the approach for some of the Oregon health insurance studies mentioned above. While we consider this a sensible approach in terms of PAP timing, it may be slightly problematic in some cases. For instance, the researcher could learn from examining the endline data that the control group had an unexpectedly low (or high) value of a certain outcome variable, and as a result choose to include (or not include) that variable as a primary outcome in the analysis. This need not be problematic, of course. Levels of this outcome may be lower than the researcher expected for both the treatment and control groups, with no implications for the treatment effect. But if the researcher has good background knowledge about what the levels of this variable *should* be, and he has identified an outcome where values are in fact anomalously low for the control group, then this might increase the odds of a spurious difference between the treatment and control groups, generating misleading inference.

An alternative proposal discussed by Olken (2015) is to remove the treatment status variable from the dataset entirely before examining the data, blinding the researcher to this critical variable. This seems to alleviate some of the concerns, although it is not perfect if, once again, examining the overall distribution of outcomes still somehow sheds light on the likely treatment effect for that variable (either overall or for a subgroup, say), and this leads the researcher to modify the PAP.

RESULTS-BLIND REVIEW AND REGISTERED REPORTS

Olken (2015) and Coffman and Niederle (2015) mention another promising way to address publication bias and specification search: results-blind review. Chris Chambers (2013) and other transparency reformers in psychology have recently and successfully championed this method, though the idea has been around since at least the 1960s. Robert Rosenthal wrote that given researchers' outcome-consciousness,

> what we may need is a system for evaluating research based only on the procedures employed. If the procedures are judged appropriate, sensible, and sufficiently rigorous to permit conclusions from the results, the research cannot be judged inconclusive on the basis of the results and rejected by the referees or editors. Whether the procedures were adequate would be judged independently of the outcome. To accomplish this might require that procedures only be submitted initially for editorial review or that only the result-less section be sent to a referee or, at least, that an evaluation of the procedures be set down before the referee or editor reads the results. This change in policy would serve to decrease the outcome-consciousness of editorial decisions. (Rosenthal 1966, pp. 35–37)

Studies that are submitted to such review are sometimes referred to as "registered reports" (RRs). It is worth describing how RRs might work in practice, since this is one of the most innovative and promising ideas for combatting *p*-hacking that has emerged in recent years. Authors first write a detailed study protocol and PAP and submit the PAP to a journal before the experiment is run or data collected. The

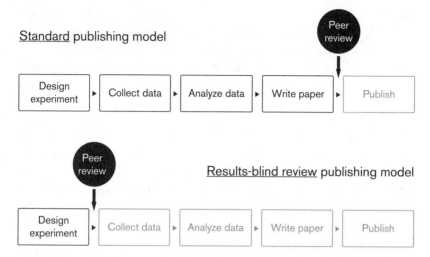

FIGURE 6.1. Comparison of the standard publishing model and the "registered reports" model with results-blind review.

journal reviews the plan for the quality of the design and the scientific value of the research question and may choose to give "in-principle acceptance" (IPA). An IPA can be thought of as akin to the standard journal "revise and resubmit" and is contingent on the data being collected and analyzed as planned. If the author follows through on the proposed design, and the data are of sufficiently high quality, the study is accepted for publication regardless of whether the results are statistically significant and conform to the expectations of the editor or referees or to the conventional wisdom in the discipline.

Social scientists regularly review research proposals for grant-making agencies and are accustomed to critiquing the substance of research design and data before seeing results. It is not a large step from those reviews to the results-blind reviewing of RRs. Figure 6.1 contrasts the timing of research and review in the standard publishing model with that for RRs. Much of the process is the same, but the timing of peer review is, crucially, far earlier in the research cycle for RRs.

Several psychology journals have begun using results-blind review, either regularly or in special issues (Chambers 2013; Chambers et al. 2014; Nosek and Lakens 2014). Beyond psychology, an issue of *Comparative Political Studies* was the first to feature results-blind review in political science (Findley et al. 2016), for both experimental and observational research studies. As of yet, no economics journals have adopted the RR format, although an RR pilot was launched in 2018 by the *Journal of Development Economics*. The rise of experimental studies and PAPs in economics (as evidenced by the rapid growth of the AEA registry discussed in Chapter 5) may facilitate the acceptance of this approach.[4]

USE OF PAPS IN OBSERVATIONAL STUDIES

An important and still open question is how widely the approach of study registration and hypothesis prespecification could be usefully applied in nonprospective and nonexperimental studies. This issue has been discussed extensively in recent years within medical research, but consensus has not yet been reached in that community. Perhaps unexpectedly, it actually appears that some of the most prestigious medical research journals, which typically publish randomized trials, are even more in favor of the registration of observational studies than the editors of journals who publish primarily nonexperimental research (Epidemiology 2010; Lancet 2010; Loder, Groves, and MacAuley 2010). What is going on, and why has consensus been so hard to find?

Dal-Ré et al. (2014) surveyed the landscape in medical research, evaluated the pros and cons, and came down on the side of requiring registration for observational studies, which would include prospective analysis plans. This is an important issue, given that, according to their analysis, there were 300,000 (!) observational studies in a single year listed in the PubMed database, compared to only 20,000 randomized controlled trials. The ratio of observational to experimental studies is likely similar in the social sciences—samples of papers from economics indicate that experiments make up 8 percent of top publications (Hamermesh 2013). Observational studies come in many shapes and sizes, and many of the pros and cons laid out below could also apply to the preregistration of meta-analyses like those described in Chapter 5.

The potential benefits of registering observational studies described in Dal-Ré et al. (2014) include

(1) "increasing transparency and credibility,"

(2) "improving the peer-review process and ethical conduct of studies,"

(3) "ensuring that the totality of evidence is publicly available,"

---

4. For an up-to-date list of journals using this format, see https://osf.io/8mpji/wiki/home/. For differing perspectives on how useful registered reports are likely to be in the social sciences, refer to Ansell and Samuels (2016) and Foster et al. (2018).

(4) "enhanc[ing] communication regarding explored, but not published, hypotheses,"

(5) "facilitat[ing] systematic reviews and research collaborations,"

(6) "reduc[ing] redundancy and funding committed to research questions for which adequate studies have already been conducted or are being performed," and

(7) "allowing published evidence to be better placed in context."

Making sure that planned studies are registered somewhere is certainly valuable. To this issue, point 4 above seems particularly important: often scholars repeat analysis previously carried out, but never published, by other researchers, and without the registration of planned observational studies there is simply no way for them to know about those earlier attempts. What is left unanswered by Dal-Ré et al. (2014) is how to incentivize scholars to register "failed" attempts. Why take the time registering— and publicizing—your "failures"? Or even beyond the perception of failure, why take the time to register analysis that one does not plan to publish, and that no one will know about in the absence of registration? The process here is totally different than the registration of a prospective experimental study, say, since later publication can be conditioned on *ex ante* registration. Since there is typically no way for others to verify when I ran my analysis with publicly available observational data, I might simply choose to register only those analyses that I ultimately choose to publish.

A few potential negatives to registering observational studies that Dal-Ré et al. (2014) mention include

(1) the burden of ongoing serial amendments resulting from "highly exploratory, hypothesis-generating research with complex, meandering analyses,"

(2) "hindrance of new idea generation,"

(3) "reduction in the analyses of end points not pre-specified because they were conceived after the study started,"

(4) potential for researchers to steal ideas from the registry and scoop others, and

(5) the difficulty of verifying that publicly available data were not analyzed or investigated prior to the registration.

The authors discount potential negatives 1–3, claiming that researchers simply need to disclose which analyses were post hoc and which were prespecified, and that this will not spill over negatively into other choices. With wide adoption of registration and a norm that registering a study results in the scholarly rights to the related intellectual claim, the authors also believe that scooping (i.e., scholars coming in to appropriate others' ideas) would not be a problem (potential negative 4). However, we are not sure. Some scholars might specialize in registering a wide range of potential analyses and ideas, but never put in the effort and work to actually realize them or get them published, somewhat akin to recent concerns over patent trolls in the U.S. software industry. And there are bound to be many controversies and cases where multiple scholars are interested in related topics; it may simply not be possible to disentangle theft of innovative ideas from the observational study registry from simple coincidence of intellectual interests.

In our view, the major concern with the preregistration of nonprospective observational studies using preexisting data—and the one that may make it infeasible for many types of studies—is that there is often no credible way to verify that preregistration took place before data were analyzed (potential negative 5). As noted above, analysis of existing publicly available data differs fundamentally from the case of prospective studies in which the data have not yet been collected or accessed, where data mining is literally impossible. Registering observational studies using preexisting data might even have severe consequences for the entire transparency agenda, if doing so creates the false impression of transparency, while actually eroding trust in entire bodies of research, due to the loopholes noted above.

What are some ways to address these concerns? For one, certain datasets could be hosted on a remote server, and access to the data could be restricted to those who register their intended study. This seems promising but is not completely airtight. Unscrupulous researchers could speak to collaborators who already have access to the data, and have others run analysis for them and thereby gain an unfair, or at least undisclosed, advantage before registering a PAP. (Just as fraudulent researchers have been known to create pseudonyms in order to conduct peer review for their own papers, researchers could create pseudonyms to download data while registering a research plan under their own name. See, for example, Patel [2014]; Ferguson, Marcus, and Oransky [2014]; and Yu et al. [2016].)

One situation where this complication does not present itself is when data do not yet exist. In other words, a prospective but nonexperimental (observational) study has many of the advantages of prospective experimental studies, in that it is impossible to examine the data and craft the PAP accordingly. The earliest economics study (to our knowledge) that used a PAP on nonexperimental data in this way was Neumark (2001).

The following account of the origins of David Neumark's (2001) study is based on conversations with our University of California, Berkeley, colleague David Levine as well as an editorial accompanying Neumark's article (Levine 2001). Alan Krueger (of Princeton) appears to have suggested to Levine, who was editor of the journal *Industrial Relations* at the time, that multiple researchers could analyze the employment effects of an announced and upcoming change in the U.S. federal minimum wage with prespecified research designs, in a bid to eliminate "author effects." The minimum wage literature was then (and remains) a highly politicized and widely discussed body of evidence in labor economics focused on the employment impacts of these wage policy changes, with widely disparate findings across scholars, sometimes even using the same data. Levine was supportive in principle and thought that this approach could create a productive "adversarial collaboration" between authors with starkly different prior views on the likely employment impacts of the policy change (Levine 2001). This concept of adversarial collaboration—two sets of researchers with opposing theories (or prior findings) coming together and agreeing on the right way to test hypotheses before observing the data—is often associated with Nobel Prize–winning economist and psychologist Daniel Kahneman (see, e.g., Bateman et al. 2005).

So what happened? The minimum wage in the United States increased in both October 1996 and September 1997. Although Krueger ultimately decided not to participate in the prespecified research activity, Neumark submitted a prespecified research design consisting of the exact estimating equations, variable definitions, and subgroups that he would use to analyze the effect of the minimum wage on the unemployment of younger workers using October, November, and December Current Population Survey data from 1995 through 1998. This detailed plan was submitted to journal editors and reviewers prior to the end of May 1997; the October 1996 data started to become available at the end of May 1997, and Neumark assured readers that he had not examined any published data at the state level prior to submitting his analysis plan. Figure 6.2 shows the timeline of relevant events in terms of the study and policy.

The verifiable time stamp of the federal government's subsequent release of data indeed makes this approach possible, but the situation

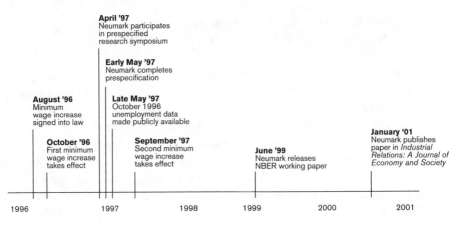

FIGURE 6.2. Timeline of events in Neumark's (2001) minimum wage study.

also benefits from the depth and intensity of the minimum wage debate prior to the study. Neumark had an extensive literature to draw upon when choosing specific regression functional forms and subgroup analyses. He tested two definitions of the minimum wage: the ratio of the minimum wage to the average wage (common in Neumark's previous work) and the fraction of workers who benefited from the newly raised minimum wage (used in David Card's earlier work, where Card had often found minimum wage impacts on employment quite different from those reported in Neumark's work; Card 1992a, 1992b). Neumark tested models with and without covariates for the employment rate of higher-skilled prime-age adults, as recommended by Deere, Murphy, and Welch (1995).

Neumark's (2001) results mostly fail to reject the null hypothesis of no effect of the minimum wage increase: only 18 of the 80 analytical specifications resulted in statistically significant decreases in employment (at the 90 percent confidence level), with estimated elasticities ranging from −0.14 to −0.3 for the significant estimates, and with others closer to zero. These estimates fall somewhere in the middle of the range of previous effects in the literature (Doucouliagos and Stanley 2009).

It is difficult to see how a researcher could reach Neumark's level of prespecified detail with a research question with which they were not already intimately familiar. It seems more likely that in cases where researchers are less knowledgeable, they might either prespecify an inadequate level of detail or choose an inappropriate statistical specification; this risk makes it important that researchers should not be punished for deviating from their PAP in cases where the plan omits important details or contains errors, as argued in Casey et al. (2012).

It seems likely to us that the majority of observational empirical work in the social sciences will continue largely as is for the foreseeable future and will not use PAPs. However, for important, intensely debated, and well-defined questions, it would be desirable, in our view, for more observational research to be conducted in a prespecified fashion, following the example in Neumark (2001). Although prespecification will not always be possible, the fact that large amounts of government data are released to the public on regular schedules, and that many policy changes are known to occur well in advance—as in the case of the anticipated federal minimum wage changes discussed above, or prespecified observational analysis of election outcomes in political science, as in Monogan (2013)—will make it possible for the verifiable prespecification of research analysis to be carried out in many settings.

LEARNING FROM OTHER RESEARCH FIELDS

Another frontier topic in this realm is the use of prespecified algorithms, including machine learning approaches, rather than exact PAPs for prospective studies. For instance, the exact procedure to be used to determine which covariates should be included in order to generate the most statistically precise estimates can be laid out in advance, even if those covariates are unknown (and unknowable) before the data have been collected. This data science approach is just now becoming better known in the social sciences but has already been used in the analysis of medical trials and in biostatistics for several years (van der Laan et al. 2007; Sinisi et al. 2007).

A proposal related to, but slightly different from, PAPs is Nobel-winning Berkeley physicist Saul Perlmutter's suggestion for the social sciences to use "blind analysis" (MacCoun and Perlmutter 2015). In blind analysis, researchers explicitly add noise to the data or conceal important features of it, while working with it and running the analysis, thus preventing them from knowing which way the results are turning out, and thus making it impossible for them to either consciously or unconsciously bias their analysis. Then, at the very end, the noise or concealment is removed from the data and the final results are produced. This technique is apparently quite common in experimental physics (Klein and Roodman 2005), but we are not aware of its widespread use in economics or other social sciences. However, the approach discussed above of examining endline data for the control group alone—or for both the control and treatment groups together without knowing any individual's treatment status (Olken 2015)—is quite similar in spirit. Clearly, strict data handling and access protocols would need to be enforced to prevent peeking at the true data by researchers.

Major differences are also beginning to emerge in the use of PAPs, and in the design and interpretation of experimental evidence more broadly, among social scientists versus scholars in other fields, especially health researchers, with theory playing a greater role in the design of social science experiments. For instance, economists often design experiments to shed light on underlying theoretical mechanisms, to inform ongoing theoretical debates, and to measure and estimate endogenous behavioral responses. These behavioral responses may shed light on broader issues beyond the experimental intervention at hand, and thus could contribute to greater external validity of the results. As a result, PAPs in economics and political science are often very detailed and make explicit reference to theoretical models. For example, Bai et al. (2017) preregistered the theoretical microeconomic model and structural econometric approach that they planned to apply to a study of commitment contracts in the Indian health sector, and they went on to successfully estimate those parameters using their endline data.

This distinction between the types of studies carried out by medical researchers and social scientists (including those working on health topics) has a number of important implications for assessing the reliability of evidence. One has to do with the quality "standards" and perceptions of the "risk of bias" in a particular design. For medical trialists accustomed to the CONSORT standards or other reporting guidelines for medical efficacy trials (discussed in Chapter 8), studies that do not feature double-blinding—and thus run the "risk" of endogenous behavioral responses to the medical intervention—are considered less reliable than studies that employ double-blinding (for a detailed discussion, see Eble, Boone, and Elbourne 2014). Although a few studies conducted by economists do feature double-blinding (e.g., Thomas et al. 2003, 2006), blinding participants to their status is either logistically difficult (e.g., if government partners are unwilling to distribute placebo treatments to some of their population) or even impossible in nearly all settings.

To illustrate, how would you provide a placebo treatment in a study investigating the impact of the distribution of cash transfers on household consumption patterns? Even in settings that might seem promising for placebo treatments, such as the community-level deworming treatments discussed in Miguel and Kremer (2004), blinding participants to their status is basically impossible: deworming generates side effects (mainly gastrointestinal distress) in roughly 10 percent of those who take the pills, so community members in a placebo community would quickly deduce that they were in fact not receiving real deworming drugs if there were few or no cases of side effects.

As noted above, endogenous behavioral responses are often exactly what social scientists set out to measure and estimate in our experiments, as described in our PAPs, and thus are to be embraced rather than rejected as symptomatic of a "low-quality" research design that is at "high risk of bias." Taken together, it is clear to us that the experimental literature in psychology, political science, economics, and other social sciences often has very different objectives than medical, public health, and epidemiological research—and, thus, different research methodologies are called for. Despite the value of learning from recent experience in biomedical research, and the inspiration that biomedical research has provided to the rise of new experimental research methods in the social sciences, social scientists have not been able to simply import existing medical trial methods wholesale. Rather, we are developing new and tailored approaches to preregistration, PAPs, reporting standards, and transparency to meet the needs of our own research fields.

SEVEN

Specification Searching Solutions

Sensitivity Analysis and Other Approaches

In Chapter 4 we discussed the problem of specification searching and discussed a few methods, such as the p-curve, that can be used to test for abuse of researcher flexibility in analysis. This chapter builds on Chapter 4, discussing methods that can be used not only to document the sturdiness (or lack thereof) of an estimate, but also approaches that construct alternative estimates by combining or averaging across many models and many analytical decisions. We especially recommend these methods when a pre-analysis plan is not a viable option, although it may also be valuable to prespecify the approach used to gauge robustness across various analytical decisions.

This chapter assumes some familiarity with sampling and bootstrapping methods. If you need a primer or refresher, please refer to Efron and Gong (1983) or Horowitz (2001).

SPECIFICATION CURVE

Social science researchers today are expected to show at least some robustness checks, or results across alternative analytical specifications, to convince readers of the validity of their results. While this practice has become more common in recent years, there remains a widespread concern that even the robustness checks that are presented could be cherry-picked from among a large set of possible alternatives. Young and Holsteen (2017), for example, looked at 60 quantitative articles published in top sociology journals, and while the average article contained about three footnotes reporting sensitivity analyses, not a single one in any article they reviewed reported a sensitivity analysis that weakened or contradicted the main findings of a paper. So, one might ask whether there is a way to carry out these checks more systematically and convincingly.

Simonsohn, Simmons, and Nelson (2015b) and Young and Holsteen (2017) offer related approaches to what the former describe as analysis of the "specification curve." These approaches are similar in spirit to Leamer's extreme-bounds analysis (discussed in Chapter 4) but extend it by testing a more exhaustive combination of analytical decisions, not just decisions about which covariates to include in the regression model. For example, if the authors of a paper had decided in the course of their analysis to (1) dichotomize one continuous variable, (2) drop a few outliers, and (3) cluster standard errors at a certain level of aggregation, the specification curve would run a version of the model with all possible combinations of those three decisions, so $2^3 = 8$ regression models at the very least. If the full exhaustive set is too large to be practical, a random subset of specifications can be used. A researcher can then construct the specification curve by plotting all the effect sizes from all the models in order of increasing magnitude, with some indication of significance level and a grid below indicating which decisions were used in a given model run.

Figure 7.1 shows the specification-curve application that Simonsohn, Simmons, and Nelson (2015b) constructed for a famous article by Bertrand and Mullainathan (2004) that estimated the effect on job application success of having a name that, in the United States, is predominantly given to whites versus a name predominantly given to blacks, as a way to quantify the extent of racial discrimination; this approach has since been adopted in hundreds of other contexts. Bertrand and Mullainathan sent out real-looking résumés in response to actual job postings. These résumés were identical in terms of individual qualifications, but the names on the résumés were randomly varied to have "white" names (e.g., Emily for women, Greg for men) or "black" names (e.g., Lakisha for women, Jamal for men) and recorded the numbers of callbacks different résumés received.

As evidence of the persistent racial discrimination in the United States, résumés with white names received a staggering 50 percent more callbacks. While higher-quality résumés (i.e., those with better educational and job qualifications) with white names received 30 percent more callbacks than low-quality white-name résumés, this effect was

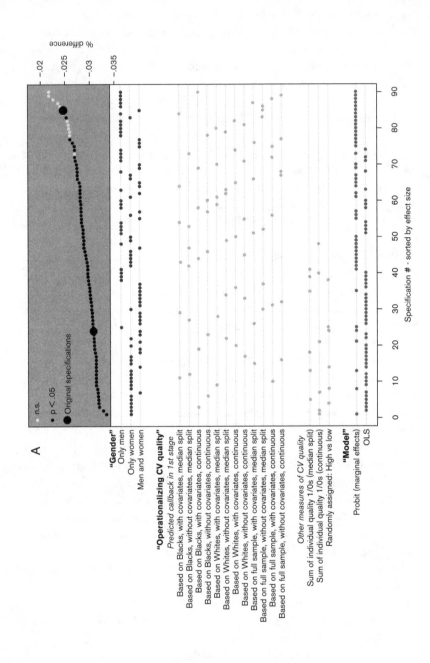

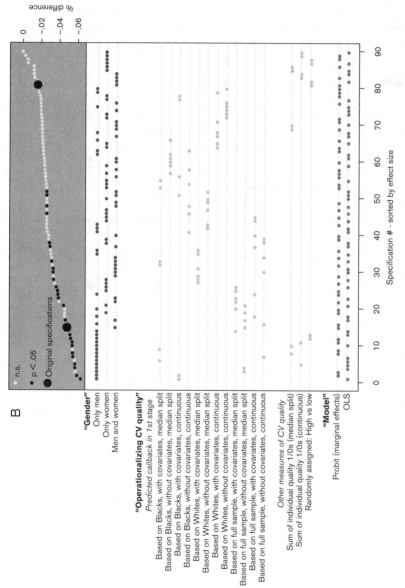

FIGURE 7.1. Specification curves of (**A**) main effects and (**B**) interaction effects from Bertrand and Mullainathan (2004). In both panels, analysis decisions are listed on the left and indicated by dots on the graph; results are sorted by effect size and plotted across the top.

smaller for résumés with black names, indicating a smaller return on human capital investments, such as education, for African Americans.

This study is widely considered to be of high quality: given its use of a randomized design, often considered the gold standard for empirical research design, it can credibly make a strong causal claim on an important question. It has been cited over 3,000 times according to Google Scholar (as of the writing of this book), a high level of influence.

That said, the study was conducted before pre-analysis plans were common or even really known in the social sciences, possibly raising some concerns about the results even though they are experimental. Just think back to the example of the Sierra Leone project (Casey, Glennerster, and Miguel 2012) discussed in Chapter 6, in which researchers were able to cherry-pick particular outcomes in order to generate different conclusions. Simonsohn, Simmons, and Nelson (2015b) applied their specification-curve approach to address this concern, focusing on key dimensions along which Bertrand and Mullainathan (2004) had some analytical leeway—namely, how to deal with heterogeneity in effects by gender, how to measure résumé quality, and which regression model to use (specifically, linear regression or probit).

Using this approach, Simonsohn and colleagues determined there were at least 90 different but reasonable analytical specifications in the original paper. Figure 7.1A presents the main estimated impact of having a distinctively black name on the likelihood of receiving an interview callback. The two original specifications in Bertrand and Mullainathan (2004) appear as large black dots along a line of mostly black dots and only a few gray dots, where the black dots indicate statistically significant specifications (at $p < .05$) and the gray dots do not meet this threshold. The bottom portion of Figure 7.1 panel A shows which analytical decisions led to each effect estimate, in terms of sample used, covariates included, and regression model. Examining patterns here could potentially illuminate analytical decisions, or combinations of decisions, that led to particularly large or small effect estimates. There do not appear to be strong patterns in panel A: in nearly every specification, there is a statistically significant effect of having a black name in reducing interview callbacks. The demonstration here that the effect is robust across scores of specifications helps convince us that this is a valid finding, and not dependent on a particular set of analytical decisions.

Figure 7.1 panel B shows the second effect mentioned above, namely the interaction effect of having a black name and candidate quality as captured in the résumé. This test is more complicated—the interaction of black names and résumé quality should actually be compared to the interaction of white names and résumé quality. A null result for the black-name interaction compared to the consistently larger and significant white-name interaction is more evidence of racial discrimination. The specification curve indicates that this finding generalizes across the range of plausible analytical specifications, few of which are statistically significant at high levels of confidence: the gray dots outnumber the black dots here. This specification-curve approach is relatively new, and one can imagine improvements in how the data are visualized in a more compact manner. In data visualization, less is often more (Tufte 1983).

A natural next step to determine analytical robustness is to permute the data. Researchers can generate shuffled samples with no true effect (by construction), and then compare the specification curves generated by these placebo samples to the specification curve from the actual data. If there are few differences between the placebo and actual data, this indicates that there is likely no true treatment effect. Permutation tests (also known as randomization tests or exact tests) are employed for data that have randomly assigned treatment status, and their close cousin, bootstrapping, is used for treatment without random assignment. For more technical information on permutation tests, which we do not discuss here for reasons of space, see Pitman (1937) or Fisher (1956a).[1] For information on bootstrapping, see Efron and Gong (1983), Efron (1992), and Horowitz (2001).

It is useful to illustrate this approach in the context of Bertrand and Mullainathan's (2004) study of racial discrimination in hiring. In a permutation test, the researcher would generate a placebo indicator variable for having a typically black name in the data. This placebo variable would be a randomly generated binary variable with the same fraction of ones and zeros as in the actual black indicator. Then the researcher would carry out the original regression analysis with these new, permuted data. Given that the placebo variable is just noise, most of the time we would not expect the estimated effect of having a black name to be statistically significant. For instance, as we saw above, in the actual data the black-name effect is statistically significant in roughly 80 out of 90 models that Simonsohn, Simmons, and Nelson (2015b)

---

1. We can't resist mentioning that permutation tests were first developed by Sir Ronald Fisher, supposedly after a discussion with a woman who claimed to be able to distinguish between tea made by pouring in the milk first (bad) versus tea made by pouring in the tea first (good). Apparently, Brits can indeed tell the difference (Powers 1988).

checked, but in permuted data we would not expect significant results by chance in more than around four or five out of 90 models.

To conduct real statistical tests, Simonsohn and colleagues recommend permuting the data 500 times and then rerunning the analysis across each of these draws of the data. Many comparisons are possible with this much data (500 draws × 90 regression models in the specification curve), but the authors argue that in practice it is useful to compare the median effect size across the actual versus placebo data, the share of results with the predicted sign, and the share of statistically significant results with the predicted sign. Another key comparison, which is conceptually analogous to the traditional p-value, is the percentage of the shuffled samples with as many or more statistically significant results than the actual data.

Bertrand and Mullainathan's (2004) study comes out of the specification-curve exercise intact: the main results are robust. Simonsohn, Simmons, and Nelson (2015b) go on to apply the specification curve to a second, more controversial study, and one that does not fare as well under greater scrutiny. That study, published in a leading scientific journal, reported a relationship between the gender of hurricane names and the number of fatalities the hurricane caused (Jung et al. 2014). The idea advanced by the study's authors is that, because of gender stereotypes about feminine "weakness," government agencies and citizens do not take female-named hurricanes (e.g., "Katrina") as seriously as male-named hurricanes ("Andrew") and do not prepare adequately as a result. We confess that we do not see this as an especially plausible theory, but it was widely shared when first published. "Scientists Discover New Source of Hurricane Danger: Sexism" read the headline in the *Los Angeles Times*.

In fact, Jung et al. (2014) presented statistical evidence that there is more damage, on average, from female-named hurricanes, and the effect was statistically significant. But their study was widely criticized upon publication by researchers who took issue with their analytical decisions (e.g., Christensen and Christensen 2014; Maley 2014; Malter 2014; Bakkensen and Larson 2014). First off, one can see in the specification-curve application by Simonsohn, Simmons, and Nelson (2015b) in Figure 7.2 that the vast majority of specifications do not generate statistically significant results, unlike the published result (the large black circle), and this is an immediate cause of concern regarding robustness. Note, too, that the largest estimates typically require one specific analytical choice, the use of a negative binomial statistical model. Now that

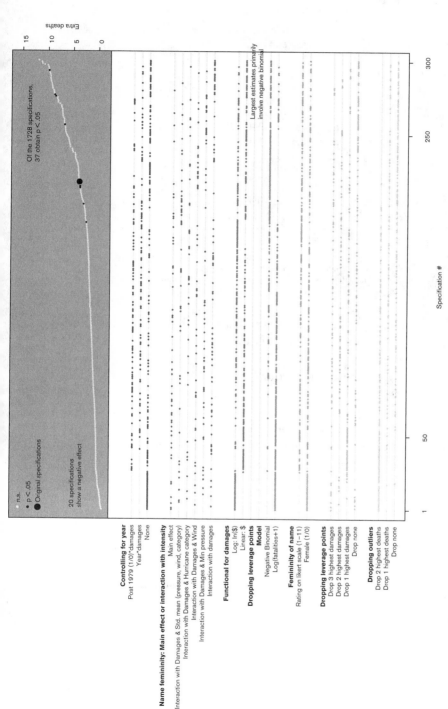

FIGURE 7.2. Descriptive specification curve of main effect from Jung et al. (2014). Each dot in the top panel (shaded area) depicts a point estimate from a different specification; the dots vertically aligned below (white area) indicate the analytic decisions behind those estimates. A total of 1,728 specifications were estimated; depicted are the 50 highest and lowest point estimates, and a random subset of 200 additional ones.

TABLE 7.1 SUMMARY OF SPECIFICATION CURVES OF JUNG ET AL. (2014) AND
BERTRAND AND MULLAINATHAN (2004)

	Observed result	p-value
	Example 1. "Female" hurricanes are deadlier	
Median effect size	1.63 additional deaths	$p = .459$
Share of results with predicted sign	1,704/1,728	$p = .156$
Share of results with predicted sign and $p < .05$	37/1,728	$p = .850$
	Example 2. "Black" names receive fewer callbacks	
Median effect size	3.1 pp fewer calls	$p < .002$
Share of results with predicted sign	90/90	$p = .125$
Share of results with predicted sign and $p < .05$	85/90	$p < .002$

NOTES: Table shows the observed results from all possible specifications, and then the fraction of curves with certain characteristics using a large number of permuted (null-effect) datasets.

might be the right analytical choice—it's debatable, as indicated by other critical researchers—but this, in itself, starts to raise important concerns about robustness.

Table 7.1 summarizes the robustness of Jung et al.'s (2014) findings as well as those of Bertrand and Mullainathan (2004), based on the specification-curve results in Figures 7.1 and 7.2. First of all, nearly half (46 percent) of the curves from permuted data show at least as large a median effect size as the original data, 16 percent show at least as many results with the predicted sign, and fully 85 percent of the permuted data results show at least as many statistically significant results with the predicted sign. These patterns look more like noise than signal. For instance, if the female-named-hurricane effect was actually zero, roughly 50 percent of the curves from permuted data would show at least as large a median effect size as the original, very close to the 46 percent reported in the table. Simply put, a true null effect appears relatively likely to be able to generate the supposedly statistically significant published results.

By contrast, regarding Bertrand and Mullainathan (2004), less than 0.2 percent of the permuted curves generate as large a median effect as the actual data, 12.5 percent of permuted curves show at least as many results with the predicted sign, and less than 0.2 percent of permuted curves show at least as many significant results with the predicted sign. This is strong evidence that the published results are unlikely to have been generated by chance.

MULTIVERSE ANALYSIS

The approach of Simonsohn, Simmons, and Nelson (2015b) takes the data as given and varies the analysis in multiple ways. An alternative method of dealing with the analytical flexibility we highlighted in Chapter 3, advocated by Steegen et al. (2016), is to also consider the many choices that go into data construction and variable creation. Steegen et al. develop the "multiverse" approach, a name inspired by the popular concept of multiple coexisting realities, which they link to different data-construction decisions.

They build their example multiverse using data from a study by Durante, Rae, and Griskevicius (2013), which concludes that ovulation has effects on females' survey answers regarding their political and social views. In particular, Durante, Rae, and Griskevicius (2013) claim that periods of high fertility (ovulation) led single (unmarried) U.S. women to be less religious and more politically liberal (supporting Barack Obama in the 2012 presidential election) while women who were married (or in a committed relationship) and in a high-fertility part of their menstrual cycle had the opposite response. These women are found to answer questions in a way that indicated they were more religious and more likely to support the conservative candidate (Governor Mitt Romney).

Steegen et al.'s idea is to create a multiverse of analysis datasets, using all reasonable combinations of data cleaning and construction decisions. Of course, there are many choices that go into data construction, and this leads to extra degrees of freedom for authors, which in turn leads to the possibility of selective reporting or cherry-picking. For example, Durante, Rae, and Griskevicius (2013) considered women on days 7 to 14 of their menstrual cycle high-fertility, and women on days 17 to 25 low-fertility. The analysis explicitly compared high-fertility to low-fertility women, dichotomizing the continuous day-of-menstrual-cycle variable and excluding women at all other points in their cycles. Since this is a key variable in the analysis, the multiverse approach constructs this variable using other plausible definitions of high and low fertility to gauge robustness:

Days 6–14 high, days 17–27 low

Days 9–17 high, days 18–25 low

Days 8–14 high, days 1–7 and 15–28 low

Days 9–17 high, days 1–8 and 18–28 low

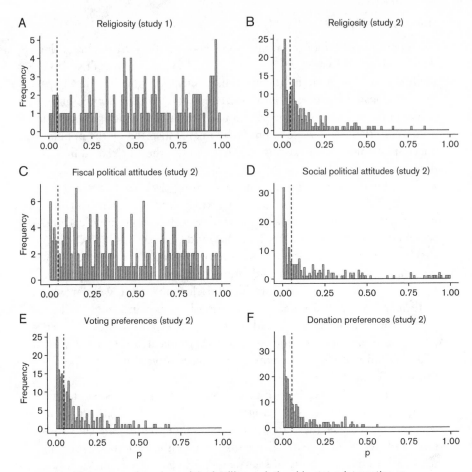

FIGURE 7.3. Histograms of *p*-values of the fertility × relationship status interaction on **(A, B)** religiosity for the multiverse of 120 datasets in Study 1 and 210 datasets in Study 2, **(C, D)** fiscal and social political attitudes for the multiverse of 210 datasets in Study 2, and **(E, F)** voting and donation preferences for the multiverse of 210 datasets in Study 2. Dashed lines indicate *p* = .05. Reprinted with permission from Steegen et al. (2016).

Interestingly, these definitions are all taken from one or another previously published paper by the lead author (K. M. Durante), which suggests they are at least sensible. Beyond this variable, other data choices regarding the definition of relationship status (e.g., how exactly do you define "single"?) and the paper's sample exclusion criteria combine to produce 120 total possible datasets in the multiverse; a second study from the same paper results in 210 datasets. Steegen et al. (2016) then conduct the original analysis on all the alternative datasets and summarize the results in two ways—via histograms of the p-values resulting under all combinations, and via grids of p-values organized by data decisions—to help discern patterns.

The histograms (Figure 7.3) reveal that two of the six main outcomes—the survey questions on religious and fiscal political attitudes from Steegen et al.'s (2016) "Study 1"—have nearly uniform p-value density, indicating wide variation in the strength of the posited association. In other words, for these two outcomes, the significant results in the paper come from only a very specific set of data choices; many other potentially reasonable data choices would have resulted in totally insignificant results. The grids reveal that only about half of analytical decisions result in statistically significant associations. Together, these results indicate that there is reason to be skeptical of the published results on the link between ovulation and political attitudes for single versus other U.S. women. This finding provides another reason for researchers to preregister their analysis plans: there may well be good reasons to favor one definition of high fertility over another, but it is difficult to separate out valid reasons from *ex post* data mining in practice in the absence of a pre-analysis plan.

Note the strong similarities with the approach of Simonsohn, Simmons, and Nelson (2015b), although along a different dimension (i.e., data decisions, rather than analytical decisions). A fuller assessment of the robustness of results could cross these two approaches, examining results along pairs of data-analysis combinations.

MODEL AVERAGING

Another way to deal with statistical model uncertainty is through Bayesian model averaging. Supporters of this approach claim it has stronger decision-theoretic foundations than the extreme bounds analysis developed by Leamer (1983) and others (see Brock, Durlauf, and West 2003). This is similar to the previous methods, but instead of simply displaying or treating all models equally, each model in the space of plausible models is assigned a probability of being true based on researcher priors and goodness-of-fit criteria. This is a key difference with specification-curve-type approaches, which effectively weight each alternative model in the space of examined specifications equally.

Averaging the resulting estimates generates a statistic incorporating model uncertainty,

$$\hat{\delta}_M = \Sigma_m \mu(m \mid D)\hat{\delta}_m , \qquad\qquad \text{Eqn. 7.1}$$

where m refers to a particular statistical model, M is the space of plausible models, $\mu(m|D)$ is the posterior probability of a model being the true model given the data D, and $\hat{\delta}_m$ is the estimated statistic from model m $\in$ M.

These weights must, of course, be chosen somehow. Cohen-Cole et al. (2009), from whom we borrow the above notation, revisited the empirical question from Leamer (1983) and studied the deterrent effect of the death penalty with a model-averaging exercise that combines evidence from Donohue and Wolfers (2005) and Dezhbakhsh, Rubin, and Shepherd (2003), using the Bayesian Information Criterion (Schwarz 1978).[2] The weighted average they generated implies a large but imprecisely estimated deterrent effect of executions on homicides in the United States. (As we saw above, even without employing explicit probability weights, simply visualizing the distribution of estimates across the entire space of statistical models can also be quite informative on its own.)

Two well-cited examples of model averaging engage in a thorough investigation of the determinants of cross-country economic growth, a core topic in macroeconomics. Sala-i-Martin's (1997) humorously titled article "I Just Ran Two Million Regressions" uses model weights proportional to the integrated likelihoods of each model (a measure of model fit). He picked all possible three-variable combinations out of 60 covariates that had been reported in the literature as being significantly related to economic growth and found that about one-third of the 60 variables can be considered robustly positively correlated with economic growth across models.[3]

This is in contrast to earlier methods employed by Levine and Renelt (1992), who concluded that very few measures were robustly correlated

2. The Bayesian Information Criterion (BIC) is a measure of model fit, defined as -2 $\ln(L)+\ln(n)k$, where L is the likelihood, n is the number of observations, and k is the number of parameters. Like the Akaike Information Criterion, the BIC has a penalty term for the number of parameters to avoid overfitting; the penalty is larger in the BIC.

3. The definition of *robustness* in this method is a bit complicated but involves the weighted cumulative distribution function of all the many coefficient estimates. Rather than focusing just on the point estimate and significance of a single estimate, imagine the distribution implied by a single coefficient estimate and its standard error. Then combine all those distributions across many models. How exactly one does this depends on the assumption of whether the distribution of coefficients is normal or not. Regardless, significance is defined as variables for which the weighted CDF(0) is larger than 0.95, which means that the vast majority of the models produce significant estimates. It's also important to mention that in regard to "CDF(0)" Sala-i-Martin (1997) is agnostic about CDF(0) and 1 - CDF(0): whether the effect is negative or positive doesn't matter; what matters is that effects are largely on the same side of zero.

with growth. (They concluded that at the very most, the average share of investment in gross domestic product seems robustly correlated with average growth rates.) Levine and Renelt's method is more along the lines of Leamer's extreme bounds analysis—take the highest and lowest significant estimate across all the models, and go to the far edge of the confidence interval of each of those estimates. Are they on the opposite side of zero? If so, then the claim is not robust.

Formally, in a set of j regressions of the form $y = \alpha_j + \beta_{xj}x + \beta_{zj}z + \varepsilon$, define the lower extreme bound as the lowest value of $\beta_{zj} - 2\sigma_{zj}$ and the upper extreme bound as the highest value of $\beta_{zj} + 2\sigma_{zj}$. To be robust, these values should lie on the same side of zero. Sala-i-Martin's method is a deliberate attempt to move away from such extreme value tests, which use less information from the distribution of each individual coefficient estimate.

Sala-i-Martin, Doppelhofer, and Miller (2004) conducted what they call Bayesian Averaging of Classical Estimates, weighting estimates using an approach analogous to Schwarz's Bayesian Information Criterion, and found that only 18 of 67 variables studied in the literature are significantly and robustly partially correlated with economic growth, once again suggesting that many findings reported in the existing empirical literature may be spuriously generated by specification searching and selective reporting. Fernández, Ley, and Steel (2001) carried out a related exercise and found results similar to those of Sala-i-Martin.

MULTIPLE TESTING CORRECTIONS

In Chapter 4 we demonstrated that testing multiple outcomes or using multiple sets of controls resulted in a higher-than-expected fraction of low p-values, even on simulated data. Aware of this, applied econometricians have recently called for increasing the use of multiple testing corrections in order to generate more meaningful inference in study settings with many research hypotheses (Anderson 2008; Fink, McConnell, and Vollmer 2014). The practice of correcting for multiple tests is already widespread in certain scientific fields. For example, genomewide association studies, which conduct a million or so tests in a hypothesis-neutral fashion, use 5×10^{-8} ($p = .00000005$) as a conventional p-value (see Benjamin et al. 2012). However, it has yet to become common across social sciences. (That said, there have been some calls to change the cutoff across the social science disciplines. Most notable is Benjamin et al. [2017], which has nearly 70 authors and recommends using .005 instead of .05 as the significance cutoff.)

Simply put, since we know that p-values fall below traditional significance thresholds (e.g., .05) purely by chance a certain proportion of the time, it makes sense to report adjusted p-values that account for the fact that we are running multiple tests, since this makes it more likely that at least one of our test statistics has a significant p-value simply by chance.

There are several approaches to multiple testing, some of which are used and explained by Anderson (2008)—namely, reporting index tests, controlling the family-wise error rate (FWER), and controlling the false discovery rate (FDR). Anderson also provides links to statistical code (in Stata) to carry out these tests. These approaches are each discussed in turn below.

Reporting Index Tests

One option for scholars in cases where there are multiple related outcome measures is to forgo reporting the outcomes of numerous tests, and instead standardize the related outcomes and combine them into a smaller number of indices, sometimes referred to as a *mean effect*. To implement this for a family of related outcomes:[4]

1. Make all signs "agree" (i.e., allow all positive values to denote beneficial outcomes).

2. Standardize all outcomes by demeaning and dividing by the control group standard deviation; denote the standardized outcomes $\bar{y}$.

3. Construct $\bar{s}_{ij}$ for individual i in family j, which is a weighted average of the $\bar{y}$ variables in a given family. The simplest way is to weight each input into the index equally; another common approach is to use the inverse of the covariance matrix to weight each standardized outcome.

4. Use $\bar{s}_{ij}$ the new index as a single outcome in a regression model and evaluated with a standard t-test.

Kling, Liebman, and Katz (2007) implemented an early index test in the "Moving to Opportunity" field experiment using methods developed in biomedicine by O'Brien (1984). There are, of course, many ways to do step 3, but O'Brien found that the inverse covariance matrix (which is an efficient generalized least squares estimator) is more statistically

---

4. We borrow notation from Anderson (2008), which has a helpful explanation of these methods.

powerful than other methods; this approach ensures that highly correlated outcomes each receive somewhat less weight while less correlated outcomes receive relatively more weight in the analysis.

This method addresses some concerns regarding the multiplicity of statistical tests by simply reducing the number of tests. A potential drawback is that the index may combine outcomes that are only weakly related, and may obscure impacts on specific outcomes that are of interest to particular scholars (but note that these specific outcomes could also be separately reported for completeness).

Controlling the Family-Wise Error Rate

The FWER is the probability that at least one true null hypothesis in a group is rejected (i.e., a type I error, or false positive). This approach is considered most useful when the "damage" from incorrectly claiming that *any* hypothesis is false is high. There are several ways to implement this approach, the simplest method being the Bonferroni correction of multiplying every original p-value by the number of tests carried out (or, identically, comparing p-values to α/n where α is the significance level and n is the number of tests or family size; Bland and Altman 1995), although this is extremely conservative, and improved methods have also been developed.

Holm's sequential method improved on Bonferroni by ordering all p-values tested and comparing the lower p-values to lower thresholds (Holm 1979). Formally, compare all p-values in a family to $\dfrac{\alpha}{n - rank + 1}$, where "rank" refers to the rank order of p-values within a family from lowest to highest. This means that the lowest p-value is compared to α/n and the highest is compared to α. This provides the same control on the FWER as Bonferroni (i.e., FWER$\leq\alpha$) but reduces the type II error rate. A related and more efficient recent method is the free step-down resampling method, developed by Westfall and Young (1993). This method improves on Bonferroni and Holm by incorporating the existing dependence between outcomes being tested.[5] When implemented by Anderson (2008), it implies that several highly cited experimental preschool interventions

---

5. Interested readers should refer to Westfall and Young (1993) or Anderson (2008) for details, but the idea of the free-stepdown resampling method is that instead of ranking and comparing p-values to $\dfrac{\alpha}{n - rank + 1}$, the data are resampled, and ranked p-values are compared to ranked simulated p-values from the resampled data. This retains the original dependence structure of outcomes.

(namely, the Abecedarian, Perry, and Early Training Project studies) exhibit few positive long-run impacts for males, while females still show significant gains.

A similar method developed by Romano and Wolf (2005) also incorporates the dependent structure of multiple tests but requires fewer assumptions. Lee and Shaikh (2014) applied this method to reevaluate the Mexican PROGRESA conditional cash transfer program and found that overall program impacts remain positive and significant but are statistically significant for fewer subgroups (e.g., by gender, education) when controlling for multiple testing. List, Shaikh, and Xu (2016) also propose a method of controlling the FWER for three common situations in experimental economics: testing multiple outcomes, testing for heterogeneous treatment effects in multiple subgroups, and testing with multiple treatment conditions.[6]

Controlling the False Discovery Rate

In situations where a single type I error is not considered very costly, researchers may be willing to use a somewhat less conservative method than the FWER approach, and trade off some incorrect hypothesis rejections in exchange for greater statistical power. This is made possible by controlling the FDR, which is the percentage of rejections that are type I errors. Benjamini and Yekutieli (2001) detail a simple algorithm to control this rate at a chosen level under the assumption that the p-values from the multiple tests are independent, though the same method was later shown to also be valid under weaker assumptions. Benjamini, Krieger, and Yekutieli (2006) describe a two-step procedure with greater statistical power, while Romano, Shaikh, and Wolf (2008) propose the first methods to incorporate information about the dependence structure of the test statistics. We generally think that the benefits of FDR make it more attractive than other approaches, including FWER, in much social science research, and currently use the algorithm described by Benjamini, Krieger, and Yekutieli (2006).

Multiple hypothesis testing adjustments have recently been used in finance (Harvey, Liu, and Zhu 2015) to reevaluate 316 factors from 313 different papers that explain the cross section of expected stock

---

6. Most methods are meant only to deal with the first and/or second of these cases. Statistical code to implement the adjustments in List, Shaikh, and Xu (2016) in Stata and MATLAB is available at https://github.com/seidelj/mht.

returns. The authors report the results of three methods of adjusting for multiple hypothesis testing (Bonferroni's; Holm's; and Benjamini, Hochberg, and Yekutieli's) and conclude that t-statistics >3.0, and possibly as high as 3.9, should be used instead of the standard 1.96, to actually conclude that a factor explains stock returns with 95 percent confidence. Index tests and both the FWER and FDR multiple testing corrections are also employed in Casey, Glennerster, and Miguel's (2012) study (discussed in Chapter 6) to estimate the impacts of a community-driven development program in Sierra Leone using a dataset with hundreds of potentially relevant outcome variables.

BOOTSTRAP REALITY CHECK

Another method that controls for, or acts as a reality check for, data snooping or data mining (running multiple tests on the same data) was developed by White (2000). The testing of multiple hypotheses, or repeated use of the same data, is a particularly central problem with time series data used over and over again by multiple scholars, such as data on stock returns, which makes this research quite important in empirical finance (for fun and profit!). Like the model averaging approach described above, the reality check requires a researcher to estimate the entire space of plausible models, but now compares the performance of the preferred model to a benchmark model (e.g., a model for stock market predictions based on the efficient market hypothesis—the hypothesis that says it's impossible to beat the market since the market always reflects all available information), and does so repeatedly with bootstrapped samples.

To assess whether a certain preferred model actually outperforms the benchmark after accounting for snooping with multiple models, the researcher first calculates the performance of the preferred model using mean squared error improvement over the benchmark, or the relative profit of the strategy. She then selects a bootstrap sample (with replacement) and calculates the mean squared error improvement (or profit) with the new sample for all of the different plausible statistical models, recording the best mean squared error improvement (or profit) across all the models. This approach can then be repeated 1,000 (or more) times, gathering the 1,000 best mean squared errors (or profits). In the final step, one must compare the original preferred model's mean squared error to the best performance from each of the 1,000 bootstraps. The p-value is the fraction of bootstrapped best fits that outperform the preferred model. (A truly predictive model would have returns higher than 95 percent of the best-performing models from each of the bootstrapped samples.)

To attempt to clarify with an example, imagine you came up with a new stock-investment strategy that you think is better than a low-cost S&P 500 fund, and found 57 competing (but less profitable) strategies that also claimed the same thing, for 58 total ways to supposedly beat the market. Take your investment strategy (call it X) and calculate how much more profit you would have made with X than with the S&P 500. Call it $Y. (If $Y is less than zero, you can stop right now and decide your strategy isn't good.) Then select a bootstrap sample (with replacement) from your stock returns data to get a slightly different set of observations. Find the best investment strategy from the 58, and record how much more it made than the S&P 500. Repeat the bootstrapping 1,000 times, calculating the best model and profit out of the 58 each time. Then compare your original $Y to the entire distribution of other best-model profits. Ideally, your strategy had higher profits than 950 or more of the best strategies from the 1,000 bootstrapped samples (i.e., 95 percent of the time, $p < .05$). If so, you might want to forget research and go code up your strategy for a hedge fund. If not, your strategy is likely just an artifact of the fact that you tested 58 different strategies on the data before picking the best one.

This method was implemented on a large number of trading rules by Sullivan, Timmermann, and White (1999), and a similar method that addresses the presence of poorly performing or irrelevant alternatives was developed by Hansen (2005).

CONCLUSION

If there's a thread connecting all the methods throughout this chapter, it's this: Test all the models with all the data, and do so transparently. As researchers, we really like to think that the final model and variables we decide on are the best, and we knew it was best all along, and it should be obvious to everyone. Unfortunately, this is unlikely to always be the case. Even if we are sincere in our view that the final model and data we chose is right, extensive robustness checks along the lines of those reported in this chapter may be necessary to convince others that researcher bias is not driving the results. When the bulk of alternative models and data provide similar answers, we can have greater confidence in our answers. When they do not agree, it opens space for useful discussion regarding the sources of these disagreements.

Of course, even the choice of a particular set of models to estimate means that there is still some scope for researcher discretion and possible cherry-picking. In such cases, specific reporting standards regarding the types of models, covariates, and data construction to report could be valuable. Reporting and disclosure standards are also valuable in allowing other scholars to better understand and build on existing research. We turn to these important issues in the next chapter.

PART FOUR

Practices

EIGHT

Reporting Standards

"Do you think that the economics discipline has a conflict-of-interest problem?" asks the filmmaker during a segment of the 2010 documentary *Inside Job.* The segment features a prominent economist who coauthored a report extolling the stability of Iceland's financial sector, not long before its meltdown threatened global markets. Of course, misjudgments happen and no one has a crystal ball. But the filmmaker points out that the very same economist collected a six-figure consulting fee for the report from the Icelandic Chamber of Commerce, a detail not mentioned anywhere in the report. The film is credited with pushing the American Economic Association to require that published articles include a disclosure statement online regarding potential conflicts of interest (Casselman 2012).

The conflict-of-interest statement is an example of a *reporting standard,* an explicit guideline about the information that researchers should present as part of their study. Reporting standards do not directly regulate how research is done. For example, rather than prohibit researchers from collecting consultant fees, conflict-of-interest disclosure requirements specify what researchers need to report to readers, and how that reporting is to be done.

Most issues covered by reporting standards are far less morally fraught than financial conflicts. For example, some guidelines indicate that studies should report the prevalence of missing data for key variables in a study. Making explicit that this should be reported can be useful for researchers who otherwise might not realize that other experts regard this as important in assessing the quality of a study. These standards can thus be useful training tools for young scholars. Standardized reporting also strengthens the promise of meta-analysis methods for aggregating results from multiple studies (see Chapter 5), by increasing the consistency of the information that these techniques can use.

Reporting standards also address the worry that mundane details might be left out of a paper for less innocuous reasons. Ideally, one would hope that a study having a large amount of missing data would make authors *more* likely to call readers' attention to the issue, but the fear is that they may sometimes be *less* likely to do so—for example, if they do not want readers to downgrade the perceived validity of the results. Reporting standards clarify expectations and reduce the latitude for researchers to shrug off keeping important details from readers.

We should be clear at the outset that we believe adherence to reporting standards can benefit researchers even when their own disciplines do not formally require it. Standards help authors anticipate information that reviewers may expect to see explicitly reported in a paper, thus boosting publication prospects. Given that standards often represent collective efforts by the research community to formulate best practices in reporting, adherence can strengthen one's scientific contribution by making study results more accurately understood by readers. They can also be helpful when reviewing other manuscripts, as a reminder of what details one should look for.

In this chapter, we discuss an especially influential set of scientific reporting standards, and then describe the broad domains that different reporting standards may cover. We will also discuss standards regarding how specific technical terms are used in research articles. Finally, we focus on writing project proposals, which should ideally provide detailed and precise descriptions of the procedures to be used in a study.

THE CONSORT STANDARD

Currently, the most prominent set of scientific reporting standards is CONSORT (Consolidated Standards of Reporting Trials), used for randomized controlled trials (RCTs) in medicine. While it has been revised several times since, CONSORT started in the mid-1990s, arising from a gathering of researchers who wished to develop a standardized scale for assessing the quality of RCTs (Begg et al. 1996; Altman et al. 2001; Schulz, Altman, and Moher 2010). The group's purpose shifted as members came to recognize how many of the elements important to

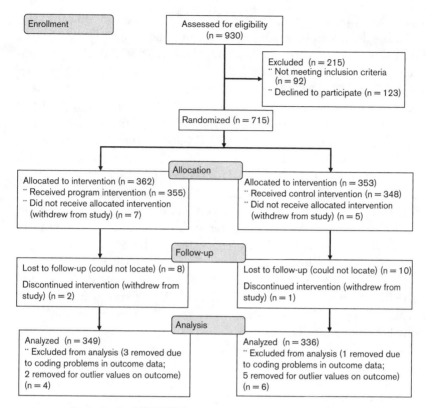

FIGURE 8.1. Example of a CONSORT flow diagram.

assessing the quality of RCTs were often simply not reported in published articles. This is a common story of standardization: demand for a collective solution rises as the costs of researchers' often haphazard ways of reporting results become clearer.

CONSORT has been a stunning success: over the past two decades there has been rapid, almost universal adoption among medical trialists. Today, let's imagine you are part of a team authoring a clinical trial that you want to submit to *JAMA (Journal of the American Medical Association),* a leading medical journal. As part of your submission, you would need to provide a completed CONSORT checklist, in which you indicate the page of your manuscript on which each of 37 different pieces of information is reported (we'll show some examples from this checklist shortly). You would also need to submit a CONSORT flow diagram, detailing the numbers of participants at different stages of recruitment, intervention, and analysis (see Figure 8.1).

While CONSORT is relatively narrowly focused on medical RCTs, RCT-style research designs have become increasingly prominent in social science (Jackson and Cox 2013), and CONSORT has been influential as a model for reporting standards for other research. One specific effort seeks to extend the CONSORT guidelines to social and psychological interventions, for example (CONSORT-SPI; Montgomery et al. 2013). A task force offering guidelines for experimental political science draws explicitly on CONSORT's flow diagrams (Gerber et al. 2014). Similarly, a task force for health economics explicitly adopted the format of CONSORT's checklist (Husereau et al. 2013).

Meanwhile, developing reporting guidelines has become a small industry in medical research, where well over 300 (yes, three hundred!) sets of guidelines have been developed for different research types. Leading examples are STROBE (Strengthening the Reporting of Observational Studies in Epidemiology; von Elm et al. 2007); SQUIRE (Standards for QUality Improvement Reporting Excellence; Ogrinc et al. 2016); and ARRIVE (Animal Research: Reporting of In Vivo Experiments; Kilkenny et al. 2010). To deal with the proliferation of reporting standards, the EQUATOR Network was established to organize guidelines and help investigators identify the standards most appropriate for their research.[1]

CONSORT is described as evidence based, in the sense of there being some grounds for asserting that following each guideline promotes a more accurate understanding of a study's results. However, as with most successful standards, the authority of CONSORT's guidelines relies heavily on their formulation by groups of experts, officially convened and oriented toward consensus, as well as endorsement by editorial teams at journals. The phrase "science by committee" is sometimes used derisively, but reporting standards provide one example where committees can bear great fruits for science.

This does not mean that all efforts toward reporting standards have to begin with large task forces or entrenched professional organizations. Early in the recent wave of concern about replicability in social psychology, for example, a small group of three collaborators wrote a brief proposal called the "21-word solution" for experimental social psychology (Simmons, Nelson, and Simonsohn 2012): "We report how we determined our sample size, all data exclusions (if any), all manipulations, and all measures in the study."

---

1. We think it's a bit of a stretch, as far as acronyms go, but EQUATOR is Enhancing the QUAlity and Transparency Of health Research.

At the time, one issue for social psychology was that the very short article length in some of its journals created a justification ("no space") for omitting details useful for assessing studies accurately. The 21-word solution was offered to demonstrate the brevity with which one could capture what the authors regarded as the most important aspects of undisclosed flexibility leading to false positive findings (see also LeBel et al. 2013):

(1) continuing or stopping data collection on the basis of one's results;

(2) running additional experimental conditions but reporting only those that "worked";

(3) dropping outliers if doing so improves results; and

(4) collecting and analyzing many measures but reporting only the "best" results.

Alongside this, the authors and others also created standardized language asking about these issues that manuscript reviewers could paste into all their reviews:

> I request that the authors add a statement to the paper confirming whether, for all experiments, they have reported all measures, conditions, data exclusions, and how they determined their sample sizes. The authors should, of course, add any additional text to ensure the statement is accurate. This is the standard reviewer disclosure request endorsed by the Center for Open Science (see http://osf.io/project/hadz3). I include it in every review.

Placing themselves in the vanguard of the movement to change norms in their research community, they wrote: "A small but energetic choir may get the entire congregation to sing along" (Simmons, Nelson, and Simonsohn 2012, p. 4).

And it worked: the journal then regarded as an epicenter of inadequate reporting, *Psychological Science,* subsequently changed its guidelines to require authors to explicitly affirm that these issues had been reported in the study, and lifted the word limitation for the methods sections of papers so that space limits did not hinder researchers from being transparent about their research design and analytical choices.

CONTENTS OF REPORTING STANDARDS

Reporting standards often distill their recommendations into a checklist. Checklists are useful for authors because they can tick through

TABLE 8.1 EXAMPLES OF ITEMS FROM CONSORT 2010 CHECKLIST

Domain	Examples
Study context	2b. Specific objectives or hypotheses.
	25. Sources of funding and other support (such as supply of drugs); role of funders.
Study design	3a. Description of trial design (such as parallel, factorial) including allocation ratio.
	4a. Eligibility criteria for participants.
Details about data collection process	8b. Type of randomization; details of any restriction (such as blocking and block size).
	11a. If done, who was blinded after assignment to interventions (for example, participants, care providers, those assessing outcomes) and how.
Data description	13a. For each group, the number of participants who were randomly assigned, received intended treatment, and were analyzed for the primary outcome.
	13b. For each group, losses and exclusions after randomization, together with reasons.
Analysis methods	12a. Statistical methods used to compare groups for primary and secondary outcomes.
	16. For each group, number of participants (denominator) included in each analysis and whether the analysis was by original assigned groups.
Results reporting	17a. For each primary and secondary outcome, results for each group, and the estimated effect size and its precision (such as 95% confidence interval).
	18. Results of any other analyses performed, including subgroup analyses and adjusted analyses, distinguishing prespecified from exploratory.
Study limitations	20. Trial limitations, addressing sources of potential bias, imprecision, and, if relevant, multiplicity of analyses.
	21. Generalizability (external validity, applicability) of the trial findings.
Materials availability	23. Registration number and name of trial registry.
	24. Where the full trial protocol can be accessed, if available.

to make sure that everything has been addressed. In doing so, checklists codify, in a practical way, a set of expectations about what *ought* to be reported. Requiring a checklist also presents an explicit opportunity for researchers to affirm—on the record—that their reporting is proper. Finally, checklists are relatively easy for others (including reviewers) to check if they wish, or at least can be made so by requiring researchers to indicate where in the manuscript each checklist item is addressed. (Of course, as the number of checklist items grows, the process of assessing compliance inevitably becomes more time-consuming.)

Reporting standard checklists commonly include items that might read like the most basic advice for writing an effective research paper. For example, STROBE guidelines for observational studies include "summarize key results with reference to study objectives" and state that the study's abstract should provide "an informative and balanced summary of what was done and what was found" (von Elm et al. 2007). One might wonder how many researchers really need all this spelled out for them, although we suspect one wonders this less the more manuscripts one reads. Many checklists are ordered roughly in terms of their typical order of appearance in a paper; together they form a useful template for putting together an empirical paper.

The meat of reporting guidelines directly engages the question of what and how specific details of studies are to be reported. As noted, many different standards have been offered for different types of research. Drawing on several of these, guidelines are naturally broken down into eight or so broad issues, which we list below along with a few associated questions. Table 8.1 also illustrates each domain with associated examples from the CONSORT checklist (available at www .consort-statement.org).

1. *Study context*—What funding sources were there? Were there potential conflicts of interest?

2. *Study design*—Who was eligible to participate? What measures were collected? How was the target sample size determined?

3. *Details about data collection process*—When were the data collected? For a randomized experiment, how were the random assignments generated and how were they implemented? How much noncompliance was there with assigned treatment status? How much attrition was there?

4. *Data description*—From how many participants were data collected? What are the means and standard deviations of key measures used in the study?[2]

---

2. For experimental work, we think it preferable to present means and standard deviations separately for treatment and control groups in the study.

5. *Analysis methods*—What statistical methods does the study use? How are missing data in the study handled?

6. *Results reporting*—What are the confidence intervals of estimates? What were the results of any sensitivity or subgroup analyses that were done?

7. *Study limitations*—What are potential weaknesses and biases of the study? What can be said about the generalizability of its findings?

8. Materials availability—Are the data and code available? Is the protocol for the data collection available? If so, where?

From these, one can adduce three broad purposes. One is *transparency,* in the straightforward sense of making as clear as possible how a study was done and what its results were. A second is *standardization,* which increases the capacity for studies to be evaluated together and to be synthesized in reviews or by formal methods of meta-analysis (see Chapter 5). A final purpose is *disclosure,* or pressing researchers to make information explicit even when it makes the findings less straightforward or persuasive than they might be if the information were withheld from readers.

Beyond this, other aspects of reporting quality may be especially important in specific social science contexts, which is one reason why different standards may be developed for different research areas. For example, when research seeks to evaluate the effectiveness of specific interventions, detailed and explicit information about the fidelity with which the intended intervention was implemented may be vital for understanding what results imply about the proposed interventions (Carroll et al. 2007; Bellg et al. 2004). Likewise, if research is evaluating an intervention as it might potentially be implemented on a larger scale, information about the cost of the intervention is important for assessing its feasibility and its cost effectiveness.

STANDARDIZING DEFINITIONS

Reporting standards can go beyond just stipulating what information is to be reported about a study, to also standardize the language used to report it. Specifically, reporting standards can provide authoritative definitions for otherwise slippery terms. For example, when presenting results from a survey, social scientists often report its *response rate.*

This term can mean many different things. For example, if telephone interviewers make dozens of calls to a number supposedly associated with an individual but never get any answer confirming that the number is in use, should the case be counted against the response rate or omitted from the calculation entirely? Given that higher response rates are usually interpreted as better, researchers have an incentive to employ the most favorable definition.

The American Association of Public Opinion Researchers (AAPOR) regularly convenes an expert panel to offer a set of *Standard Definitions* for the field (AAPOR 2016). These provide specific definitions for specific types of response rates that can be referred to by name, as well as definitions for how response rates differ from related quantities like *completion, participation, consent,* or *recruitment* rates. Researchers can refer to these definitions to indicate how they are using a specific term. AAPOR's flagship journal *Public Opinion Quarterly* requires manuscripts to use these terms as defined in *Standard Definitions*.

AAPOR is in a strong position to offer these guidelines because, while researchers in many fields use surveys, AAPOR is recognized as a central professional organization among survey methodologists. Other terms are deployed across disciplines in ways that make it hard to imagine who might claim jurisdiction, or how any large group might come to consensus on specifics. As one example, in Chapter 9, we will discuss the term *replication,* which has many distinct definitions across disciplines.

In recent years, broad concerns have emerged about null hypothesis significance testing, and the precise circumstances under which researchers should be able to describe findings as "statistically significant." The American Statistical Association, for the first time in its history, convened a task force in 2015 and offered an official statement about a particular statistical practice—the assignment and interpretation of p-values (Wasserstein and Lazar 2016). The guidelines repeated several common points about their limitations and suggested that "proper inference requires full reporting and transparency." Nonetheless, the statement's guidance was very general, perhaps even to the point of being vague, and, as a result, it is hard to imagine how such a statement on its own might gain much traction in actual research practice.

A group of over 70 social scientists have since tried to address this by specifically proposing to replace the commonplace use of *significant* to describe findings of $p < .05$ in non-confirmatory research with a new standard of $p < .005$ (Benjamin et al. 2017). They proposed that findings below $p < .05$ but not below $p < .005$ instead be referred to as *suggestive*.

A problem here is that virtually every research methodologist, including those arguing for $p < .005$, would agree that ideally, if null hypothesis testing is to be used, the significance level would vary based on details of the study—such as the expected effect size and the cost of collecting sample subjects, as well as on the practical consequences of false positive vs. false negative findings. Lakens et al. (2017) raise this counterargument to the $p < .005$ proposal at length. They quote from R. A. Fisher (1956b), who invented the terms *null hypothesis* and *significance test* in the first place, as writing that "no scientific worker has a fixed level of significance at which, from year to year, and in all circumstances, he rejects hypotheses; he rather gives his mind to each particular case in the light of his evidence and his ideas." But, of course, the reality is that much social and medical research currently does fixate on conventional cutoff values (and especially $p < .05$). So one counter-counterargument would be that, given how strongly rooted having some conventional cutoff for significance tests is, changing that convention to $p < .005$ would at least be a pragmatic improvement. Lakens et al. (2017), on the other hand, advocate discarding the term *statistically significant* altogether.

In other words, it is much easier to get methodologists to agree that there are serious problems with how *p*-values are typically used than it is to agree on any policy proposal for what should be done instead. This illustrates a broader paradox that often emerges from the academic politics of reporting standards. It is easier for standards to gain broad endorsement when they represent a consensus, but the path to obtaining such consensus often involves being less specific. Yet being less specific may then reduce the usefulness of the standard.

Reporting standards, even the best-known ones like CONSORT, are relatively new. One concern is that the gain in standardized reporting may come at a cost, for instance in terms of the creativity authors show when analyzing or describing data. There may be a tendency to simply write papers in the standard template without giving much thought to issues not explicitly covered in the reporting standards. Innovative papers with unusual research designs, data, or methodological approaches may not "fit" neatly with standard checklists, hurting their publication prospects. It will be important that reporting standards are regularly updated, as CONSORT has done, to reflect the evolution of approaches and needs in their research fields.

PROJECT PROTOCOLS

Being able to provide all of the information about a study specified by a reporting standard requires keeping track of those details in the first place. A *project protocol* is a detailed recipe or instruction manual that is useful for researchers while also enabling others to reproduce a data collection project. Project protocols can be part of a pre-analysis plan, as discussed in Chapter 6. However, keeping track of details of a project is important regardless of whether information is posted prior to data collection, and the full record of a project may include many details that were not foreseen at the outset.

Protocols are commonplace in the medical literature, as in areas of lab science, which are rife with examples of experiments failing to replicate because of supposedly minor changes such as the brand of bedding in mouse cages, the speed at which one stirs a reagent, or the packaging of culture dishes (Sorge et al. 2014; Hines et al. 2014; Perkel 2015). Examples also exist in social science, such as when small changes in the wording of a survey question, or its location on a survey, can lead to dramatic differences in the distribution of responses. Many social science lab experiments are premised on the idea of subtle situational differences leading to substantial behavioral differences, underscoring the importance of a careful record of experimental details.

When researchers collect their own data, they should aim to provide comparably detailed descriptions of what they did. A 33-item checklist of suggested items is contained in the SPIRIT (Standard Protocol Items: Recommendations for Interventional Trials) statement (Chan et al. 2013). This includes details on the participants, interventions, outcomes, assignment, blinding, data collection, data management, and statistical methods, among other things.

We encourage protocols to include as much "raw materials" information as possible. For example, an employer audit study may involve sending fake résumés to employers. The project protocol should provide these résumés in full. Or an experiment may involve seating respondents either in a clean or a messy office environment. Rather than simply describing the environment, the protocol should include photographs. Studies using surveys can include all of the question wordings, as well as any scripts or letters used in recruiting respondents. The nearly limitless capacity for online supplements nowadays leaves little reason for restraint in making design details available to interested scholars.

Reporting Details about Randomization

One area of experimental design in which experimental social sciences can improve involves reporting details of randomization. For example, Bruhn and McKenzie (2009) document the lack of clear explanation pertaining to how randomization was conducted in RCTs published in economics journals.

In the simplest case, which we call *pure randomization,* each observation is assigned to an experimental condition independently and without any reference to the process of assignment for any other observation. With pure randomization, the treatment and control groups have the same distribution on any covariate in expectation, but in practice substantial imbalance on some covariate can happen by chance, especially if sample sizes are small. Researchers can reduce this risk by stratifying (or "blocking") on key variables. For example, a design might assign equal numbers to each condition within each combination of age group, race/ethnicity, and sex. More elaborate techniques exist, like drawing a large number of potential random allocations and using the one that produces the best overall balance across a large set of covariates. The point is that researchers should be sure to report exactly what approach, with what variables, their study used.

In addition, there seems to be some disagreement in both medicine and the social sciences over the appropriateness of including baseline covariates in regression analysis of a randomized trial. In expectation, both approaches yield the same estimated treatment effect, although including controls may do so with more statistical precision. Controls may also adjust for random imbalance between conditions. At the same time, one can worry about specification searching, in which models with different combinations of baseline covariates were fit and the reported results are the ones showing the largest treatment effects. If baseline variables are to be included, researchers can indicate which variables (or the criteria they will use to determine this) as part of a pre-analysis plan.

The medical literature also exhibits much greater concern over the blinding and concealment of randomized assignment than some of the social science literature. Sometimes, blinding is impossible or irrelevant in a social science field experiment: for example, the recipient of a cash transfer needs to know that they received cash in order for the program to have any effect. In any event, tales of trials ruined through carelessness with the original randomization assignment, as well as tips on how to avoid the same problem, are described in Schulz and Grimes (2002).

When researchers use administrative or secondary data, much of the work of a project protocol is implicit in sharing one's code along with either the raw data or (if that's not possible) explicit information about the source and version of the raw data. The statistical code can make transparent all the steps involved in going from the raw data the researcher obtained to the reported results. We discuss this process in further detail in Chapters 9 and 11.

The advantage of secondary data in this respect is that (hopefully) those responsible for the original data collection have taken responsibility for documenting all of these details. For example, when someone uses one of the U.S. National Longitudinal Studies of Youth (NLSY79 or NLSY98), the online documentation includes extremely detailed information about how sampling was done and how interviews were conducted, to which a user can easily refer.

We are primarily thinking of protocols as supplemental materials, but some medicine and science journals have begun to publish the protocols themselves. The advantages of publishing a protocol related to the development of a new procedure (e.g., "We invented CRISPR, here's how it works") are likely obvious, but the advantages of publishing protocols for randomized trials still underway may be less so. *BioMed Central* and *BMJ Open,* among others, now publish protocols of trials planned or ongoing, with the hopes that this will reduce later publication bias, allow patients to see trials in which they might like to enroll, allow funders and researchers to learn of work underway to avoid duplication, and allow readers to compare the research originally proposed to what was actually completed when results are later published.[3] *BMJ Open* suggests, but does not require, that its published protocols include the checklist items from the SPIRIT reporting standard for protocols (www.spirit-statement.org). Social scientists could similarly publish their pre-analysis plans, and journals publishing registered reports (see Chapter 6) represent a step in this direction.

In any event, open protocols are not a perfect solution for the concerns giving rise to the advance registration of studies. Even when protocols are published or otherwise public, studies have found important differences between protocols and published results in medical journals. Chan et al. (2004) found that 60–71 percent of outcomes described in protocols went unreported in the paper, while 62 percent of the studies

---

3. As an example of guidelines for publishing protocols, see http://bmjopen.bmj.com /site/about/guidelines.xhtml#studyprotocols.

had major discrepancies between primary outcomes in the protocols and in the published papers, though there was a relatively even mix of these discrepancies favoring significant or nonsignificant results. Another study found that the appropriate level of statistical detail is often lacking in protocols, again raising the issue of researcher degrees of freedom, and there are often discrepancies between protocols and published results (Saquib, Saquib, and Ioannidis 2013). While 31 percent of published papers had some sort of prespecified plan for their regression adjustments (i.e., specifying which baseline covariates would be controlled for), only 53 percent of the plans matched what was published in the ultimate paper. That said, the existence of registries and protocols allows us to quantify these discrepancies and, hopefully, provide further impetus for the research community to address them.

Some of the problems point to ways in which reporting standards more generally are imperfect solutions, especially in terms of how they are carried out in practice. For example, Ben Goldacre and colleagues launched a project auditing papers published in high-profile medical journals to determine whether they had analyzed outcomes differently from how they had planned to do so, without reporting the departure in the paper (as per CONSORT guidelines). Some journals published corrections as a result of the audits. The *New England Journal of Medicine (NEJM)*, which has the highest impact factor of any medical journal, flatly refused to do so (Goldacre 2016). Although *NEJM* had endorsed the CONSORT guidelines, the deputy editor replied that the journal "finds some aspects of CONSORT useful but we do not, and never have, required authors to comply with CONSORT." Official endorsements of reporting standards, in other words, can still leave some ambiguity about whether authors are actually expected to take them seriously, or whether some aspects of the guidelines remain optional. This may be troubling when endorsements of a standard may lead a reader to believe that a study would report something—like departing from registered analysis plans—if it had happened, but authors are not actually expected to do so in practice.

CONCLUSION

The backstage of the research process is often messy. Writing a paper involves extracting and ordering details of that mess. Reporting standards offer guidelines about how research should be reported. We have offered some examples here from medical research, in which adherence to some reporting standards is required, although this remains unusual in most social science fields where standards are newer and are generally optional. Reporting standards offer a road map of what researchers are expected to present. Codifying reporting standards can also reduce instances in which researchers who would not explicitly commit fraud might nevertheless be tempted to selectively omit details that could make their findings less persuasive. This is one of their most valuable contributions to the quality of the resulting research.

Another important advantage of reporting standards is the greater clarity they bring to other researchers attempting to interpret or replicate the analysis. It is to this latter issue that we turn in the next chapter.

NINE

Replication

In 1998, the prestigious medical journal *The Lancet* published an article that appeared to present evidence linking certain vaccines and autism (Wakefield et al. 1998). We know now that the study's conclusion was wrong: vaccines do not cause autism. We know this because of the many, many subsequent studies that found no association between vaccination and autism (Maglione et al. 2014; Jain et al. 2015). Subsequent investigation also revealed that even the original data do not support the findings reported in the *Lancet* (Deer 2011). If you look up the article online now, the word *RETRACTED* appears in giant red letters on every page.[1]

The *Lancet* article is considered a public health tragedy insofar as it inspired some parents not to vaccinate their children. Partly as a result, there have been needless outbreaks of measles and mumps. The tragedy points to one of the key values of science: the importance of replication. Broadly speaking, replication is scientific work directed toward establishing the reliability of previous results. Replication enables science to be self-correcting, so that even when individual studies get it wrong, scientific communities eventually get it right.

In this chapter, we begin by presenting some of the key distinctions drawn in defining replication and related activities. We describe the incentive problems that have led to deep concerns that replication studies are undertaken far less frequently than they should be. Then we discuss some

---

1. See https://doi.org/10.1016/S0140–6736(97)11096–0.

major developments in ongoing efforts to assess and improve the replicability of social science.

WHAT IS REPLICATION?

The term *replication* can refer to a few distinct research activities, and its use differs across social science disciplines, making discussions of replication across fields even more challenging (Freese and Peterson 2017). Psychological research, for instance, is dominated by experiments, often conducted on low-cost groups of participants like local college students. For such research, the obvious way to interrogate the stability of an experimental result is by conducting additional experiments. In this context, replication is understood to involve different data than the data used in the original study.

By contrast, many studies in economics and sociology involve large data sources that are often very expensive to produce and may be uniquely authoritative for the specific research question that a study poses. Analyses typically involve many intricate steps, with researchers having to use their judgment to make many decisions along the way. Here, questions about the stability of results frequently involve reexamining the same data used in the original study. Accordingly, even though these fields recognize that replication can involve new data, in practice the term has referred more often to studies that use the same data.

The other important way that the use of *replication* varies is whether it refers to activities narrowly focused on the question of whether the specific results of the original study can be reobserved, or more broadly focused on whether conclusions drawn from those findings are robust. The former is uncontroversially considered replication, while somewhere in the latter is a fuzzy and debated boundary separating replication from studies that simply build upon past work. Similar to Clemens (2017), when the same data are used as in the original study, we refer to this as a distinction between *verification* and *reanalysis*. When work uses new data, we refer to this as a distinction between *direct replication* and *extension*. The different types of replication are summarized in Table 9.1.

TABLE 9.1   TYPES OF REPLICATION

Compared to original study	Focused on repeating procedures	Focused on introducing key difference(s)
Same data	Verification	Reanalysis
Different data	Direct replication	Extension

VERIFICATION AND REANALYSIS

Verification at its simplest asks whether the original data can be used to generate the same results as those presented in the original study. Mistakes happen. A high-profile finding that was used to recommend governmental austerity policies turned out to be an artifact of an Excel error (Herndon, Ash, and Pollin 2014). Findings from a study reporting the benefits of workplace diversity could not be reproduced, for indeterminate reasons that may have included the author treating numbers meant to indicate missing values as if they were real values (Stojmenovska, Bol, and Leopold 2017).

Even when results can be verified, they might not provide the best characterization of what the data actually indicate. Reported results may be dependent on decisions that appear arguable or arbitrary, perhaps due to specification searching (see Chapter 4). For example, Freese and Powell (2001) reanalyzed data from a study that reported support for a sociobiological hypothesis about parenting behavior, and they found that the significant results disappeared when any of a variety of alternative, plausible analytic decisions were made. If findings depend on decisions that are not justified, then the findings themselves are not justified.

Reanalysis may also proceed from an argument that there is a better way to analyze the original data than what was reported in the original study. For example, Breznau (2015) questioned the model specification of a study by Brooks and Manza (2006) that found that public opinion influenced how much rich democracies spent overall on social welfare programs. Specifically, he argued cogently that the model's inclusion of an interaction term while omitting a corresponding "main effect" term entailed implausible assumptions in order to be justified. When he fit the model with the missing main effect included, the key result of the study disappeared.

In addition, reanalysis can be a way of making a more general case for the value of new methods, by providing a concrete demonstration of a case in which using the new method makes a difference by revising an existing result. For example, King et al. (2001) sought to discourage political scientists from using listwise deletion for missing data—that is, simply omitting cases with any missing data—in favor of using multiple imputations. One way they made their argument was to reanalyze data from a study of Russian elections that had used listwise deletion and failed to find significant relationships between attitudes and how people voted. King et al. showed that using multiple imputation on the same data led to significant results, which were more consistent with what political scientists would expect.

Almost always, reanalysis projects will involve verification as a first step. Only by verifying that one is following procedures that led to the same results as the original study can one demonstrate conclusively that subsequent changes in results are due to changes in the analysis.

Direct Replication

A direct replication tries to follow the procedures of the original study in collecting data as closely as circumstances allow. Unlike verification, where investigators might expect to be able to obtain exactly the same results as the published study, direct replications in fields that rely on statistical analyses are not undertaken with the expectation that results will be exactly the same. Even in the best circumstances, chance variation will lead to some difference in results no matter how closely the original procedures were followed, at least when dealing with human or animal subjects.[2]

Going further, direct replications are never exact replications of the original study, no matter how close they may seem. Even when researchers collect the same measures of the same people, they are not measuring the same people at the same time in the same place. Just as the Greek philosopher Heraclitus famously said that "no man ever steps in the same river twice"—because the second time, it is neither exactly the same river nor exactly the same man—no research study is ever done twice.

Perhaps this seems like just a philosophical point, but it has an important implication for how direct replication often plays out in practice (Freese and Peterson 2017). To illustrate, we can take a now notorious case from social psychology, in which prominent Cornell researcher Daryl Bem (2011) published a paper in one of his field's top journals (the *Journal of Personality and Social Psychology*) providing evidence for the paranormal phenomenon of precognition. For example, in one experiment, subjects were asked to press one of two buttons. Afterward, depending on what button they chose, they would be shown either an ordinary photo or a repulsive one. The link between button and photo was randomly determined—and only *after* the button was pressed—so neither the participants nor anyone else had any way of

---

2. Perhaps molecules, atoms, or particles might be expected to behave sometimes in exactly the same manner in a direct replication, as far as humans are able to observe.

knowing which button would invoke the repulsive photo. Nevertheless, Bem's results indicated a slight—yet, by conventional standards, statistically significant—tendency for respondents to select the button that averted being shown the repulsive photo, as if they could somehow unconsciously "sense" what would happen.

We take it for granted that precognition is not real, but this makes it useful for thinking about replication. After the study was published, various researchers conducted direct replication studies of the experiment, and no evidence of a better-than-chance pattern of replication subsequently emerged (Galak et al. [2012] provide a meta-analysis). For now, just consider hypothetically the case of an investigator collecting new data to replicate the abovementioned experiment and failing to find an effect. We would interpret this as evidence against precognition, but we were already inclined toward that conclusion to begin with. Someone who did believe the original results might offer an alternative interpretation, namely that the null effect in the replication study was due to differences between the original study and the purported replication. Because there are always differences between replications and the original study, some version of this argument can always be made, and, logically speaking, there is some possibility that it might be right.

The implication that has been observed time and again in the history of science is that, when findings from new data diverge from those of the original study, debates about whether it truly counts as a failed replication can be protracted and difficult to resolve decisively (Collins 1992). Indeed, they are often never fully resolved in the sense of the scientists who are directly involved finally agreeing, but instead scientific consensus may occur by one side or the other being increasingly marginalized and left behind. To paraphrase physicist Max Planck, science advances one funeral at a time.

Nevertheless, we can see that a replication study that sought to repeat procedures from Bem's experiment as closely as possible would provide the strongest challenge to the original findings if it failed to observe similar results. The more design differences there are between the original and the new experiment, the more reasons there are that the results from the new experiment might differ. For example, if the repulsive photos used in our hypothetical failed replication of Bem's experiment were different from the ones Bem used, someone might posit that the reason the new experiment did not observe the same results is that perhaps the occurrence of precognition depends somehow on the content of the photos. Maximizing similarity to the original study allows a replication to speak most directly to the question of whether a study's findings should be taken at face value.

Extension

Imagine someone is given a choice between (a) having a painful experience for 60 seconds or (b) having a painful experience for 60 seconds followed by a merely uncomfortable experience for 30 seconds. Put that way, we might think any non-masochist would choose (a), but a psychology experiment that administered both conditions to participants by having them place their hands in very cold water found that respondents recalled (b) as the less negative experience (Kahneman et al. 1993). The theoretical conclusion drawn from the finding was that how people recall an experience often places very little weight on actual durations and high weight on how the experience ends. Subsequently, the researchers showed that a similar result could be observed using unpleasant sounds instead of cold water, and also in an applied setting in which the extremely uncomfortable experience of a colonoscopy was rated less negatively when it was followed by the less uncomfortable experience of leaving the colonoscope stationary for a short time at the end (Redelmeier, Katz, and Kahneman 2003).

The subsequent studies strengthen the credibility of the underlying theory by providing positive evidence from multiple distinct ways of testing it. As far as that theory goes, one can argue that these different studies provide stronger evidence in its favor than a set of direct replications of the original study would, as simply showing that the same experiment yields the same result does little to resolve questions about alternative explanations or limits to generalizability. As opposed to direct replication, this work deliberately introduces differences to the original study to see if results consistent with the original study's conclusions hold despite these differences in context.

Extensions that involve using a different analytical approach to test the same theory have sometimes been called "conceptual replications." These studies have the advantage of seeming more creative and broadly instructive than simply trying to follow the original study as closely as possible. Nevertheless, the relationship between conceptual replication and replication has become controversial in recent years. The concern is that the introduced differences produce a built-in asymmetry. Conceptual replications are taken as evidence supporting a theory when results are consistent with the original study, but results that are not consistent are readily attributable to design differences that may be dismissed as not pertinent to the theory. If so, then the contribution of conceptual replication to the potential self-correction of science, which is a reason conventionally cited for what makes replication so important, is uncertain. As Chambers (2017, p. 16) puts it, "Conceptual replications thus force science down a one-way street in which it is possible to confirm but never disconfirm previous findings."

Edge Cases and Hybrids

Of course, as with most typologies, not every study fits neatly into one of our four types. An example that mixes reanalysis and extension involves a highly influential finding that foreign aid only helped stimulate economic growth in developing countries that had a favorable mix of fiscal, monetary, and trade policies (Burnside and Dollar 2000). The data spanned the period 1970–93. Subsequently, Easterly et al. (2004) were able to update these data to 1997 and also add some additional countries, which expanded the total number of available observations from 275 to 356. Easterly et al. fit the same models as Burnside and Dollar, but the coefficient for the key result changed substantially in the updated data and was no longer significant. The study involved a combination of the same data and new data, and, by otherwise following the same analysis procedures, Easterly et al. were able to demonstrate persuasively that the original study's conclusions did not follow in the expanded data.

REPLICATION'S INCENTIVE PROBLEM

The standing paradox of replication is that its central role in science in principle occurs alongside the infrequency of replication studies in actual practice. For a long time, this was thought to raise the puzzle of why science worked so well despite so seldom undertaking replication studies (e.g., Hacking 1983). More recently, however, many fields have become concerned that their findings may not be as replicable as previously believed, and that more replication work needs to be undertaken.

Incentives to undertake replication work are often low. Science prizes originality, and trying to replicate someone else's research is seen as not original, and even as being "beneath" leading scholars. After the Bem experiments on precognition were published in social psychology's top journal, one group of researchers repeated experiments as closely as they could and found no evidence of precognition (Ritchie, Wiseman, and French 2012). The article was immediately rejected by the same journal and a couple of other major journals on the grounds that, per policies at that time, the journals published only novel studies and not replications (Yong 2012).

The episode ignited controversy because faith in science as self-correcting is hard to reconcile with findings of paranormal activity being publishable in a field's top outlet and research that calls those findings into question being hard to publish at all. Recent years have seen a strong push for journals to explicitly indicate their openness to considering well-executed replication studies, with considerable if still only partial success (Nosek et al. 2015; Duvendack, Palmer-Jones, and Reed 2015). This has included entreaties for journals to recognize that they have a special obligation to serve as an outlet for replication work connected to studies they have published.[3]

Not only have there usually been weak incentives to conduct replication work, but the incentives that exist may encourage biased work. The value of independent replication has long been recognized—at least in the abstract—given the many reasons scientists might be biased toward affirming their past work. Physicist Richard Feynman (1974) once wrote about scientific integrity that "the first principle is that you must not fool yourself—and you are the easiest person to fool."

Yet scientists who take it upon themselves to conduct an independent replication study may be especially motivated to do so when they are dubious of a finding. So they may be vulnerable to fooling themselves by making decisions that confirm their own prejudices against a finding (Freese and Peterson 2017). Moreover, direct replication studies get the most attention—and have the best publication prospects—when they call the published finding into question. One consequence may be that investigators give less attention to meticulously following details of the original experiment that might genuinely be key to successfully replicating the original results. Some literatures show evidence of a "Proteus phenomenon" in which the tendency for an initial study to overestimate effect size is followed by the second study tending to be biased in the opposite direction (Ioannidis and Trikalinos 2005).

As discussed in Chapter 6, preregistering studies with pre-analysis plans reduces the opportunity for some types of biased analysis and

3. This has been referred to as the "Pottery Barn rule," by analogy to the store policy "You break it, you own it." As a footnote to this footnote, Pottery Barn has no such rule, and the quote on which the analogy appears to be based refers to a "pottery store" (Friedman 2003), which is a very different thing.

reporting, and direct replication studies that involve new data collection could also usefully be preregistered, for the same reasons as other studies. Journals offering the possibility of results-blind peer review can enable replication studies to be embarked upon without their publication prospects being tied to their bottom-line results. This idea has been extended to the possibility of "crowdsourcing" replication, which we describe later in this chapter.

Prespecification of a plan regarding the experiment also allows investigators to obtain feedback about their experiment from the authors of the original study. This allows the investigators a constructive opportunity to clarify any details that they believe to be important, and thus gives the replication the best chance of corroborating the original study. It also reduces the leeway for the authors of the original study to argue that a replication was poorly conceived if it ends up producing divergent results. Of course, that the authors of the original study might have useful input for a replication attempt does not abrogate their responsibility to make as much information as they can available when the study is originally published.

IMPROVING REPLICABILITY

Initiatives to improve the replicability of research fields have involved changes on many fronts. Many involve basic principles of increased transparency and attention to reproducibility that we describe throughout this book. In this section, we discuss three specific developments. First are replication audits, which seek to provide systematic evidence of the extent of replicability problems by conducting larger-scale investigations of sets of studies. Second is the use of "crowdsourcing" to provide open invitations to investigators to join collective replication projects. Third is recognition that measures to improve the replicability of a field need to begin prior to the publication of original findings in the first place.

Replication Audits

The desire to understand whether broad replicability problems exist in an area have led to efforts to collect systematic information by pursuing replication over a sample of articles, which we call *replication audits*. In Chapter 10 we describe a pioneering replication audit regarding verification that sought to obtain data and code to verify all papers published in an economics journal in a multiyear period in the early 1980s

(Dewald, Thursby, and Anderson 1986). Problems with obtaining data in a similar effort that focused on the *American Economic Review* led directly to that flagship economics journal strengthening its data-sharing policies (McCullough and Vinod 2003; Bernanke 2004).

The idea has more recently been extended to direct replication studies. A large effort, called the Reproducibility Project: Psychology (RP:P), sought to conduct direct replications of 100 experiments that had been published in three high-ranking psychology journals in 2008 (Open Science Collaboration 2015). This effort later inspired a team of economists to conduct direct replications of all 18 papers using laboratory experiments that had been published in two leading economics journals over a three-year period (Camerer et al. 2016).

Replication audits offer a summary of how many experimental results were successfully replicated. Deciding what counts as "success" versus "failure" is often not clear-cut, even when investigators are just considering replication results for a single study. When summarizing results of a replication audit, there is still no single, agreed-upon best way to measure success.

The most straightforward criterion is to deem a direct replication successful if its results are statistically significant and in the same direction as the results of the original study. By this criterion, however, replication results can be failures even when effect sizes are much closer to the original study's results than they are to zero (e.g., if the replication study is statistically underpowered, as in Figure 9.1 panel A). This problem can be addressed by having replications be well powered for smaller effect sizes than were reported in the original study, which in practice means that direct replications are to be conducted on samples that are larger, perhaps much larger, than those of the original study.

High-powered replications do raise a different question, which is whether direct replication studies should be considered successes if effect sizes are different from zero but significantly smaller than those reported in the original study. If a study of an after-school reading program gains interest because it found large positive effects, then it seems misleading to say its findings were successfully replicated by a high-powered study that found only a very small positive effect, even if the latter is statistically significant (as in Figure 9.1 panel B). One may instead define a direct replication as successful only if the magnitude of the key result in the replication study is not significantly different from the original study. But even then, there are likely to be different perspectives on what counts as a qualitatively similar result—say, from the point of view of the relevant theory.

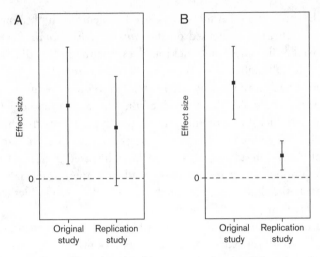

FIGURE 9.1. Examples of ambiguous cases for classifying replication studies as a success or failure. In example **A,** the point estimates are similar but differ in statistical significance; in **B,** the estimates are both significantly different from zero but also significantly different from one another.

But this is not necessarily preferable in all contexts. For example, worrying about effect sizes in Bem's precognition experiments seems beside the point, for any consistently observable positive result would upend the laws of physics. One measure reported in the RP:P involved researchers subjectively assessing whether the effect was replicated, and one can imagine researchers offering a subjective—but explicit—criterion beforehand as to what results would constitute success or failure for that study.

Results from replication audits are obviously instructive. The main finding of the RP:P was that the majority of study results (across various metrics) were not successfully replicated, and attempts by some to argue that this is not a cause for alarm seem wishful, at least to us. At the same time, concerns familiar to every social scientist regarding the drawing of inferences from samples do not go away just because we are talking about a sample of articles rather than a sample of people. For example, in contrast to the results of the RP:P, most results from the replication audit in experimental economics did successfully replicate. While this may mean that the experimental economics literature is more replicable than the experimental psychology literature, it could also reflect differences in the selectivity or representativeness of the specific journals that defined the samples (or, for that matter, differences in how the replications were executed that have no necessary bearing on the truth of findings of the original study). In either case, far more replication audits will be necessary to get a better handle on just how reliable most empirical social science findings truly are.

Crowdsource Replication

What we call *crowdsource replication* projects publicly announce a protocol to conduct a direct replication and allow other investigators to join the project by following the protocol to collect their own data. The RP:P provides an example, in which the target sample of studies was announced and investigators were invited to sign up for the specific study they would try to replicate. A related initiative, called Many Labs, selected 13 classic and more recent experimental findings that could easily be implemented on a web-based platform, and then invited labs to conduct the experiments (Klein et al. 2014). Doing so not only provided a high-powered effort to assess whether the specific effects could be successfully replicated, but also permitted investigation of whether there were systematic differences among labs.

Crowdsourcing has given rise to an entirely different publication type, called the registered replication report (RRR; Simons, Holcombe, and Spellman 2014). Investigators submit a detailed description to a journal of how they plan to conduct a replication study and how they plan to analyze the data. The journal then seeks feedback from reviewers, including the authors of the original study. If the journal accepts the proposal, it is then publicly posted, and other labs are given the opportunity to participate by using the agreed-upon protocol to conduct their own replication studies. As long as the protocol is followed, the journal commits to publishing all the study results together, regardless of how the results turn out.

Crowdsourcing is not without its critics. One concern is that its emphasis on experiments that can be readily implemented on a broader scale may result in a focus on simpler, weaker, or less important experiments. A high-profile RRR found overall null results for a study of the psychological phenomenon of ego depletion, in which acts of self-control are proposed to deplete mental resources and temporarily impair subsequent self-control (Hagger et al. 2016). Ego depletion is most closely associated with a series of experiments by Baumeister et al. (1998), but the crowdsource project selected an experiment by Sripada, Kessler, and Jonides

(2014). Baumeister and Vohs (2016) responded to the null results by arguing that Sripada and colleagues' procedure provided a dubious test of their theory. Acknowledging that they had approved the RRR in advance, they said that this was only after several different procedures they had suggested had been rejected as incompatible with the limitations of crowdsourcing. "Under the circumstances," they write, "we understood our approval to mean 'Sure, go ahead' and not 'Yes, that's a definitive test of the phenomenon we've been studying all these years'" (Baumeister and Vohs 2016, p. 574).

A different sort of crowdsourcing involves inviting groups of researchers to analyze the same dataset. In one example, investigators recruited 29 teams of researchers to look at the same set of soccer data, which included information on players' skin color, to analyze whether darker-skinned players were more likely to get red cards than lighter-skinned players (Silberzahn and Uhlmann 2015; Silberzahn et al. 2017). Most teams did find evidence of a modest association, corresponding to a 30 percent increase in the odds of a red card for those in the darkest skin-tone category compared to those with the lightest skin tones. However, some analysts found no association, and some found much larger associations (corresponding to point estimates of a change of 100 percent or more in the odds). In other words, had we relied on only one group's analysis—as, of course, is usual for published papers—the conclusion might have ranged from "no bias" to "huge bias," even though data are the same.

Interventions before the Initial Publication

As concerns about research replicability have grown, so too has recognition that improving replicability begins before publication. As we discuss in Chapter 10, scientists are understood to have some ethical obligation to help other researchers who seek to replicate their work, but, in practice, compliance with requests after publication is often weak. Researchers may feel they have little to gain from taking the time to help, and they may feel like they are just putting themselves at risk of whatever reputational harm might ensue if replication efforts fail. Even investigators willing to help may find that it is hard to locate materials or to reconstruct their work, especially as more time has passed, given many other time-consuming research and teaching commitments.

The best practice for ensuring long-term replicability are journal policies that press authors to maximize the extent to which data and other materials needed to replicate findings are available as a condition for journal publication (Freese 2007). Beyond this, journals can also seek to ensure that results are independently verified before they are published. The *American Journal of Political Science,* for example, contracts with a third party to take code and data provided by an accepted paper's authors and verify that the results can be obtained from these materials before publishing the article.[4] Note that they do not try to determine that there are no mistakes in the code, which would be stronger but would also dramatically increase the workload and professional judgment involved.

Authors who replicate their own findings before the paper is published can increase the prospects that later verification and replication by others will succeed. For example, projects that involve multiple data analysts can have them work independently to see if they obtain the same results and reconcile any differences. Of course, this is more work. In Chapter 4, we recounted a case in which social psychologists who thought they had made a new discovery (about the identification of the color gray by political extremists) conducted a direct replication before trying to publish it, and found out that the original result was just a fluke (Nosek, Spies, and Motyl 2012). Not only was doing so more work for the authors, but the extra work ended up leaving them without anything to publish. The perverse incentives this introduces are obvious.

One can urge investigators to undertake internal replication as part of their commitment to seeking to get things right, but broader improvement may need to result from internal replication being expected as part of what makes results publishable. For example, in behavior genetics, early work using molecular genetic data turned out to involve a startling number of findings that subsequently failed to replicate in other datasets. In response, the editor of *Behavior Genetics* published an editorial announcing that the journal would expect novel findings involving specific genetic variants to be accompanied by a direct replication study from a different data source (Hewitt 2012). In social psychology, concerns about rigor in the late 1970s and '80s led to a rise in the number of related experiments expected to be presented in an article, which served as a sort of replication (Greenwald 1976; Wegner 1992). At the same time, researchers publishing a study with multiple experiments may have conducted even more experiments and only published the ones that "worked" as intended, perhaps concluding—and perhaps

---

4. The policy statement is available at https://ajps.org/ajps-replication-policy/.

reasonably—that the failed experiments had problems in design or execution. As discussed in Chapter 6, by preregistering a replication experiment before conducting it, researchers can demonstrate that the replication was planned as such and not plucked from a larger set because it produced the right results.

CONCLUSION

Replication is the secret sauce of science. It's how scientists realize when past work was wrong and, in so doing, help better and sturdier findings be built. By the same token, successful replications help address the fallibility of any one researcher and establish findings as reliable products of a scientific community.

Yet just because research communities understand the importance of replication does not mean that the needed work will get done, or get done right. Scientific institutions often pose many disincentives that reduce the frequency or quality of replication studies. We have described some of these in this chapter, and highlighted some of the ongoing efforts to improve.

TEN

Data Sharing

In 2012, two social psychologists resigned after investigations suggested that they had fabricated data in some of their studies. Both episodes began when Uri Simonsohn (2013) noticed that different experimental conditions reported standard deviations more similar to one another than would be expected by chance. Simonsohn followed up by asking the researchers for the raw data. His subsequent analyses of these data raised further questions that ultimately led to official investigations, echoing the Stapel fraud case discussed in Chapter 1.

In his subsequent account of these incidents, Simonsohn noted that there was a third researcher whose work had similarly suspicious reported results. That researcher, however, had eluded further investigation because Simonsohn had been unable to obtain the raw data. "The main author reported losing them," wrote Simonsohn (2013), "and the coauthors of the article did not wish to get involved."

Obviously it is disconcerting that this researcher, who may have committed fraud, went unexposed because they were savvy enough to recognize that "Oops, I lost the data" would effectively thwart additional inquiry. Had this researcher been required to make their data public in order to publish the article in the first place, this convenient excuse would not have been available. A major fraud scandal in political science, for example, was uncovered precisely because the journal required the data to be posted, allowing suspicious anomalies in those data to be discovered (Broockman, Kalla, and Aranow, 2015).

Data sharing serves at least two distinct scientific purposes, one evaluative and the other generative. The *evaluative* purpose of sharing data is to increase the credibility of findings by allowing the evidence to be directly verified and interrogated by others. This is not just about combating fraud, but also about allowing others to assess the consequences of analytic decisions other than those reported in a study. The *generative* purpose is to enable other investigators to pursue new questions and thereby maximize the total potential research contribution of data.

This chapter considers data sharing from both policy and practical standpoints. The key policy question is how and when researchers should be required to share research data with others. As we discuss, researchers may have good reasons to be reluctant to share certain types of data. Creating effective data-sharing policies involves thoughtfully balancing different considerations. Beyond this is the practical question of how those wishing to make data available to others for posterity can best do so.

WHY ARE DATA-SHARING POLICIES NECESSARY?

The Insufficiency of Norms

The idea that science needs anything so formal as a "policy" regarding data sharing is relatively new. Until recently, data availability was understood more in occasional and ethical terms. For example, the American Sociological Association's Code of Ethics has long stated that, once a study is published, researchers are to "permit [its] open assessment and verification by other responsible researchers," as far as safeguarding protections to research participants allows.[1] Similarly, to the extent possible, researchers should "make their data available after the completion of a project or its major publications." That is, the code presents data sharing as a matter of norms: researchers have an ethical obligation to allow colleagues to verify results and, if possible, to make their dataset broadly available after they have finished with it.

While making norms explicit is useful, ethical exhortations often fall short in practice. For instance, even when researchers write multiple papers from a given data collection effort, they often have ideas for yet more papers they would like to write. As a result, projects may live on indefinitely without the researcher regarding them as complete. Worse,

---

1. The American Sociological Association's Code of Ethics is available at http://www.asanet.org/code-ethics.

once a paper is published, the incentive to respond to requests to provide information is lower, and the ability for researchers to reconstruct what they did may erode with time. Researchers can just say, "I lost the data" or "I don't have time," or fail to respond altogether, without direct consequences most of the time.

Evidence makes it clear that professional norms are not sufficient to motivate broad compliance with requests to share data after publication. In 2006, a group of Dutch psychologists sought to obtain data for all empirical studies published in two issues of four major psychology journals. They were successful only 27 percent of the time (Wicherts et al. 2006). Additionally, the studies for which authors did not share data were more likely to report weaker evidence and contain simple reporting errors (e.g., internally inconsistent χ^2 and p-values), raising the possibility that declining to share data may signal lower research quality (Wicherts, Bakker, and Molenaar 2011).[2]

Sociologist Cristobal Young had students request replication materials for sociology articles whose analyses they wished to try to reproduce (Young and Horvath 2015). Only 15 of 53 requests (28 percent) were successful. Political scientist Thomas Carsey conducted a similar exercise and reported that students "often come away from this assignment frustrated, shocked, and rather disappointed" (Carsey 2014).

The most pioneering effort to systematically assess the availability of research data is from economics. In 1982, the *Journal of Money, Credit, and Banking (JMCB)* began requesting data and code for papers published in the journal as part of a National Science Foundation initiative (Dewald, Thursby, and Anderson 1986). In principle, this request was just an extension of the existing policy that authors would share their data if asked. Yet they were able to get data from only 78 percent of papers published in the journal after the new policy was instituted, and from only 34 percent published prior to that. (The submitted data were also frequently an unlabeled and undocumented mess, and researchers were often unable to reproduce the published results.)

JMCB's initiative, incidentally, did not do much to change data-sharing policies in economics. Ten years later, only two additional journals had adopted similar policies, and *JMCB* discontinued requesting data for a few years in the 1990s. In 2003, McCullough and Vinod wanted to examine the sensitivity of published analyses to differences across

---

2. These statistical errors can be checked for with the statcheck package in R (see Nuijten et al. 2016).

statistical packages and sought to do so by reanalyzing the data from eight empirical articles published in one issue of the *American Economic Review (AER)*. Despite *AER* ostensibly obliging authors to respond to such requests, McCullough and Vinod (2003) were able to obtain data and code for only four of the eight papers. In response, the editor of *AER*—future Federal Reserve Chairman Ben Bernanke—changed the official policy to require submission of data and code as a condition of publication (Bernanke 2004).[3]

Reasons for Reluctance

The mysterious psychologist who claimed a loss of data in response to a query about suspicious results exemplifies one reason researchers might not want to share their data: *maybe they have something to hide*. If that were the only reason not to make data public, then the science policy question would be easy—all data should always be available upon publication.

But other reasons for reluctance exist, and two are especially important. The first is that sharing data may be perceived as undermining the incentive for researchers to undertake the work of collecting data themselves. Years ago, a political scientist reacted to a data-sharing proposal by warning about the rise of "data vultures," predicting that "generations of scholars will be raised to mine existing datasets, not to collect data on their own" (Gibson 1995). More recently, a controversial editorial in the *New England Journal of Medicine* described a worry that "the system will be taken over by what some researchers have characterized as 'research parasites'" (Longo and Drazen 2016). Just as patent rights give pharmaceutical companies incentive to undertake the enormous investment required to develop new drugs, rights over data may be viewed as necessary to spur the ambitious data collection efforts that science needs to make progress.

The second is that social science benefits from data that cannot be broadly shared for legitimate reasons. For example, some of the best data for studying income inequality are data from individual tax returns. The data require authorization to obtain and can only be analyzed in accordance with agreements. Researchers are not legally or ethically

---

3. There is heterogeneity in how economists comply with this policy, from posting only the final data file and final code used in analyses to posting the whole workflow from raw data to all supplemental analyses.

allowed to provide the data to others. If social scientists could only publish using data that could be published on websites, we would know far less about social inequality and countless other topics than we do.

PROTECTING INCENTIVES TO COLLECT DATA

Scientists sometimes get carried away when referring to "their" data. Even when a dataset absolutely would not exist without a scientist's effort, it often depends crucially on many other people as well. Data collection is often funded by grants from governments or foundations. Large projects often involve the work of many staff, as well as tools and protocols developed by earlier scholars. Research participants answer survey questions and consent to clinical trials. We are not trying to discount all the work, perseverance, and creativity required to spearhead data collection, but discussions of data ownership must be kept in perspective.

Of course, data are the lifeblood of empirical science, and it would be a perverse consequence of a data-sharing policy if it reduced the amount of important data collected. Below, we discuss three measures to protect incentives: extract sharing, data embargoes, and data citation.

Extract Sharing

Journals' interest in mandating data sharing stems primarily from what we called the evaluative purpose of data sharing—assessing the validity of the specific findings published in the journal. This purpose is partly served by having researchers share only an extract that includes the specific variables required to reproduce a paper's results. Typically, when researchers plan to write multiple papers using the same data, different papers involve at least a few different variables. Extract sharing therefore allows researchers to prevent being "scooped" by allowing them to hold back data that are not used in a specific paper.

Unfortunately, sharing of extracts does not address potential concerns about specification searching. One might worry that some variables left out of the extract were in fact analyzed by the researcher, and were not included in the analysis because they weakened or complicated the presented results. For example, perhaps a study asking whether conservatives or liberals are more tolerant of opposing views actually included many different measures of tolerance, but reported only those for which statistically significant differences were observed.

One might identify the problem here as pertaining more to the researchers' lack of disclosure about what they did—and the corresponding results—than to incomplete data sharing per se. Reporting guidelines could explicitly request that all associated analyses be reported or that all observations and variables analyzed in a project be included in an extract whether used in the final analyses or not. Making full project documentation, including original survey instruments, publicly available would address some of these concerns. Also, for projects that lend themselves to preregistration and prespecified analysis plans, researchers may specify that different variables were intended for different studies even when all are nested within a larger data collection effort.

Data Embargoes

In Chapter 3 we described the Time-sharing Experiments for the Social Sciences (TESS) platform. Researchers propose survey experiment projects to TESS, and successful proposals are fielded at no cost to investigators, using a nationally representative survey platform. While TESS makes all its data publicly available, it would not be fair to the investigators who proposed an experiment if someone else could swoop in and publish their experiment before the investigators themselves were able to do so. At the same time, some investigators never publish the results of their TESS experiments. TESS's solution is to post data one year after TESS delivers the data to investigators, so that investigators have sufficient—but not indefinite—"data patents" and the opportunity to avoid being scooped.

Genetic research provides a larger-scale example. Many projects that collect genomic data with funding from the U.S. National Institutes of Health have agreements to deposit the data in the repository dbGaP (which stands for "database of Genotypes and Phenotypes"). A given data collection effort may have the potential to spawn many, perhaps hundreds, of papers. The originating research team retains exclusive rights to generate as many publications as it can during an initial embargo period (often one year). The embargo retains the incentive for genetics researchers to launch ambitious data collection efforts while adding to their incentive to write up results quickly (which has value for the rest of the scientific community). At the same time, having a mandated and centralized mode of data-sharing aids replicability and ensures that other researchers may generate additional findings from the same datasets.

Data Citation

A traditional way for researchers to ensure that they will receive credit when other scholars use their data to generate new findings is to allow others to use their data only in a coauthorship arrangement. In many cases, this may seem appropriate given the effort that data collection requires. However, drawbacks include the implication of permanent ownership of data, barriers to others' using data in ways that are unorthodox or that challenge earlier findings, and a disincentive to making data more public than required.

Short of requiring coauthorship, citation standards help ensure that researchers making a dataset public receive some recognition for it. Yet style guides traditionally have provided elaborate information on how to cite all manner of sources for the literature review of a paper—but have provided no information about how to cite *data* that are used. The *American Sociological Review* is one journal that has adopted data citation guidelines. The example citation provided on the journal's website is as follows:[4]

> Deschenes, Elizabeth Piper, Susan Turner, and Joan Petersilia. Intensive Community Supervision in Minnesota, 1990–1992: A Dual Experiment in Prison Diversion and Enhanced Supervised Release [Computer file]. ICPSR06849-v1. Ann Arbor, MI: Inter-university Consortium for Political and Social Research [distributor], 2000. doi:10.3886/ICPSR06849.

Data citation is valuable not only for recognizing those responsible for leading data collection, but also for providing systematic information about the version of a dataset and its distributor. Popular repositories, including Harvard's Dataverse, automatically create digital object identifiers (DOIs) for all data and provide examples of how to cite the data they archive. These repositories are described in more detail later in the chapter.

PRIVATE DATA

Data use may be restricted for many reasons, the most prominent of which is to protect the privacy of participants. Social scientists often seek information about participants that could be uncomfortable, embarrassing, or even harmful if shared with the wrong person. A key

---

4. See https://us.sagepub.com/en-us/nam/american-sociological-review/journal201969#submission-guidelines.

distinction drawn for protecting such data is between confidentiality and anonymity. Data are *confidential* when researchers have information about the identity of participants but agree to keep identities private. Data are *anonymous* when researchers themselves do not know respondents' identities.

Data posted publicly are, by definition, not confidential. Social science data that involve private information can therefore be made available to other investigators only under two broad conditions:

1. Investigators accessing the data may be bound formally to keep the data confidential themselves.

2. Shared data may be anonymous, meaning that, as far as can be determined, researchers who use the data will not be able to identify individuals.

As we discuss at length below, however, whether data that appear to be anonymous actually are anonymous is increasingly difficult to judge, and even when data are indeed anonymous there can still be issues regarding subjects' privacy.

Restricted-Access Data

The steps investigators must take to access confidential data vary. In the simplest scenario, investigators must sign an agreement that they will use the dataset only for research purposes and not share it with anyone else. Often, the researchers (and their institution) must also agree to analyze the data under secure conditions—for example, by using an encrypted drive on a locked computer not connected to the Internet.

For extremely sensitive data, like our earlier example of personal tax returns, researchers can analyze the data only at special approved sites, staffed by government employees. No output can be taken off these sites unless it has been checked and approved. The U.S. Census Bureau, in collaboration with a few other statistical agencies such as the Centers for Disease Control and Prevention's National Center for Health Statistics, operates a series of these facilities called Federal Statistical Research Data Centers (FSRDC) nationwide.[5]

For journals that otherwise mandate data availability, an exception for such data can be made by asking the researchers to be explicit that such restrictions exist upon article submission. Editors can affirm and

5. See https://www.census.gov/fsrdc for more information.

approve the restriction. Also, if allowed, researchers can still make available all of the code they used to analyze the data, and carefully describe the process by which they gained access. That code could then be used by anyone else who gains permission to use the same data.

Anonymizing Data

Direct identifiers are variables that obviously identify individuals, including names, email addresses, and social security numbers. Of course, these must be removed in order for the resulting dataset to be anonymous. But just because direct identifiers have been removed does not mean the data are truly anonymous.

A famous example occurred in the 1990s when the State of Massachusetts announced that it would make some information from medical records publicly available to researchers, with identifying information removed to protect confidentiality (Heffetz and Ligett 2014). Within days, Latanya Sweeney—then a computer science graduate student at MIT, now a professor at Harvard—showed that one could quickly identify the governor of Massachusetts in the data and thus obtain his private medical information. The governor was the only man with his birthdate who lived in his zip code, and these variables were included in the supposedly de-identified data.

Using other information to deduce identities from data stripped of direct identifiers is called *re-identification,* and it scares the daylights out of those responsible for curating "public use" versions of confidential data. The possibilities that configurations of variables may identify participants leads to many examples of datasets that require very useful variables to be artificially coarsened (in other words, noise is added to the underlying data).

For example, consider the biggest data collection projects that the National Science Foundation funds in sociology and political science: the General Social Survey (GSS), which includes detailed (three-digit) codes for respondents' occupations; and the American National Election Studies (ANES), which include the states where respondents reside. GSS does not provide the state of residence, but only the region of the country, while ANES provides occupation only as coded into very broad categories. These projects have effectively chosen different solutions for the problem that, when combined with information like a person's sex, age, and marital status, an unusual occupation paired with a sparsely populated state may well uniquely identify someone.

The large amount of other information available about individuals today makes re-identification challenges increasingly severe. As an example, Netflix once sponsored a contest in which data scientists were given information about how users had rated some films and asked to predict how those users would rate others.[6] The dataset included only seemingly minimal information: a random ID number for individuals, the film, the date of the rating, and the number of stars given.

But some people who watch movies on Netflix also rate movies on other sites, like the Internet Movie Database (IMDB). Narayanan and Shmatikov (2008) demonstrated that one could use correspondences in the dates of reviews between the Netflix data and the IMDB site to match some IDs in the Netflix data to IMDB usernames, and some IMDB usernames could then be easily connected to people's real identities. Ratings on IMDB are a public matter, but being able to match to the Netflix data meant that one could learn what other movies those people had watched and not rated on IMDB. Perhaps having other people know what movies you watched is unlikely to have severe personal consequences—although scenarios that could get some people in trouble are not that hard to envision[7]—but the larger point is that thinking about re-identification simply in terms of the information provided in a dataset can miss how someone could combine that information with data available elsewhere.

DIFFERENTIAL PRIVACY

Inspired by some of these examples, *differential privacy* is an emerging concept that speaks to the challenge of balancing the interests of social science with individual privacy (Dwork and Smith 2009; Heffetz and Ligett 2014). Differential privacy is, firstly, a property of the statistics produced from data—and the algorithms that produce those statistics. The working scenario is one in which an analyst has full access to private data but is tasked with protecting privacy when they report on those data. We describe differential privacy below using a hypothetical example.

---

6. At the time, Netflix asked users to rate movies on a 1–5 "star" scale. They have since moved to asking users only to indicate whether they liked the movie or not.

7. For instance: "Honey, why does the Netflix data say you were watching romantic movies on all these evenings that you said you had to work late at the office?"

Basic Ideas

Imagine that there is an outbreak of a new and dangerous sexually transmitted disease. A state tests high school students for the disease and determines that there is a compelling public interest in providing information about the rate of positive tests by school. At the same time, the state recognizes that the privacy of any individual's test result must be protected.

We will consider privacy in terms of one student, Veronica, in the very small town of Riverdale. Riverdale tested 83 students and 12 of them tested positive. If the state reported a rate of 14.5 percent, someone who knew that Riverdale had 80–100 students could figure out from this that there were 12 positive tests. Worse, say that some Riverdale students are openly showing others their test results (that is, there is *auxiliary information* about outcomes at Riverdale that is available to others beyond what the state provides). Some students want to prove to others that they are disease free; some with the disease decide they want to be public about it and post their test-result letters on Facebook or a similar platform. If Veronica wishes to keep her own result secret, her privacy should not depend on what others choose to divulge about theirs. Yet if people know that Veronica was tested, and if enough other students in her town reveal their test results, someone could eventually figure out Veronica's.

At this point, we need to divide into two parts the information that an aggregate statistic, like a prevalence rate, provides about an individual. The first is what we could infer about someone without their being in the dataset. Had Veronica been absent when others were tested, the school would have had 82 tests, with either 11 (13.4 percent) or 12 (14.6 percent) positive results, depending on whether Veronica herself had the disease. If this rate was unusual in comparison to other schools, we would be in a better position to guess Veronica's result than we were without this information. As a result, Veronica could still feel that the school-level statistic intruded upon her privacy, but—this is the key part—the loss of privacy would not be *due to Veronica's inclusion in the dataset,* because we are talking about what we learn from data in which Veronica is not included.

The second part is whatever additional information is provided about Veronica's disease status *as a result* of her being part of the data from which the rate was calculated. This is the "difference" in differential privacy: the specific additional loss to an individual's privacy as a result of being present in a dataset instead of absent. Protecting the privacy

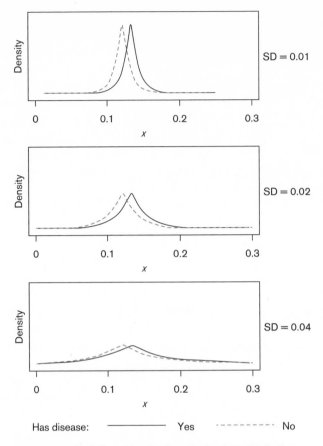

FIGURE 10.1. Statistics with noise from the Laplace distribution. For our example of a school with 83 persons, these graphs show how distributions of reported prevalance rates differ depending on whether a single individual has the disease or not and the amount of noise added to the reported rate. The more noise we add to the graph (i.e., higher SD), the more they overlap, which reduces the capacity to infer which distribution the statistic came from.

of the specific individuals in a study involves this second aspect but not the first.

We can then consider Veronica's differential privacy as protected to the extent that the reported statistics are the same regardless of whether or not Veronica is included in the dataset.[8] In the terminology that has

8. Or, if Veronica's participation in the dataset is known, the extent to which reported statistics are the same whether Veronica's true status is used or is swapped with a randomly selected value instead. From the standpoint of differential privacy, knowing

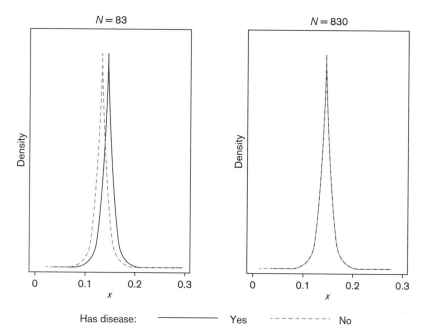

FIGURE 10.2. Differential privacy and sample size. The histograms indicate the overlap in the probability distributions of potential estimates of prevalence rates when adding the same amount of statistical noise to schools of different sizes. The greater overlap when $N = 830$ indicates the greater similarity in these distributions regardless of whether an individual student included in the data has positive or negative disease status.

been developed, two datasets that are the same except for one observation are called *adjacent datasets* (or *neighboring datasets*). Differential privacy is protected if reported statistics add negligibly to one's ability to tell whether the statistics were based on one adjacent dataset versus another. We can accomplish this by adding random noise to the statistic before reporting it. In Figure 10.1, we add random noise from a Laplace distribution with different standard deviations. The more noise we add, the more similar are the probabilities of observing a given result if Veronica's test result was negative versus positive.

We can quantify this difference in probabilities, yielding a specific, demonstrable estimate of how differentially private our algorithm for adding noise makes Veronica's information. Specifically, differential privacy usually defines as parameter ε the maximum difference in multipli-

---

the precise sample size on which a statistic is based would be the same as knowing Veronica's participation, since her participation could be inferred if everyone else at Riverdale divulged whether they had participated.

cative terms between the probability of observing a given output in two neighboring datasets (Heffetz and Ligett 2014). ε quantifies how much Veronica's inclusion in a dataset increases the ability to predict Veronica's disease status. ε is always positive, with differential privacy increasing as ε approaches zero. As we have shown, the amount of noise we add decreases ε, and ε also decreases as the potential influence that a given observation has on the statistic decreases. As shown in Figure 10.2, if Riverdale High had tested 830 students instead of 83, the same amount of random noise would result in much more similar probabilities of observing the same result, regardless of Veronica's own status.

Strengths and Weaknesses

Differential privacy shifts the question of how much statistics reveal about individuals from a matter of broad intuition to one of quantified parameters backed up by mathematical proof. The precision of the differential privacy framework allows it to be extended to scenarios in which one wishes to generate multiple statistics from a dataset, like the means for a set of variables and their correlations. Each new statistic revealed reduces the overall privacy, which means more noise would need to be added to maintain the same degree of privacy. If the precision of some statistics is more important than that of others, researchers could introduce relatively less noise to the former, akin to making different allocations from an overall "privacy budget."

That said, differential privacy implies an extremely demanding standard. It is intended to guarantee a specific level of privacy even from an adversary who has access to all auxiliary information about everyone else that might be available online or commercially (or possibly even in government administrative records). The noise needed to ensure high levels of privacy could conceivably be so great that it undermines the usefulness of the data. One line of work to make differential privacy's insights more useful in practice is trying to determine when and how much one may reduce the amount of noise that needs to be added if the availability of some level of auxiliary information may be deemed implausible (Machanavajjhala et al. 2008). In our example, if it could be judged implausible that more than half of the other students at Riverdale High, say, would publicly divulge their test results, then the amount of noise needed to achieve a given ε for Veronica's privacy would be less extreme. Exercises like this make it clear that fully open social science data may have important social costs and consequences.

Differential Privacy and Microdata

The Longitudinal Business Database (LBD) contains tax and other confidential information for more than 20 million U.S. businesses over more than three decades. The data can be analyzed only under the very strong restrictions of the FSRDC system mentioned above. This makes access to the database very costly in terms of time and other resources, which limits its use.

To increase the use of LBD, Kinney et al. (2011) have developed a synthetic version of the dataset for more open use. The researchers first created a series of models from the actual restricted-use data that allow them to simulate observed values with noise. Then the model estimates are used to simulate observations consistent with those values, and this dataset of simulated observations is made public.

The idea is not that the synthetic data can serve as a substitute for the real LBD in all cases. The authors write, "It is expected that high-level analyses involving large groups will be well preserved, while analyses involving small groups or high-dimensional inferences will require access to the confidential data" (Kinney et al. 2011). Even for more fine-grained analysis, the synthetic data can be used to generate code and fix ideas to make analyses of the real data more efficient and confirmatory.

All this implies that some analysts still have access to the full data. One might imagine some types of data that could be obtained if researchers were able to ensure privacy even from the researchers themselves. An old technique for measuring sensitive questions in surveys, known as *randomized response,* involved giving respondents some means of randomization, like a coin they could flip without showing the interviewer the result (Greenberg et al. 1969). A respondent would be presented with two questions, one of which was sensitive while the other was not. Respondents were instructed to answer the first question if the coin was heads and the second question if tails. Since it wasn't known to anyone but the respondent which question they were answering, the information for either item could not be discerned with certainty for any individual. Yet population parameters could still be estimated once surveys from many respondents were combined, albeit with more statistical uncertainty than if the information were measured directly.[9]

---

9. A variant of this approach often goes by the name *list experiment.* A person is given a list of four or five propositions, randomized so that they might or might not include a controversial proposition. Individuals do not indicate directly whether they agree with any particular proposition, but instead just indicate the number of propositions they agree with.

Randomized response has more recently inspired methods for software and consumer technology companies to obtain useful aggregate information about users while protecting individual privacy (Erlingsson 2014). Many technology products transmit usage information to companies, which raises questions about the security and privacy of this information. One method to increase privacy is for the software to sometimes transmit true information and at other times transmit information based on a random draw from a known probability distribution. Analyses of data from many users will be able to adjust for this noise, and yet the actual data from any individual user can be shown to be private to a degree quantifiable within the differential privacy framework. In our view, these techniques are likely to become increasingly useful in a world in which new auxiliary online information and "big data" further erode our ability to maintain individual privacy even in datasets that are formally anonymous.

MAKING YOUR DATA AVAILABLE

While this chapter has mostly been focused on larger policy and conceptual questions about data sharing, we also want to give attention to the nuts and bolts of how researchers can share data. Happily, sharing your own data keeps getting easier because of all the simple-to-use resources that have been developed to help. Indeed, the biggest advice we have regarding how to do data sharing is to *take advantage of existing resources*. Researchers have often made data public by simply posting a file on their personal websites, but this is far from best practice nowadays. Personal websites come and go, whereas data archivists' jobs require them to think in terms of posterity.

In the first part of this section, we discuss sharing data in terms of preparing a "replication package" associated with a single paper, by which we mean an easily downloadable set of files from which published analyses can be reproduced. Afterward, we discuss the broader scenario of having a dataset that you'd like to share apart from a specific project's replication package.

Creating a Replication Package

We believe it is useful to prepare and provide replication packages for journal articles whether they are required by journals or not. Correlational data indicate that papers that deposit data are more likely to be cited (Piwowar and Vision 2013). Also, approaching a data analysis project in anticipation of sharing your data and documentation as part of the end product avoids so much potential for confusion and trouble down the line. Your collaborators and future self will be glad you did.

As for specifics, different journals have articulated different guidelines, but they overlap enough that adopting a thorough approach at the outset would make it relatively simple to adjust for any single journal's specific requirements. What we cannot belabor enough is how much easier it is if you keep reproducibility in mind throughout your project's workflow, as opposed to trying to retro-organize a mess of files at a project's end, let alone years later.

If top refereed journals in your field already require replication packages, you can look at them to see exactly how they are organized. For instance, one admirably clear and thoughtful description of what should go in a data replication package has been provided by the *American Journal of Political Science* (*AJPS*; Jacoby and Lupton 2016). Their guidelines break the work of assembling a replication package into four components: README file, analysis datasets, software commands, and information to reconstruct analysis dataset.

README File

The README file walks the user through the contents of the replication package and how they relate to the contents of the paper. We think this is most effectively organized by presenting the data files to be used first, and then referring to each table, figure, or result in the paper and indicating the command file (or header within a larger command file) used to generate each one.

While economists often provide README files as PDF files of Word or LaTeX documents, *AJPS* recommends plain text. Regardless of whether it's readme.txt, readme.doc, or readme.pdf, what's most important is that your README file is named "readme," so that readers used to this convention will immediately find it.

Analysis Datasets

Analysis datasets are usually acceptable in whatever formats are commonly used in a field. For example, a cursory examination of the archives of a couple economics journals suggests that Stata data (.dta) files are the most common format there. For proprietary formats, some advocate also including a plain-text (e.g., .csv) file of the same data.

AJPS requires data to be accompanied by a codebook that indicates what different variables in the dataset are and what their values mean. Granted, data formats like Stata's or SPSS's make it easy for this sort of information to be preserved as part of the data file. This may make the generation of this specific information as a codebook largely superfluous, but, on the other hand, it is also easy to automatically generate a codebook from these files, so you might as well do so. When possible, automatically generating codebooks is more efficient and likely less error prone than trying to create this documentation separately. Data documentation should also include or reference any additional information needed to understand what the data are.

Statistical analysis may involve many intermediate datasets generated from code in the course of a project, such as a series of imputed datasets when multiple imputations for missing data are used. An alternative to including all these intermediate datasets in the replication package is to make sure that the code is provided for generating these datasets, so that others will be able to reproduce them. For example, if randomization is involved, the code should include random number seed values.

Software Commands

We present advice about organizing analysis workflow in Chapter 11. The practices we advocate there also help make the code in replication packages easier for others to follow and use. Code should fully reproduce results in the paper from the analysis datasets, and comments should make it clear what code reproduces what result. We encourage the use of a clearly documented master command file that executes all the individual command files in a project from beginning to end, which a project's README file can then reference.

We emphasize the value of documenting the versions of software packages used, especially anything used to produce results. As we discuss in Chapter 11, we do not mean just the version of the statistical package itself (e.g., Stata 15.2) but also the versions of user-written packages (e.g., gologit2.ado). Changes to these can result in failures to reproduce results exactly by someone using an alternate version. User-written packages are not always archived when newer versions are released, so you may want to include the versions of user-written packages that you used as files within your replication package to ensure that results remain reproducible.

Information to Reconstruct Analysis Dataset

AJPS uses the heading above to distinguish between the analysis dataset and the larger or multiple-source datasets from which the analysis dataset is constructed. In addition to the ability to reproduce results from the analysis dataset, software commands and any other information should be provided to reproduce the analysis dataset from its sources. Ultimately, the code in the replication package should connect the original data sources used in the paper to all the specific results that the paper presents.

If source data have different versions, be sure to record which version is used. Even when there is not an official version number, recording the date on which the data were obtained can be very useful. With large-scale survey data, for example, users often do not appreciate that those data are sometimes updated by the organization generating the data. We have observed collaborators baffled and upset by not being able to get the same results from the same code, when it turned out they were simply using different versions of the data.

Archiving Datasets

You may want to make your data publicly available apart from the specific replication package that you put together for any particular paper. You might also have a replication package for a working paper that you want to make available before it is published, or for a paper in a journal that does not have its own process for handling replication packages.

Once again, our central advice is to use a high-quality archiving platform rather than simply posting on your own website. Social scientists have access to many repositories for their data. We will highlight three prominent current options here, recognizing that this is a dynamic sector and that additional options may emerge in the coming years.

ICPSR/OpenICPSR

The Inter-university Consortium for Political and Social Research (ICPSR) at the University of Michigan has been in the business of archiving and distributing data since the early 1960s. The organization has data-archiving professionals and, usually at a cost, offers professional data-curation services like reviewing data and documentation for problems and generating versions of data documentation that meet certain standards. In addition, ICPSR has launched openICPSR, which is free and allows you to upload a set of files and make them publicly available; openICPSR can also distribute restricted-use data, which others must apply to access and can analyze only using a secure online system (ICPSR's Virtual Data Enclave).

Dataverse

Dataverse has been developed by Harvard's Institute for Quantitative Social Science. It is an open-source platform that institutions and individuals can install to have their own "dataverses" (i.e., collections of data resources) on their own servers. But anyone can also deposit datasets or replication packages onto Harvard's dataverse, or even create a dataverse for free within Harvard's dataverse. Prominent journals such as *AJPS* and the *Review of Economics and Statistics* use this option for the papers they publish, rather than separately posting data on a journal website. You can specify custom terms of use for users to access the data, require that you grant permission in order for files to be accessed, and create a customized form that users need to fill out when they access data. Dataverse converts data from many formats into a common format, which makes it easy to download in different formats (including the original) and also analyze data online through a platform integrated with Dataverse software.

Open Science Framework

Open Science Framework (OSF, https://osf.io) is maintained by the Center for Open Science. As with Dataverse and openICPSR, if you have a replication package for a finished paper that you want to make immediately available, you can use this platform. But OSF is also more broadly designed to be an environment in which you can (privately) store project files and work on them with research collaborators, and then make materials publicly available at a project's conclusion. You can "register" versions of your project along the way, so that you can have time-stamped analysis plans and easy integration with various systems for preregistering studies.

These platforms are all easy to use: you can create an account and do everything needed to make your data publicly available online in minutes. Creating the replication materials and data documentation that you want to post is the hard part. They are all free to use, up to a reasonably large individual project size (currently several gigabytes, although this will surely increase). All automatically assign a DOI to your data so that it has a permanent reference and is easy for other scholars to cite. All also make it easy to integrate links to your data from your own web page.

ELEVEN

Reproducible Workflow

The era of massive mainframe computers taking days to run a single regression are long gone. Nowadays there is more computing power in everyone's smartphone (and possibly everyone's toaster) than all of NASA had access to when they put a man on the moon![1] Social science research has changed accordingly. Empirical social science often requires thousands, or tens of thousands, of lines of code, little or none of which presently make it into the resulting published article. Accordingly, the idea known as Claerbout's principle has developed: "An article about computational science in a scientific publication is not the scholarship itself, it is merely advertising of the scholarship. The actual scholarship is the complete software development environment and the complete set of instructions which generated the figures" (Buckheit and Donoho 1995).

We see no reason to stop at just the figures or graphics. The same principle applies to our analysis tables, coefficients, standard errors, statistical tests, and so on. Thus, to do transparent work, in our view researchers must adopt both the reproducible statistical and methodological techniques discussed throughout this book, *as well as* workflow and software practices that make their work easily reproducible by other scholars. The goal of this chapter is to introduce you to the most important of these practices.

---

1. It's true. See https://history.nasa.gov/computers/Ch2-5.html.

There are several major tools that researchers can use to make sure their work is reproducible. Below, we discuss four major topics in this area: workflow practices, coding practices, version control, and dynamic documents. By using these tools, a researcher will move closer to the reproducibility ideal of "one-click workflow": she will be able to rerun the entire analysis (carried out earlier by another researcher) from the ground up with a single click or the execution of a single script file.

WORKFLOW PRACTICES

Computer code is just one aspect of a larger structure we refer to as "workflow" (after Long 2008), by which we mean the combination of data, code, organization, and documentation. Everything from file and variable names to folder organization to data storage to efficient and readable programming is part of workflow.

A natural starting point to describe a good workflow is to describe a basic digital folder structure (on your computer or server), which might look something like Figure 11.1. Of course, the specifics will vary for different types of research and different scholars' tastes, but many projects may have a file structure similar to the basic organization shown here. First off, you need to create a single master folder with a short but descriptive name for the project, a name that is meaningful for you as well as your collaborators. (But please don't name the folder with your coauthor's last name; that won't be a very useful project name for them, will it?)

Inside that folder, you will need to create separate folders for all of your programming script files (.R, .py, .do., .SAS, etc.), one for the untouched raw data (the data that comes in the very first format in which you acquire it), one for any edited data that you build from the raw data (probably using the scripts), one for output such as tables and figures, and one for the actual paper or article text.

Then, the way to use this setup is to never, ever, ever directly edit or write over any of the data in the raw data folder. Instead, generate any new datasets (and all your output) using your scripts, and save these new data files in the separate "data" folder.[2] This way, if you discover an error in any stage of your data processing, you can fix and then reproduce everything because your scripts and raw data are intact. (Also, you know this already, but are you backing up all your files regularly? Cloud storage and declining hard disk prices leave you with no

---

2. For more on data storage, see Hart et al. (2016).

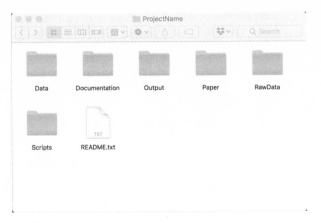

FIGURE 11.1. Example of project folder structure.

excuse for not backing up your files—also see the section on Git and Git collaboration services below for additional backup methods.)

Second, inside the project folder, write up a README file that lists and describes the contents of each of the folders and gives the installation and operating instructions for how an interested researcher should go about reproducing your analysis. The README is usually a simple text file (making it easy to open on any operating system without any proprietary software) that is the first thing a new user will open.

As the project is being conducted, researchers should maintain a written record of their work. There are multiple ways to do this: in a central research log, in individual script files, or with Git. With a central research log or lab notebook, a researcher writes a record of research activities daily, or as often as work on the project is being done (not weekly or monthly after the fact) in a single central file. This doesn't have to be a particularly enjoyable thing to read or look at, but you should write down which research team member writes what code, produces what output, edits which files, and when.

To the extent that research involves editing script files, the research log could be accomplished by adding the summary of changes (a summary of who edited which part of which file when, and why) in a comment section at the top of each script file. Alternatively, good use of Git, described below, can accomplish much of this record keeping without a separate file and without describing changes made in the script file itself, since Git log files record changes made to files, by whom, and when (see Ram 2013). This is an aid to future researchers, but also to your future self (Bowers 2011; Bowers and Voors 2016). Some journals can take six months (or more!) to referee a paper, so a good README file, along with a daily research log, can go a long way to helping you know where to pick back up when you get a "revise and resubmit." You may not remember where to find the statistical code that generates table 7, the table that reviewer 2 needs you to change in order to get your paper published, but it will be written down in your research log.

One more organization suggestion: Do not use spaces in directory names or filenames, as it complicates referring to them in certain software or operating systems. All lowercase with underscores will avoid other cross-operating-system issues.

CODING PRACTICES

Before we offer specific details on how to write reproducible code, we should likely mention the more important overarching rule: Write code. Write code instead of working by hand in your preferred statistical programming environment. By this we mean:

1. Do not modify data by hand, such as with a spreadsheet. Which is to say, don't use Microsoft Excel if it can be avoided.

2. Do not rely on the command line, drop-down menus, or point-and-click options in statistical software (such as SPSS or Stata).

3. Instead, do absolutely everything with scripts.

The simple reason for this is reproducibility. Modifying data in Microsoft Excel or any similar spreadsheet program leaves no record of the changes made to the data, nor any explanation of the reasoning or timing behind any changes. Although it may seem easy or quick to do a one-time-only cleaning of data in Excel, or make "minor" changes to get the data into a format readable by a researcher's preferred statistical software, unless these changes are written down in excruciating detail, this approach is simply not reproducible by other researchers.[3] It is better to write a programming script that imports the raw data, does all

---

3. When a situation arises that truly necessitates that something be done by hand or in Excel, then the process should be described in exact detail, down to which menus and buttons were clicked in which order, so that someone completely unfamiliar with the project would be able to do the identical task. Think of it as writing code, except for a human to run instead of a computer. For practical suggestions on using spreadsheets reproducibly, see Broman and Woo (2018).

necessary changes, with comments in the code that explain those changes, and saves any intermediate datasets used in analysis. Then, a researcher can share their initial raw data and code, and other researchers can reproduce their work exactly. Don't forget, that other researcher might be you in a few months' time.

Though we understand that a fair amount of research has been done using pull-down menus in SPSS or Stata, we strongly advise against this. A bare minimum, if one insists on going this route, is to use the built-in command-logging features of the software. In Stata, this involves the `cmdlog` command; in SPSS, it involves using the paste button to add to a syntax file. At least in that case, others can see the commands that you executed, even if they cannot readily reproduce them.

The research transparency ideal is to make everything, including changes like rounding and formatting, done with scripts. Even downloading of data from websites can be done through a script. For example, in R, the `download.file()` function can be used to save data from a website. In Stata, the `copy` command does the same. Of course, this opens the possibility that the data file will change online. In some situations, such as when using government administrative data that may be updated, you might want to simply point to the URL where the most current version is hosted. When reproducing results from a given dataset (or exactly reproducing a paper) is more important than getting the most recent data from a specific source, researchers should download their raw dataset once and never save over it, instead saving all modified intermediate datasets in a separate location. Another way to prevent unintentional changes to data is to always set the seed for random number generators whenever any random numbers are to be used (for example, the command `set.seed()` in R, `set seed ()` in Stata, and so on).[4]

Finally, here are two general organizing principles:

1. Consider not saving statistical output, instead just saving the code and data that generate it. Obviously, this would be unrealistically time consuming for large projects (especially ones where analysis takes days to run), but the idea is that you should

---

4. Another reason to avoid Excel if possible is that, as far as we can tell, you can't set the seed for the random number generator without building a macro and using Visual Basic's RANDOMIZE function. Rumor has it that the seed has something to do with system time, but Microsoft does transparently state (in the author's version 16.13.1 of Microsoft Excel for Mac) that they use the Mersenne Twister pseudorandom number generator.

be able to reproduce all the steps of your analysis from scratch anytime.[5]

2. What would happen if you, or your laptop's hard drive, were hit by a bus? How easily would anyone else be able to reproduce your work? Hopefully the probability is greater than zero. The more thoroughly you comment your code, and the more you describe the contents of every script file—and the more you make sure to back everything up—the better your chances.

Statistical Package Management

The casual programmer might naively assume that advanced software packages will always produce the exact same answer, across multiple versions of software and platforms, but this is often not the case. This is also *definitely* not the case with user-written packages. (For an example from economics demonstrating how important this issue can be with nonlinear numerical estimation, see McCullough and Vinod [2003].) At the very least, researchers should always include information on which version of a software they used to run their programs. Information about the software version can be determined using the `session.info()` command in R, and Stata users should include the `version number` command in scripts to ensure that users with newer versions of Stata use the same algorithms. Unfortunately, this is still no guarantee, since outdated or incorrect algorithms are not reproduced within newer versions of Stata. Information on the computer processor and operating system should also ideally be included, as these can produce different answers.

R users can use the `packageVersion()` command, and can run old versions of packages (archived at CRAN—the Comprehensive R Archive Network—the large collection of servers worldwide that store R and its many packages). Since R (and other open-source languages) require numerous packages, manually recording packages is not recommended. Instead, for reproducibility, users can obtain every necessary package from a specific point in time by using the checkpoint package, and can more easily store different versions of packages using the

---

5. A practical step here, if using knitr in R Studio and your analysis takes a long time to run, is to use the cache feature. Caching can be turned on globally with `knitr::opts_chunk$set(cache = TRUE)`; before sharing with others, deleting the `_cache` folder will remove all intermediate objects.

packrat package.[6] When writing code, tell checkpoint the date the code was written; then, when others run the code, checkpoint will search CRAN for the versions of all packages as they existed on that date. Stata users can use the `viewsource` command for any .ado they use, but since Statistical Software Components unfortunately does not archive old versions, reproducibility may be lost, so ideally researchers would also include the actual code for the version of the user-written .ado along with their publicly archived data and code files.[7]

The movement toward open-source (i.e., freely available) software such as R and Python is an important development, and one that has many advantages—namely, equal access to the software (independent of ability to pay) and the existence of virtual communities that contribute to an increasingly rich programming environment. Perhaps because of their open-source nature, these particular programming software packages are also quite nimble; they can tackle larger and larger datasets, web-scraping, natural language processing, text analysis, and other general programming tasks better than most canned software programs.

That said, we appreciate that many social science disciplines have long traditions of using proprietary software, including SAS, SPSS, and Stata, and learning a new programming language may be an undesirable additional burden in established researchers' already busy lives. In this chapter, we thus present specific coding suggestions and sometimes commands in both R and Stata, in order to be relevant to the greatest number of scholars.

General Coding Suggestions

There are several general coding rules that all researchers should use when organizing and implementing their analysis, and here we offer some specific workflow organization suggestions that should be valid regardless of code or operating system.

---

6. For more information, see https://cran.r-project.org/web/packages/checkpoint/vignettes/checkpoint.html and https://rstudio.github.io/packrat/.

7. Though SSC and the `netinstall` command are the most popular way to install user-written commands in Stata, E.F. Haghish has written a `github` command that would download and install specific versions of Stata commands from GitHub and allow the authors to archive old versions of the software there. For more information, see https://github.com/haghish/github.

1. Make sure that your script files are self-contained. That is, don't write a program that works only if you first run a group of other files in a specific order and then leave things hanging in a certain precarious way. You should be able to run intermediate steps of the workflow without disrupting things downstream.

2. Include tests in your code. This can alert you if output ever changes unexpectedly. For example, if merging intermediate datasets and dropping unmatched observations, you could write code to throw an error and alert you if the number of observations changes (see the Stata example below).

3. You can never comment your code too much. Comments should truly explain what the code is doing rather than merely transliterating—it is more useful to describe x<-1 with "initialize the population count to 1" than "set x equal to 1." Comments should also be checked to make sure they convey no inaccurate information and don't go out of date.

4. Indent your code. (We are too smart to weigh in on the spaces vs. tabs debate.)

5. Once you post or distribute code or data (within your team or to others), any changes at all require a new filename (or a version control system in place; see below).

6. Separate your data cleaning and analysis files; don't make any new variables that need saving (or that will be used by multiple analysis files) in an analysis file. It is better to only create a variable once so you know that it is identical when used in different analysis files.

7. Never name a file "final"—it won't be, and why do you want to tempt fate? Instead, add a date and author initials or version number.

8. Name binary variables "male" instead of "gender," such that 1 = Male and 0 = Not, so that the name is more informative to someone who comes across it in the future.

9. Don't leave clutter around—delete temporary or unnecessary intermediate values. You can use a prefix such as x_ or temp_ so you know which files or variables can easily be deleted later. Stata also has tempfile and tempvar functionality.

10. Every variable should have a label (if this is accommodated in the software you are using). If not, create a good data dictionary.

11. Use relative directory paths (such as "./Data" and not "C:/Users /Garret/Documents/Project/Data") so that users on other comput- ers do not have to rename every single reference to a file and can instead just change or assign a global directory once.

Stata-Specific Suggestions

The authors of this book have primarily used Stata over their careers and have noticed a few ways that Stata programming can easily be more reproducible. Readers not familiar with Stata may find the specific com- mands used here a bit confusing, but the basic principles apply to other statistical packages. Here is a partial list:

1. Accurately and concisely capture missing values. There are multiple reasons why a value might be blank. To fully convey this, use the full set of missing values available to you (".a"–".z", not exclusively ".") in order to distinguish between "don't know" and "didn't ask" or other distinct reasons for missing data.

2. Make sure code always produces the same result, and that merging and sorting are reproducible. When sorting or merging datasets, be sure to uniquely specify observations, because if you don't, Stata can do something arbitrary and not repeatable. So instead of just sorting or merging on "ID" when there are multi- ple observations per ID, sort by "ID" and "name" or whatever additional variables it takes to uniquely specify observations. You can use the `duplicates` command to test whether the varlist you use uniquely identifies observations. The `sort, stable` command can also be used, though it is slower and may not solve your problem, since it only keeps observations in the same relative order as you had prior to sorting. The `egen rank, unique` command has similar issues with ties.

3. Also ensure that code produces the same results by running simple "if" tests to alert yourself when results change. For example, when you merge two intermediate datasets that may change over the course of the project, and you know there are 74 observations that aren't matched, and you want to make sure that doesn't change, you can explicitly test that with this code:

```
count if _merge!= 3
if r(N)!= 74 {
display "Unmatched observations changed!"
this isn't a command-will throw error to get
your attention

}
```

4. Don't use abbreviations for variables (which may become unstable after adding variables) or commands (beyond reason).

5. Use global macros to define directory paths so that collaborators can readily work across different computers.

6. Use local macros for varlists to ensure that long lists of variables include the same variables whenever intended.

7. Use computer-stored versions of numerical output instead of manually typing in numbers or copying and pasting. For example, instead of copying and pasting the mean after a summ command, refer to r(mean). Use the return list command to see a full list of stored values after a regular command, and the ereturn list after estimation commands.

8. If you have a master .do file that calls other .do files, and each has its own .log file capturing output, you can run multiple log files at the same time (so you end up with a master .log file).

9. Use the label data and notes commands to label datasets and help yourself and other researchers easily identify the contents.

10. Use the notes command for variables as well for identifying information that is too long for the variable label.

11. Validate data sources to ensure consistency. Data sources sometimes change over time, and collaborators (and other new scholars) should ensure that the data they are using are the same data over time. This is particularly useful when downloading data from external sites at different times. To check for data consistency, use the datasignature command to generate a hash or checksum and help ensure that the data are the same as before, or that you and a colleague are using the same dataset. For example, you can try this yourself with a dataset one of the authors obtained through a Freedom of Information Act request by downloading the data from Harvard's Dataverse: http://dx.doi.org/10.7910/DVN/ZZOTRV. Make sure

and download it in tab format. Then import that data into Stata (with the simple `import delimited 15F0425_Doc_01_DRS85998.tab` command). When you run `datasignature`, you should get back 255362:8(48980):2957852276:2008891936, which should (for all practical purposes) uniquely identify your dataset. (Try it—make any changes to the data, run `datasignature` again, and you'll get different results.) You can use the extensions `datasignature set, datasignature confirm,` and `datasignature report` to save the signature, and then test a current signature against saved values.[8]

12. In addition to labeling your variables, you should also use value labels for all categorical variables. Include the numerical value in the label, however, since without it, it can be hard to tell what numerical value is actually meant by a given category. This is easily done with the `numlabel [lblname-list], add` command.

13. Even though Stata is case sensitive, don't use capital letters in variable names since not all software packages are case sensitive.

14. Make your files as nonproprietary as possible. (Use the `saveold` command to enable those with earlier versions of Stata to use your data.) This is why trusted data repositories like Harvard's Dataverse are so useful: they'll do this for you.

VERSION CONTROL

We assume that everyone learns early on in the course of their computer education what the "Save As" button is for. The underlying principle here is that you shouldn't save over important documents. The way most people learn to do this is with Save As—sort of like Figure 11.2.

Carefully using Save As is a good start, but there's a better way: actual version control software. This is a tool developed by software

---

8. The `datasignature` command just runs a checksum, a neat algorithm that condenses entire files into short and (for all practical purposes) unique strings, which you can (and should) sometimes use for computer security reasons. For example, when downloading large files such as the latest LaTeX distribution, a checksum ensures that nothing was corrupted during transfer (see http://www.tug.org/mactex/downloading.html). This is fairly simple to check on most computers by typing `openssl md5 pathtofile` from the command line on Mac/Unix, or `CertUtil -hashfile pathtofile MD5` on Windows. You could also do this yourself outside of Stata with whatever data file you want to check if the content is the same.

FIGURE 11.2. *Piled Higher and Deeper* by Jorge Cham. www.phdcomics.com.

programmers, but social scientists have recognized its benefits. Version control software is designed to maintain detailed record keeping of changes to statistical code among multiple collaborators. There are several such packages. Early centralized systems, such as Subversion (http://subversion.apache.org), are perhaps more straightforward to use, but in recent years distributed forms of version control such as Mercurial, and especially Git, have become far more widely used and are well supported by a user community.[9]

The most famous such system is Git—which we'll introduce with another comic (Figure 11.3). Git definitely has a steep learning curve. It was developed by the allegedly prickly technology personality Linus

9. Git was created in 2005. GitHub, the popular website that hosts projects maintained with Git, was launched in 2008.

Torvalds, who maintains the Linux kernel. If you can get over some of its quirks, the tool is very powerful. Git was originally built as a command line tool, but there are several popular graphical user interface (GUI) applications that can simplify many tasks, all while retaining the same information record as the command line.[10]

Git projects are organized into folders called *repositories*. Instead of changing the name of a file in a repository to keep track of versions, in Git a user keeps the same filename and tells Git when to record versions of the file. This is a two-step process: users first *add* whatever files they wish to the *staging area,* then *commit* everything in the staging area. Every commit requires a message describing what change is being made, facilitating better recall of why particular changes were made.

Git has the ability to jump back in time to the state of the repository at the time of any commit. More impressive is that Git can selectively undo

10. The original documentation and the book *Pro Git* by Chacon and Straub (2014) are available at https://git-scm.com/doc. Many other beginner-oriented resources are available as well. We recommend the tutorials from Atlassian (https://www.atlassian.com/git/tutorials) and Software Carpentry (https://swcarpentry.github.io/git-novice/). A list of GUI applications for different platforms is at https://git-scm.com/downloads/guis.

earlier commits (changes made to files) while preserving changes made in later commits, at least in certain circumstances. So, if you write and commit excellent code on Monday, write and commit terrible code on Tuesday, and write and commit excellent code on Wednesday, on Thursday you can *revert* Tuesday's changes without losing Wednesday's work.

In practice the ability to use this functionality is limited, because Git on its own is unable to determine which edition of a specific line of a file should take precedence. In other words, if you're working on completely different lines of a file on Monday versus Tuesday, this works, but if not, you create a *conflict,* which Git will make you *resolve* manually by showing you the two conflicting versions and letting you decide which to keep.

Beyond computer code alone, Git can also display the differences between any two versions of any text file. Some of Git's magic is limited to text files: it can store all your versions of binary files such as Microsoft Word .docx files or PDFs, but it can't easily display the differences between them for you as it can for text files.[11] Users can also *branch* their repository (which explains the "tree model" reference in Figure 11.3). If you need to have a working version of your code but would also like an experimental version for testing new code, you can easily create an unlimited number of branches and then *check out* (as if from a library) one branch at a time, eventually merging branches to bring in the most desirable parts from each branch.

While Git is useful for solo authoring, it is especially useful for collaboration. Repositories can be hosted on any server (the *remote* repository), and each user has a *local* repository on their own machine. Users can then *push* and *pull* changes into and out of the remote repository, respectively (*push* is to send changes from your local machine to the remote repository; *pull* is to bring the changes from the remote repository to your local machine). Users can have copies (called *clones*) of the remote repository on any number of machines, making it useful as a backup.

Git also enables a neat model for open-source collaboration, which allows you to make your code public even in cases where you don't know (or trust) everyone to freely edit the code. In this case, users host their code publicly on a platform like GitHub.com,[12] and when others

11. Some non-text files, like images, can be easily compared with Git. See https://help .github.com/categories/working-with-non-code-files/.

12. Bitbucket.com and GitLab.com are similar hosting services offering varying levels of free storage for nonpaying users. Typically, public repositories are free, whereas larger teams must pay for private repositories, with discounts available for academic /educational users.

want to make contributions, they create their own copy (called a *fork*) of the code, make and commit changes, and then issue a *pull request* (i.e., they request that the owner merge, or *pull*, those changes into the main version of the code). Code owners then decide whether to accept or reject the changes.

Several large programming libraries that have hundreds of contributors—such as D3 (the visualization library for Javascript), Ruby on Rails, Matplotlib for Python, and Jupyter Notebook for interactive computing—are all hosted on GitHub, which means that Git is definitely powerful enough to manage your (relatively) itsy-bitsy research project.

DYNAMIC DOCUMENTS

Beyond code, researchers can also make preparation of articles and manuscripts more reproducible. The principle is to automate the production of tables and figures, so that any modification of the analysis will automatically be reflected in the output. Also, code and the manuscript itself can be written together in a single document so that the code is more easily understood and the details of the analysis in the manuscript are more transparent.

The best tools to use are likely to change with time, but one widely used option is LaTeX, which (like many powerful tools) has a steep learning curve but has the advantage of eventually automating a large portion of the work.[13] There are a number of time-savers in LaTeX. For one, instead of numbering tables and figures by hand, and constantly having to go through and renumber items as their order changes, LaTeX handles the numbering automatically. You give anything you like a label, and by referring to that label you can have LaTeX automatically print the appropriate number given the current order (e.g., table~\ ref{tab:regressions} becomes "table 6"). Footnotes and citations are similarly automated. Whenever the writer wants to cite a paper inline, she just refers to the citekey of a given article, then tells LaTeX where the master list of all references is (called a bibtex file). LaTeX then automatically formats the inline citations, and compiles a list of references at the end if desired. Since each field (e.g., author name and title) is stored separately, any reference style (MLA, APA, Chicago) can be

---

13. OK, now a little nerd snobbery: the "X" in LaTeX is meant to represent the Greek letter χ, so you can pronounce it "lay-tek" or "lah-tek" but not like the name of rubber hospital gloves.

obtained by changing one line of code in the call to create an appropriately formatted references section.

More than that, LaTeX is designed to easily include other files in the final output. So instead of copying and pasting a figure or table (from Stata output, say), users call the filename that contains the latest version of that table or figure. If that figure gets updated, the figure is automatically updated the next time the LaTeX document is compiled. Using this method, researchers can reproduce an entire paper in two clicks: one click to execute your code to produce all your figures and tables, and one to compile your LaTeX document. Stata users can use `estout` or `outreg2` to output their journal-formatted regression tables in LaTeX, while R users can use the stargazer package. The files produced by these packages are then called in your LaTeX document. You'll never forget to update a table or make a copy-and-paste mistake again.

More recently, programmers have developed "dynamic documents" that allow scholars to write statistical analysis code and the final paper all in a single master document. This makes it possible, in some cases, to reproduce an entire project with a single mouse click (rather than the two-click method we just described). Dynamic documents are a way to implement the concept of "literate programming" introduced by Knuth (1984, 1992). The basic idea is that "programs [should] be *works of literature*. . . . Instead of imagining that our main task is to instruct a *computer* what to do, let us concentrate rather on explaining to *human beings* what we want a computer to do" (Knuth 1984; emphasis in original). Simply put, code should be written in as simple and easily understood a way as possible, and should be very well commented, so that researchers other than the original author can more easily understand the goal of the code.

The knitr package for R, in conjunction with R Studio (www.rstudio .com), makes this relatively easy to implement (Xie 2013, 2014). Authors alternate between chunks of code and bits of the document, as shown in Figure 11.4. The gray lines are code (starting with three backticks ` ` `r{} and ending with three more backticks ` ` `) and the white is the actual document. The document portion is written with Markdown syntax. Markdown is quite simple (think of how you might mark up text in an email or SMS to try and emphasize certain words— asterisks for bold, underscores for italics; see more at http://rmarkdown .rstudio.com/) but powerful enough to handle all the citations, figures, and tables that you might want to include in a final research paper.

The code chunks can be set up to spit out just the code, just the results, neither, or both into the final output (that's what the commands

```
1   ---
2   title: "Simple Example"
3   author: "Garret Christensen"
4   date: "June 30, 2017"
5   output: pdf_document
6   ---
7
8   ```{r setup, include=FALSE}
9   knitr::opts_chunk$set(echo = TRUE)
10  ```
11
12  ## R Markdown
13
14  This is an R Markdown document. Markdown is a simple formatting syntax for
    authoring HTML, PDF, and MS Word documents. For more details on using R
    Markdown see <http://rmarkdown.rstudio.com>.
15
16  When you click the **Knit** button a document will be generated that includes
    both content as well as the output of any embedded R code chunks within the
    document. You can embed an R code chunk like this:
17
18  ```{r cars}
19  summary(cars)
20  ```
21
22  ## Including Plots
23
```

FIGURE 11.4. A simple example of an R Studio R Markdown file.

echo and include are about), and the bits of the document are spit out, so what results from compiling one R Markdown (.Rmd) file is the final paper—PDF, Word .docx, slides, or HTML.[14] Writing code and the paper like this, you'll never need to copy and paste, and you'll also never need to wonder "Where the heck is the code that generated table 7?" after getting back a revise and resubmit after several months, because the code and the output are seamlessly woven together in a single document—a big plus.

Using Jupyter Notebook (http://jupyter.org) also simplifies interactive sharing of computational code with over 40 popular open-source programming languages (Shen 2014). Many programs that accommodate these approaches, including R, Python, and Julia, are open source, making it easier for members of the research community to look under the hood and possibly reduce the risk of the kinds of software computational errors documented in McCullough and Vinod (2003).[15] Computational aspects of reproducibility, which is the notion of getting the same results across different operating systems and processor chips, are discussed at length in Stodden, Leisch, and Peng (2014).

Documents produced with these tools can be posted and shared easily on the Internet: HTML output is native to the web, any Markdown

14. The behind-the-scenes conversion to other formats is done by Pandoc, a useful tool in its own right. See http://pandoc.org/.

15. The recommendations regarding checking the conditions of Hessians for nonlinear solving methods proposed by McCullough and Vinod (2003) are quite detailed and were modified after omissions were brought to light. See Shachar and Nalebuff (2004), McCullough and Vinod (2004a, 2004b), and Drukker and Wiggins (2004).

file hosted on GitHub is automatically rendered, and RPubs is a free hosting service by R Studio. For Stata users, dynamic documents have been less well developed, but user-written packages (e.g., MarkDoc and Weaver)[16] allow users to write their .do files in such a way that the log files output by Stata are formatted and readable in Markdown, HMTL, or LaTeX, and support for dynamic documents is now built into Stata (for more details, see http://www.stata.com/new-in-stata/markdown/).

CONCLUSION

It is a truism that the world is becoming more and more data oriented. Every generation of future quantitative social science researchers will need to learn more programming, and when they do so, it makes sense to adopt the best practices of computer programmers and data scientists.

You have likely gotten pretty far in life already using your current methods, such as the date-and-initial method of saving files and tracking versions that is common among many of our coauthors. But as economists Matthew Gentzkow and Jesse Shapiro point out, "not one piece of commercial software you have on your PC, your phone, your tablet, your car, or any other modern computing device was written with the 'date and initial' method" (Gentzkow and Shapiro 2014, p. 12). We agree with their advice:

> If you are trying to solve a problem, and there are multibillion-dollar firms whose entire business model depends on solving the same problem, and there are whole courses at your university devoted to how to solve that problem, you might want to figure out what the experts do and see if you can't learn something from it. (p. 5)

Experts have already done all the heavy lifting in developing these tools; we just need to use them.

ADDITIONAL RESOURCES

For book-length treatments of this subject, we strongly recommend that Stata users read Long (2008) and that R users refer to Gandrud (2016) for workflow recommendations both in general and specific to their respective programming language. Our suggestions here borrow heavily from their work. *The Practice of Reproducible Research* (Kitzes, Turek,

16. See http://www.haghish.com/statistics/stata-blog/reproducible-research/packages.php.

and Deniz 2017) is a helpful collection of case studies from across disciplines and across software tools.

Another excellent, more concise take on these issues is Matthew Gentzkow and Jesse Shapiro's manual on code and data referred to above (Gentzkow and Shapiro 2014). They come from the same background as the three of us: they aren't professional coders and didn't take many programming classes as undergrads. But once their research datasets became massive, and their programming problems were increasingly challenging (especially given large collaborative work teams), they figured they should listen to the full-time programmers and database managers who had spent years solving these problems. Their manual adapts many of these solutions to data-based social science research. For those wondering where to start, there is also the useful "Good Enough Practices" (Wilson et al. 2017), and for those already doing significant programming and computation, "Best Practices" (Wilson et al. 2014).

We also refer undergraduate instructors and others who may be interested to Richard Ball and Norm Medeiros's Project TIER (Teaching Integrity in Empirical Research), which is a "protocol for comprehensively documenting all the steps of data management and analysis that go into an empirical research paper." They teach a specific standard file organization using the Open Science Framework, which teaches students good habits and allows their instructors to exactly reproduce the work of every student. Of course, these practices should allow students to reliably replicate their own analysis, too.

TWELVE

Conclusion

TAKING STOCK

Congratulations on making it through the book! We hope this tour of major topics in research transparency and reproducibility has been useful to you. You'll recall that we started by painting a picture of the ideal scientific ethos to which we should all aspire. We then discussed some of the root problems and shortcomings plaguing social science research today. The second half of the book introduced a wide range of ideas, tools, and approaches that have the potential to address many of these concerns—some are already doing so. We think of this book as a kind of Swiss Army knife for open science research methods, with different techniques coming in handy depending on the situation.

This book is being written at a particularly exciting time for social science research. When we were starting out as graduate students (between the mid-1990s and mid-2000s), the research being carried out in economics, political science, psychology, sociology, and related fields looked very different than it does today. For one, randomized controlled trials (RCTs) were largely unknown outside of lab experiments in psychology or economics—and they were highly controversial and widely criticized when introduced. (For an intellectual history of the rise of experimental and quasi-experimental methods in economics, and their critics, see Angrist and Pischke [2010]). The types of data used in empirical research were limited and often of dubious quality. Sharing data with the rest of the research community was rare, and the concept of preregistration unknown.

In a mere decade or two, the landscape has been transformed: experimental techniques and other scientific approaches to hypothesis testing are now ubiquitous in many (though not all) social science fields, massive administrative datasets have been digitized, genetic and biological markers are available for entire populations, new forms of "big data" are being scraped from the web every day, and researchers are relying on cutting-edge statistical and data science approaches such as machine learning with greater regularity—aided, of course, by significant advances in computing technology (the Internet!). Some of the methodological and theoretical conservatism that characterized our fields two decades ago has broken down. New subfields—including behavioral economics, which blends insights from sociology and psychology within economic frameworks, and social science genomics, which integrates biological data—are ascendant.

The movement toward more open social science came out of this dynamic milieu. While there was no identifiable "research transparency" or "open science" community in the social sciences even five or six years ago, it is now a flourishing area of both research inquiry and activism within our fields. Researchers' exploding interest in transparency and reproducibility further reflects broader trends, as citizen-advocates push for transparency in government and corporations around the world. Considering this momentum, we believe the movement is on track to outlast earlier bursts of interest in research transparency, such as the (unfortunately) fleeting excitement generated by Rosenthal's (1979) and Leamer's (1983) famous articles on the file drawer problem and specification searching.

ACHIEVING LASTING CHANGE IN SOCIAL SCIENCE RESEARCH

How do we turn the current movement into something durable? This book is intended to be part of the push for lasting change. We believe that teaching open science ideals and practices to the next generation of scholars—as well as to more seasoned researchers interested in these topics, and to policymakers and other consumers of research output—is a promising way to begin to change attitudes in our fields. The ideas speak for themselves: once you've absorbed the importance of Mertonian norms for scientific inquiry, and begun to understand the new methods that have been developed to help us move closer to attaining them, it is difficult to go back to business as usual. Many individuals who have participated in seminars, training institutes, and online courses on these topics have gone on to adopt and teach open science approaches themselves within their own research communities, further propagating the movement.

But changing norms alone may not be enough to achieve rapid change. Greater institutionalization of these ideals, practices, and approaches is also needed. Thankfully, this is another area where there has been dramatic progress over the past few years. A notable example is the American Economic Association RCT Registry, which since 2013 has rapidly attracted over 2,100 studies (at the time of this writing), many employing pre-analysis plans (which, you'll recall, were unheard-of a few years ago). The existence of the registry has facilitated the rise of pre-analysis plans in economics and beyond, and especially in development economics, where large research centers—including the Jameel Poverty Action Lab, Innovations for Poverty Action, and the Center for Effective Global Action—are advocating their adoption by grantees and affiliates. Adoption of pre-analysis plans appears to be particularly high among Ph.D. students and younger faculty (at least anecdotally), suggesting that there may be a generational shift at work. Other registries in political science, through the Evidence in Governance and Politics (EGAP) group, and in psychology (AsPredicted), are playing a similar role and accelerating the change in norms in those fields.

The Berkeley Initiative for Transparency in the Social Sciences (BITSS) is another organization that has emerged in recent years to promote dialogue and build consensus around research transparency practices. Since its inaugural meeting in December 2012, BITSS has provided grants for research in this area, engaged with policy organizations interested in bringing reproducibility practices into their own workflow, and established an active training program for the next generation of social scientists. BITSS has also established an award to recognize emerging leaders, the Leamer-Rosenthal Prize for Open Social Science, named after scholars who were well ahead of their time on these issues, and whose work you are familiar with from this book.[1]

Other specialized organizations have also emerged, most notably the Center for Open Science (COS), which has quickly become a focal point for innovation, coordination, and software development in this area. The Replication Network aims to promote the publication of replication

---

1. See http://www.bitss.org. Miguel is a founder of BITSS and currently its faculty director, and Christensen was a research scientist at BITSS. BITSS is an initiative of the Center for Effective Global Action at the University of California, Berkeley.

8 MODULAR STANDARDS

Citation Standards Describes citation of data	**Data Transparency** Describes availability and sharing of data
Analytical Methods Transparency Describes analytical code accessibility	**Research Materials Transparency** Describes research materials accessibility
Design and Analysis Transparency Sets standards for research design disclosures	**Preregistration of Studies** Specification of study details before data collection
Preregistration of Analysis Plans Specification of analytical details before data collection	**Replication** Encourages publication of replication studies

ACROSS 3 TIERS

1 DISCLOSURE: the final research output must disclose if the work satisfies the standard

2 REQUIREMENT: the final research output must satisfy the standard

3 VERIFICATION: third party must verify that the standard is being met

FIGURE 12.1. Transparency and Openness Promotion (TOP) Guidelines for evaluating journal submissions.

studies; Project TIER has developed a curriculum to teach computational reproducibility to undergraduates; MAER-Net has developed guidelines for economics meta-analysis; and so on.

One still outstanding question is how to most effectively—and rapidly—shift professional norms and practices within our research communities, beyond simply advocating alternative approaches to doing research. Changing journal standards, for example, and making tweaks to funder policies (say, to mandate open data) may be powerful tools for speeding the adoption of new practices. Policymakers could further raise the bar by using only evidence that meets the highest standards of reproducibility and transparency in their own decision making. Yet the relative importance of these approaches has not been tested.

One exciting development in the area of journal standards has been the introduction of the Transparency and Openness Promotion (TOP) Guidelines, a set of modular standards that journals can use to evaluate submissions along eight different dimensions of transparency and reproducibility (Figure 12.1).[2] For each of the eight modular standards, journals can require different tiers of compliance, from tier 0 (no requirement, which is not represented in the figure) to tier 3 (third-party verification of compliance required).

2. For more information on the guidelines, see https://cos.io/our-services/TOP-guidelines/.

For example, in the area of data transparency, a journal could have no data policy at all, which would place it at tier 0. For tier 1 compliance, the journal could require that articles state whether or not data are available, and if so, where. For tier 2, it would designate where the data must be posted. Tier 3 compliance would mean requiring that the posted data and code be "verifiable," meaning it successfully produces the analysis described in the paper prior to publication.

Not all types of research or journals lend themselves to such prepublication verification, and that is fine. At least the TOP Guidelines give reviewers, authors, and readers an idea of what to expect from articles in a particular journal. Since the development of the guidelines in 2015 (Nosek et al. 2015), over 5,000 journals have signed on to the principle of rewarding transparency in research and have pledged to adopt them as appropriate within one year. Under the leadership of its editor-in-chief, Dr. Marcia McNutt, *Science,* one of the world's leading research journals, began implementing the standards in 2017 (McNutt 2016).

We hope that researchers will study the adoption of these and other guidelines. It may seem like navel-gazing for academics to do research on other academics, but the study of how transparency norms evolve in social science research communities is fascinating in its own right. This is a topic we hope will also be the subject of greater scholarly inquiry in the coming years.

LOOKING FORWARD

Our work to achieve more reliable, reproducible, and credible social science research is not yet halfway done. Throughout the book, we have highlighted many open questions, and we are relying on you—the next generation of research transparency scholars and supporters—to solve them.

For one, the role that pre-analysis plans and study registration could or should play in observational empirical research—which comprises the vast majority of empirical social science work, even a couple of decades into the shift toward experimental designs—remains only barely explored. Parallel debates exist regarding the appropriate reach of these methods into other types of research, including qualitative, historical, and theoretical work.

There is also a key unanswered question about the impact that the adoption of these new practices will ultimately have on the reliability of social science research findings. Adopting transparent practices is attractive conceptually, if you accept Merton's norms—but will the use of study registries, pre-analysis plans, disclosure statements, and open data and materials really lead to measurably improved bodies of evidence? To this point, the presumption among advocates (including ourselves, admittedly) is that while these changes will eventually lead to improved research, measuring these effects in a rigorous way will be critical to determining which practices are most effective, which are (or are not) worth their adoption costs, and ultimately how best to build support for their uptake in our fields. In doing so, we hope that our fellow social scientists will continue to seek inspiration and insights from other research domains.

We'll close with the reflections of Nobel Prize–winning physicist Richard Feynman, who laid out his thoughts on the importance of research transparency when he delivered the 1974 Commencement Address at Cal Tech, where he taught. It's an amusing read, and it touches on many of this book's central themes: the problems of publication bias and selective reporting, the need for replication, and how scholars too often fall short of the scientific ideal—mainly in Feynman's world of physics. But here we'll quote from his discussion of first principles:

> [There is an] idea that we all hope you have learned in studying science in school—we never explicitly say what this is, but just hope that you catch on by all the examples of scientific investigation. It is interesting, therefore, to bring it out now and speak of it explicitly. It's a kind of scientific integrity, a principle of scientific thought that corresponds to a kind of utter honesty—a kind of leaning over backwards. For example, if you're doing an experiment, you should report everything that you think might make it invalid—not only what you think is right about it. . . . Details that could throw doubt on your interpretation must be given, if you know them. . . .
>
> But this long history of learning how to not fool ourselves—of having utter scientific integrity—is, I'm sorry to say, something that we haven't specifically included in any particular course that I know of. We just hope you've caught on by osmosis. The first principle is that you must not fool yourself—and you are the easiest person to fool. So you have to be very careful about that. After you've not fooled yourself, it's easy not to fool other scientists. (Feynman 1974)

We hope that the material in this book will provide the basis for courses like the one Feynman spoke of decades ago, and for lectures in other research methods courses. For it doesn't matter how sophisticated the statistics, the model, the design, or the data are if our research practices allow us to continue fooling other social scientists—or ourselves. And that's no joking matter.

Appendix

Power Calculation

An important part of the design of any study, and particularly any experiment, is its statistical power. We will provide a brief overview here; most intro statistics textbooks will have a section on statistical power, and short primers such as Cohen (1992) are available, but for more in-depth book-length treatments, see Cohen (1988) or Murphy, Myors, and Wolach (2014). The power of a statistical hypothesis test is the probability that the test correctly rejects the null hypothesis when it is false. In layman's terms, if there's a real effect, what's the likelihood you'll detect it? In type I and type II error terms (type I is a false positive, type II is a false negative), power is usually referred to as $1-\beta$, where β is the false negative rate.

In practice, this concept can be used to determine the sample size required to detect an effect of a certain size. Before a study is conducted, a researcher can state how large they believe an effect will be and, based on that, calculate the sample size necessary to confidently detect that effect most of the time (usually 80 percent or 90 percent of the time). By "detect that effect," we mean finding an effect statistically different from zero at a certain significance level denoted α.

Let's assume we have a randomized trial studying a real treatment effect: Does the drug in question increase life span? (Here we present results with a one-sided test, but all these formulas can be relatively easily adjusted for two-sided tests.) That means the treated population mean μ (sample mean $\bar{Y}$, standard deviation σ) is greater than some comparison value μ_o. The effect is real, so how often will a statistical test reject the null hypothesis? That depends on the sample size, n, our desired significance level, α, and a host of other things. With a sample mean of $\bar{Y}$ (and remembering that for large samples the Z and Student's t distributions are nearly identical), the probability is Power $= 1 - \beta = \Pr(\bar{Y} \geq \mu_o + z_{1-\alpha} \sigma/\sqrt{n}|H_1 : \mu > \mu_o)$, which can be rearranged using a little algebra:

$$= 1 - \Pr(\bar{Y} < \mu_0 + z_{1-\alpha}\frac{\sigma}{\sqrt{n}} | H_1)$$

$$= 1 - \Pr\left(\frac{\bar{Y} - \mu}{\frac{\sigma}{\sqrt{n}}} < \frac{\mu_0 + \frac{z_{1-\alpha}\sigma}{\sqrt{n}} - \mu}{\frac{\sigma}{\sqrt{n}}} | H_1\right)$$

$$= 1 - \Pr\left(\frac{\bar{Y} - \mu}{\frac{\sigma}{\sqrt{n}}} < \frac{\mu_0 - \mu}{\frac{\sigma}{\sqrt{n}}} + z_{1-\alpha} | H_1\right)$$

$$= 1 - \Phi\left(\frac{\mu_0 - \mu}{\frac{\sigma}{\sqrt{n}}} + z_{1-\alpha} | H_1\right)$$

$$= \Phi\left(\frac{\mu_0 - \mu}{\frac{\sigma}{\sqrt{n}}} - z_{1-\alpha} | H_1\right)$$

Hopefully one can tell immediately that statistical power increases with a larger true effect and with a larger sample size. Similarly, power decreases with noisier data.

Figure A.1 illustrates the concept: the control group density is on the left, with a rejection region in the upper tail to the right of the vertical line. The experimental density is on the right, but there is some overlap. The region of the curve on the right that is beyond the critical value of the left curve is the statistical power $(1-\beta)$. Panels B and C are set up the same, but in panel B the standard errors are smaller (the distributions are less noisy) and power is greater. In panel C the treatment effect $(\mu-\mu_o)$ is larger (the control and experimental distributions are farther apart), which again means more power.

The formula can also be rearranged to solve for either the desired sample size or the effect size, the latter of which is sometimes referred to as the minimum detectable effect (MDE), in that this is the smallest effect one can expect to detect with a given level of statistical power. In a one-sided test of proportions (where P is the proportion that the event occurs, as opposed to a continuous variable as above), that works out to

$$\text{MDE} = (t_\beta + t_\alpha) \cdot \sqrt{\frac{1}{P(1 - P)}} \sqrt{\frac{\sigma^2}{n}}.$$

Another important aspect is referred to as the "design effect" of a study. When a study is anything other than the simplest individual-level randomized trial (such as a study with repeated observations or when the treatment is clustered at a group level) the standard error of the estimate changes, so researchers must take this into account. Stratified random sampling (e.g., to ensure that equal proportions of men and women fall into the treatment group) can improve precision, but clustering usually increases standard errors.

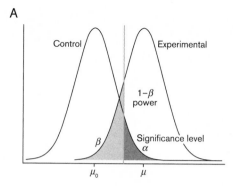

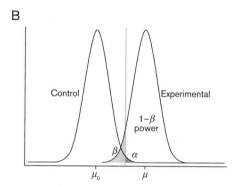

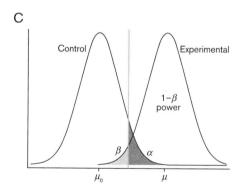

FIGURE A.1. Power $(1 - \beta)$ in three situations. Compared to panel **A**, panel **B** has less variation, and thus more power. Panel **C** has a large effect size, and thus more power.

An example of clustering in an experiment would be a study in which randomization was done at the classroom level, such that all students in a given classroom either received the treatment or did not. With clustering, for example, the larger the groups (holding the total sample size constant) and the larger the intracluster correlation (the proportion of the overall variance from within groups), the larger the design effect (Duflo, Glennerster, and Kremer 2007). Often with clustering, researchers assume that clusters are of equal size, but this need not be the case; incorporating the coefficient of variation of cluster size yields a tractable analytical solution (but in our experience, this has not made a huge difference in practice in our experiments; Hayes and Bennett 1999; Eldridge, Ashby, and Kerry 2006).

Another interesting consideration is maximizing power subject to a budget constraint. All else equal, power in an experiment is maximized when a study sample is equally split between treatment and control groups. But often all is not equal; sometimes studying the treatment group is significantly more expensive than the control (e.g., in cases where the treatment group receives a costly intervention). In this case, a researcher might want to consider maximizing power subject to a budget constraint. In a simple case of a test of proportions, the ratio of subjects in treatment and comparison groups should be proportional to the inverse of the square root of their respective costs. So, if allocating cases to the treatment group was four times as expensive as allocating them to the control group (due to intervention costs), maximum power for a fixed budget would involve assigning twice as many cases to the control group than the treatment group (see Duflo, Glennerster, and Kremer 2007: section 4.1).

In practice, power calculations require a significant amount of guesswork. Beyond clustering, there may be complicated ways that observations are related to one another, and no clear analytical solution for power or sample size. In this case, simulations are a reasonable method to consider. For example, see Arnold et al. (2011), which includes both Stata and R examples and discusses a factorial treatment intervention with treatments randomized at different levels. This type of treatment is difficult or impossible to solve analytically, but any such structure can be simulated as long as you have a way to estimate the various correlation parameters. More generally, there are numerous web applications designed to help researchers with these calculations. In R, researchers may use the `pwr` package, while in Stata, the command is `sampsi`.

Bibliography

AAPOR (American Association for Public Opinion Research) (2016). Standard Definitions: Final Dispositions of Case Codes and Outcome Rates for Surveys, 9th ed. http://www.aapor.org/Standards-Ethics/Standard-Definitions-(1).aspx

Abreu, M., De Groot, H. L. F., and Florax, R. J. G. M. (2005). "A meta-analysis of β-convergence: the legendary 2%." Journal of Economic Surveys, 19(3), 389–420.

Alatas, V., Banerjee, A., Hanna, R., Olken, B. A., and Tobias, J. (2012). "Targeting the poor: evidence from a field experiment in Indonesia." American Economic Review, 102(4), 1206–1240. https://doi.org/10.1257/aer.102.4.1206

Allcott, H. (2015). "Site selection bias in program evaluation." The Quarterly Journal of Economics, 130(3), 1117–1165. https://doi.org/10.1093/qje/qjv015

Allcott, H., and Taubinsky, D. (2015). "Evaluating behaviorally motivated policy: experimental evidence from the lightbulb market." American Economic Review, 105(8), 2501–2538. https://doi.org/10.1257/aer.20131564

Altman, D. G., Schulz, K. F., Moher, D., Egger, M., et al. (2001). "The revised CONSORT statement for reporting randomized trials: explanation and elaboration." Annals of Internal Medicine, 134(8), 663–694.

Anderson, M. L. (2008). "Multiple inference and gender differences in the effects of early intervention: a reevaluation of the Abecedarian, Perry Preschool, and Early Training projects." Journal of the American Statistical Association, 103, 1481–1495. https://doi.org/10.1198/016214508000000841

Anderson, M. S., Martinson, B. C., and De Vries, R. (2007). "Normative dissonance in science: results from a national survey of U.S. scientists." Journal of Empirical Research on Human Research Ethics, 2(4), 3–14. https://doi.org/10.1525/jer.2007.2.4.3

Angrist, J. D., and Pischke, J.-S. (2010). "The credibility revolution in empirical economics: how better research design is taking the con out of econometrics." Journal of Economic Perspectives, 24(2), 3–30. https://doi.org/10.1257/jep.24.2.3

Ansell, B., and Samuels, D. (2016). "Journal editors and 'results-free' research: a cautionary note." Comparative Political Studies, 49(13), 1809–1815. https://doi.org/10.1177/0010414016669369

Arnold, B. F., Hogan, D. R., Colford, J. M., and Hubbard, A. E. (2011). "Simulation methods to estimate design power: an overview for applied research." BMC Medical Research Methodology, 11, 94. https://doi.org/10.1186/1471-2288-11-94

Arnold, B. F., Null, C., Luby, S. P., Unicomb, L., et al. (2013). "Cluster-randomized controlled trials of individual and combined water, sanitation, hygiene, and nutritional interventions in rural Bangladesh and Kenya: the WASH Benefits Study design and rationale." BMJ Open, 3(8), e003476.

Ashenfelter, O., and Greenstone, M. (2004). "Estimating the value of a statistical life: the importance of omitted variables and publication bias" (Working Paper No. 105). Princeton University, Department of Economics, Center for Economic Policy Studies. http://search.proquest.com/econlit/docview/56626726/1A493319C9B3407FPQ/4?accountid = 14496

Ashenfelter, O., Harmon, C., and Oosterbeek, H. (1999). "A review of estimates of the schooling/earnings relationship, with tests for publication bias." Labour Economics, 6(4), 453–470.

Bai, L., Handel, B., Miguel, E., and Rao, G. (2017). "Self-control and demand for preventive health: evidence from hypertension in India" (Working Paper No. 23727). National Bureau of Economic Research. http://www.nber.org/papers/w23727

Baicker, K., Finkelstein, A., Song, J., and Taubman, S. (2014). "The impact of Medicaid on labor market activity and program participation: evidence from the Oregon health insurance experiment." American Economic Review, 104(5), 322–328. https://doi.org/10.1257/aer.104.5.322

Baicker, K., Taubman, S. L., Allen, H. L., Bernstein, M., et al. (2013). "The Oregon experiment—effects of Medicaid on clinical outcomes." New England Journal of Medicine, 368(18), 1713–1722. https://doi.org/10.1056/NEJMsa1212321

Bakkensen, L. A., and Larson, W. (2014). "Population matters when modeling hurricane fatalities." Proceedings of the National Academy of Sciences, 111(50), E5331–E5332. https://doi.org/10.1073/pnas.1417030111

Bateman, I., Kahneman, D., Munro, A., Starmer, C., and Sugden, R. (2005). "Testing competing models of loss aversion: an adversarial collaboration." Journal of Public Economics, 89(8), 1561–1580. https://doi.org/10.1016/j.jpubeco.2004.06.013

Baumeister, R. F., Bratslavsky, E., Muraven, M., and Tice, D. M. (1998). "Ego depletion: is the active self a limited resource?" Journal of Personality and Social Psychology, 74(5), 1252–1265. https://doi.org/10.1037/0022-3514.74.5.1252

Baumeister, R. F., and Vohs, K. D. (2016). "Misguided effort with elusive implications." Perspectives on Psychological Science, 11(4), 574–575. https://doi.org/10.1177/1745691616652878

Beaulieu, E. (2016). "Electronic voting and perceptions of election fraud and fairness." Journal of Experimental Political Science, 3(1), 18–31. https://doi.org/10.1017/XPS.2015.9

Becker, B. J. (2005). "Failsafe N or file-drawer number." In Rothstein, H. R., Sutton, A. J., and Borenstein, M. (Eds.), Publication Bias in Meta-analysis: Prevention, Assessment and Adjustments (pp. 111–125). New York: Wiley.

Begg, C., Cho, M., Eastwood, S., Horton, R., et al. (1996). "Improving the quality of reporting of randomized controlled trials: the CONSORT statement." JAMA, 276(8), 637–639. https://doi.org/10.1001/jama.1996.03540080059030

Bellavance, F., Dionne, G., and Lebeau, M. (2009). "The value of a statistical life: a meta-analysis with a mixed effects regression model." Journal of Health Economics, 28(2), 444–464. https://doi.org/10.1016/j.jhealeco.2008.10.013

Bellg, A. J., Borrelli, B., Resnick, B., Hecht, J., et al. (2004). "Enhancing treatment fidelity in health behavior change studies: best practices and recommendations from the NIH Behavior Change Consortium." Health Psychology, 23(5), 443–451.

Bem, D. J. (2011). "Feeling the future: experimental evidence for anomalous retroactive influences on cognition and affect." Journal of Personality and Social Psychology, 100(3), 407–425. https://doi.org/10.1037/a0021524

Benjamin, D. J., Berger, J., Johannesson, M., Nosek, B., et al. (2017). "Redefine statistical significance." PsyArXiv. https://doi.org/10.17605/OSF.IO/MKY9J

Benjamin, D. J., Cesarini, D., Chabris, C. F., Glaeser, E. L., et al. (2012). "The promises and pitfalls of genoeconomics." Annual Review of Economics, 4(1), 627–662. https://doi.org/10.1146/annurev-economics-080511–110939

Benjamini, Y., Krieger, A. M., and Yekutieli, D. (2006). "Adaptive linear step-up procedures that control the false discovery rate." Biometrika, 93(3), 491–507. https://doi.org/10.1093/biomet/93.3.491

Benjamini, Y., and Yekutieli, D. (2001). "The control of the false discovery rate in multiple testing under dependency." The Annals of Statistics, 29(4), 1165–1188.

Berge, L. I. O., Bjorvatn, K., Galle, S., Miguel, E., et al. (2015). "How strong are ethnic preferences?" (Working Paper No. 21715). National Bureau of Economic Research. http://www.nber.org/papers/w21715

Bernanke, B. S. (2004). "Editorial statement." American Economic Review, 94(1), 404.

Bertrand, M., and Mullainathan, S. (2004). "Are Emily and Greg more employable than Lakisha and Jamal? A field experiment on labor market discrimination." American Economic Review, 94(4), 991–1013. https://doi.org/10.1257/0002828042002561

Bhattacharjee, Y. (2013). "Diederik Stapel's audacious academic fraud." The New York Times, April 26. http://www.nytimes.com/2013/04/28/magazine/diederik-stapels-audacious-academic-fraud.html

Bland, J. M., and Altman, D. G. (1995). "Multiple significance tests: the Bonferroni method." BMJ, 310, 170.

Borenstein, M., Hedges, L. V., Higgins, J. P. T., and Rothstein, H. R. (2009). Introduction to Meta-analysis. New York: Wiley.

Borsboom, D., and Wagenmakers, E. J. (2013). "Derailed: the rise and fall of Diederik Stapel" [Review of: D. Stapel (2012), Ontsporing]. APS Observer, 26(1). http://www.psychologicalscience.org/observer/derailed-the-rise-and-fall-of-diederik-stapel

Bowers, J. (2011). "Six steps to a better relationship with your future self." The Political Methodologist, 18(2), 2–8.

Bowers, J., and Voors, M. (2016). "How to improve your relationship with your future self." Revista de Ciencia Política, 36(3). http://www.redalyc.org/resumen.oa?id = 32449207011

Breznau, N. (2015). "The missing main effect of welfare state regimes: a replication of 'Social policy responsiveness in developed democracies' by Brooks and Manza." Sociological Science, 2, 420–441. https://doi.org/10.15195/v2.a20

Brock, W. A., Durlauf, S. N., and West, K. D. (2003). "Policy evaluation in uncertain economic environments." Brookings Papers on Economic Activity, 2003(1), 235–322. https://doi.org/10.1353/eca.2003.0013

Brodeur, A., Le, M., Sangnier, M., and Zylberberg, Y. (2016). "Star wars: the empirics strike back." American Economic Journal: Applied Economics, 8(1), 1–32.

Broman, K. W., and Woo, K. H. (2018). "Data organization in spreadsheets." The American Statistician, 72(1), 2–10. https://doi.org/10.1080/00031305.2017.1375989

Broockman, D., Kalla, J., and Aranow, P. (2015). "Irregularities in LaCour (2014)." Unpublished manuscript, Stanford University. http://stanford.edu/~dbroock/broockman_kalla_aronow_lg_irregularities.pdf

Brooks, C., and Manza, J. (2006). "Social policy responsiveness in developed democracies." American Sociological Review, 71(3), 474–494. https://doi.org/10.1177/000312240607100306

Bruhn, M., and McKenzie, D. (2009). "In pursuit of balance: randomization in practice in development field experiments." American Economic Journal: Applied Economics, 1(4), 200–232.

Buckheit, J. B., and Donoho, D. L. (1995). "WaveLab and reproducible research." In Antoniadis, A., and Oppenheim, G. (Eds.), Wavelets and Statistics (pp. 55–81). New York: Springer. https://doi.org/10.1007/978-1-4612-2544-7_5

Buhaug, H., Nordkvelle, J., Bernauer, T., Böhmelt, T., et al. (2014). "One effect to rule them all? A comment on climate and conflict." Climatic Change, 127, 391. https://doi.org/10.1007/s10584-014-1266-1

Burke, M., Hsiang, S. M., and Miguel, E. (2015). "Climate and conflict." Annual Review of Economics, 7(1), 577–617. https://doi.org/10.1146/annurev-economics-080614-115430

Burnside, C., and Dollar, D. (2000). "Aid, policies, and growth." American Economic Review, 90(4), 847–868.

Bush, S. S., Erlich, A., Prather, L., and Zeira, Y. (2016). "The effects of authoritarian iconography: an experimental test." Comparative Political Studies, 49(13), 1704–1738. https://doi.org/10.1177/0010414016633228

Camerer, C. F., Dreber, A., Forsell, E., Ho, T.-H., et al. (2016). "Evaluating replicability of laboratory experiments in economics." Science, 351, 1433–1436. https://doi.org/10.1126/science.aaf0918

Card, D. (1992a). "Do minimum wages reduce employment? A case study of California, 1987–89." Industrial & Labor Relations Review, 46(1), 38–54. https://doi.org/10.1177/001979399204600104

———. (1992b). "Using regional variation in wages to measure the effects of the federal minimum wage." Industrial & Labor Relations Review, 46(1), 22–37. https://doi.org/10.1177/001979399204600103

Card, D., and Krueger, A. B. (1995). "Time-series minimum-wage studies: a meta-analysis." American Economic Review, 85(2), 238–243.

Carey, B. (2011). "Noted Dutch psychologist, Stapel, accused of research fraud." The New York Times, November 2. http://www.nytimes.com/2011/11/03/health/research/noted-dutch-psychologist-stapel-accused-of-research-fraud.html

Carney, D. R., Cuddy, A. J. C., and Yap, A. J. (2010). "Power posing: brief nonverbal displays affect neuroendocrine levels and risk tolerance." Psychological Science, 21(10), 1363–1368. https://doi.org/10.1177/0956797610383437

———. (2015). "Review and summary of research on the embodied effects of expansive (vs. contractive) nonverbal displays." Psychological Science, 26(5), 657–663. https://doi.org/10.1177/0956797614566855

Carroll, C., Patterson, M., Wood, S., Booth, A., et al. (2007). "A conceptual framework for implementation fidelity." Implementation Science, 2(1), 40.

Carsey, T. M. (2014). "Making DA-RT a reality." PS: Political Science & Politics, 47(1), 72–77.

Casey, K., Glennerster, R., and Miguel, E. (2012). "Reshaping Institutions: evidence on aid impacts using a preanalysis plan." The Quarterly Journal of Economics, 127(4), 1755–1812. https://doi.org/10.1093/qje/qje027

Casselman, B. (2012). "Economists set rules on ethics." The Wall Street Journal, January 9. http://www.wsj.com/articles/SB10001424052970203436904577148940410667970

Chacon, S., and Straub, B. (2014). Pro Git. New York: Apress. https://git-scm.com/book/en/v2

Chambers, C. D. (2013). "Registered reports: a new publishing initative at Cortex." Cortex, 49, 609–610. http://dx.doi.org/10.1016/j.cortex.2012.12.016

———. (2017). The Seven Deadly Sins of Psychology: A Manifesto for Reforming the Culture of Scientific Practice. Princeton, NJ: Princeton University Press.

Chambers, C. D., Feredoes, E., Muthukumaraswamy, S. D., and Etchells, P. J. (2014). "Instead of 'playing the game' it is time to change the rules: registered reports at AIMS Neuroscience and beyond." AIMS Environmental Science, 1(1), 4–17. https://doi.org/10.3934/Neuroscience.2014.1.4

Chan, A.-W., Hróbjartsson, A., Haahr, M. T., Gøtzsche, P. C., and Altman, D. G. (2004). "Empirical evidence for selective reporting of outcomes in randomized trials: comparison of protocols to published articles." JAMA, 291(20), 2457–2465. https://doi.org/10.1001/jama.291.20.2457

Chan, A.-W., Tetzlaff, J.M., Gotzsche, P.C., Altman, D.G., et al. (2013). "SPIRIT 2013 explanation and elaboration: guidance for protocols of clinical trials." BMJ, 346, e7586–e7586. https://doi.org/10.1136/bmj.e7586

Christensen, B., and Christensen, S. (2014). "Are female hurricanes really deadlier than male hurricanes?" Proceedings of the National Academy of Sciences, 111(34), E3497–E3498. https://doi.org/10.1073/pnas.1410910111

Claerbout, J., and Karrenbach, M. (1992, October). "Electronic documents give reproducible research a new meaning." http://sepwww.stanford.edu/doku.php?id = sep:research:reproducible:seg92

Clark, W. (2006). Academic Charisma and the Origins of the Research University. Chicago, IL: University of Chicago Press.

Clemens, M.A. (2017). "The meaning of failed replications: a review and proposal." Journal of Economic Surveys, 31(1), 326–342. https://doi.org/10.1111/joes.12139

Coffman, L.C., and Niederle, M. (2015). "Pre-analysis plans have limited upside, especially where replications are feasible." Journal of Economic Perspectives, 29(3), 81–98.

Cohen, J. (1988). Statistical Power Analysis for the Behavioral Sciences, 2nd ed. Hillsdale, NJ: Routledge.

———. (1992). "Statistical power analysis." Current Directions in Psychological Science, 1(3), 98–101. https://doi.org/10.1111/1467-8721.ep10768783

Cohen-Cole, E., Durlauf, S., Fagan, J., and Nagin, D. (2009). "Model uncertainty and the deterrent effect of capital punishment." American Law and Economics Review, 11(2), 335–369. https://doi.org/10.1093/aler/ahn001

Collins, H.M. (1992). Changing Order: Replication and Induction in Scientific Practice. Chicago, IL: University of Chicago Press.

Cooper, H.M., Hedges, L.V., and Valentine, J.C. (Eds.) (2009). The Handbook of Research Synthesis and Meta-analysis, 2nd ed. New York: Russell Sage Foundation.

Cuddy, A. (2012). "Your body language shapes who you are." https://www.ted.com/talks/amy_cuddy_your_body_language_shapes_who_you_are

———. (2015). Presence: Bringing Your Boldest Self to Your Biggest Challenges. New York: Little, Brown.

Cuddy, A., Schultz, S., and Fosse, N. (2018). "P-curving a more comprehensive body of research on postural feedback reveals clear evidential value for power-posing effects: reply to Simmons and Simonsohn (2017)." Psychological Science, 29(4), 656–666. https://doi.org/10.1177/0956797617746749

Cumming, G. (2014). "The new statistics: why and how." Psychological Science, 25(1), 7–29. https://doi.org/10.1177/0956797613504966

———. (2017). Understanding the New Statistics: Effect Sizes, Confidence Intervals, and Meta-analysis. New York: Routledge.

Dahl Rasmussen, O., Malchow-Møller, N., and Barnebeck Andersen, T. (2011). "Walking the talk: the need for a trial registry for development interventions." Journal of Development Effectiveness, 3(4), 502–519. https://doi.org/10.1080/19439342.2011.605160

Dal-Ré, R., Ioannidis, J.P., Bracken, M.B., Buffler, P.A., et al. (2014). "Making prospective registration of observational research a reality." Science Translational Medicine, 6, 224cm1. https://doi.org/10.1126/scitranslmed.3007513

De Angelis, C., Drazen, J.M., Frizelle, F.A., Haug, C., et al. (2004). "Clinical trial registration: a statement from the International Committee of Medical Journal Editors." New England Journal of Medicine, 351(12), 1250–1251. https://doi.org/10.1056/NEJMe048225

Deer, B. (2011). "How the case against the MMR vaccine was fixed." BMJ, 342, c5347. https://doi.org/10.1136/bmj.c5347

Deere, D., Murphy, K.M., and Welch, F. (1995). "Employment and the 1990–1991 minimum-wage hike." American Economic Review, 85(2), 232–237.

DeLong, J.B., and Lang, K. (1992). "Are all economic hypotheses false?" Journal of Political Economy, 100(6), 1257–1272.

Denton, F.T. (1985). "Data mining as an industry." The Review of Economics and Statistics, 67(1), 124–127. https://doi.org/10.2307/1928442

DerSimonian, R., and Laird, N. (1986). "Meta-analysis in clinical trials." Controlled Clinical Trials, 7(3), 177–188. https://doi.org/10.1016/0197-2456(86)90046-2

Desposato, S. (Ed.) (2015). Ethics and Experiments: Problems and Solutions for Social Scientists and Policy Professionals. New York: Routledge.

Dewald, W.G., Thursby, J.G., and Anderson, R.G. (1986). "Replication in empirical economics: the Journal of Money, Credit and Banking project." American Economic Review, 76(4), 587–603.

Dezhbakhsh, H., Rubin, P.H., and Shepherd, J.M. (2003). "Does capital punishment have a deterrent effect? New evidence from postmoratorium panel data." American Law and Economics Review, 5(2), 344–376. https://doi.org/10.1093/aler/ahg021

Dominus, S. (2017). "When the revolution came for Amy Cuddy." The New York Times, October 18. https://www.nytimes.com/2017/10/18/magazine/when-the-revolution-came-for-amy-cuddy.html

Donohue, J.J., and Wolfers, J. (2005). "Uses and abuses of empirical evidence in the death penalty debate." Stanford Law Review, 58(3), 791–845.

Doucouliagos, C. (2005). "Publication bias in the economic freedom and economic growth literature." Journal of Economic Surveys, 19(3), 367–387.

Doucouliagos, C., and Laroche, P. (2003). "What do unions do to productivity? A meta-analysis." Industrial Relations: A Journal of Economy and Society, 42(4), 650–691. https://doi.org/10.1111/1468-232X.00310

Doucouliagos, C., Stanley, T.D., and Giles, M. (2012). "Are estimates of the value of a statistical life exaggerated?" Journal of Health Economics, 31(1), 197–206. https://doi.org/10.1016/j.jhealeco.2011.10.001

Doucouliagos, H., Ioannidis, J.P., and Stanley, T. (2017). "The power of bias in economics." The Economic Journal, 127, F236–F265.

Doucouliagos, H., and Stanley, T.D. (2009). "Publication selection bias in minimum-wage research? A meta-regression analysis." British Journal of Industrial Relations, 47(2), 406–428. https://doi.org/10.1111/j.1467-8543.2009.00723.x

———. (2013). "Are all economic facts greatly exaggerated? Theory competition and selectivity." Journal of Economic Surveys, 27(2), 316–339. https://doi.org/10.1111/j.1467-6419.2011.00706.x

Doucouliagos, H., Stanley, T.D., and Viscusi, W.K. (2014). "Publication selection and the income elasticity of the value of a statistical life." Journal of Health Economics, 33, 67–75. https://doi.org/10.1016/j.jhealeco.2013.10.010

Drukker, D.M., and Wiggins, V. (2004). "Verifying the solution from a nonlinear solver: a case study: comment." American Economic Review, 94(1), 397–399. https://doi.org/10.1257/000282804322970896

Duflo, E., Glennerster, R., and Kremer, M. (2007). "Using randomization in development economics research: a toolkit." In Schultz, T.P., and Strauss, J. A. (Eds.), Handbook of Development Economics 4 (pp. 3895–3962). London: Elsevier. http://www.sciencedirect.com/science/article/pii/S1573447107040612

Durante, K.M., Rae, A., and Griskevicius, V. (2013). "The fluctuating female vote: politics, religion, and the ovulatory cycle." Psychological Science, 24(6), 1007–1016. https://doi.org/10.1177/0956797612466416

Duvendack, M., Palmer-Jones, R., and Reed, R.W. (2015). "Replications in economics: a progress report." Econ Journal Watch, 12(2), 164–191.

Dwork, C., and Smith, A. (2009). "Differential privacy for statistics: what we know and what we want to learn." Journal of Privacy and Confidentiality, 1(2), 135–154.

Easterbrook, P.J., Gopalan, R., Berlin, J.A., and Matthews, D.R. (1991). "Publication bias in clinical research." The Lancet, 337, 867–872. https://doi.org/10.1016/0140-6736(91)90201-Y

Easterly, W., Levine, R., and Roodman, D. (2004). "Aid, policies, and growth: comment." American Economic Review, 94(3), 774–780.

Eble, A., Boone, P., and Elbourne, D. (2014). "On minimizing the risk of bias in randomized controlled trials in economics" (SSRN Scholarly Paper No. ID 2272141). Rochester, NY: Social Science Research Network. http://papers.ssrn.com/abstract = 2272141

Efron, B. (1992). "Bootstrap methods: another look at the jackknife." In Kotz, S., and Johnson, N.L. (Eds.), Breakthroughs in Statistics (pp. 569–593). New York: Springer. https://doi.org/10.1007/978-1-4612-4380-9_41

Efron, B., and Gong, G. (1983). "A leisurely look at the bootstrap, the jackknife, and cross-validation." The American Statistician, 37(1), 36–48. https://doi.org/10.1080/00031305.1983.10483087

Eldridge, S.M., Ashby, D., and Kerry, S. (2006). "Sample size for cluster randomized trials: effect of coefficient of variation of cluster size and analysis method." International Journal of Epidemiology, 35(5), 1292–1300. https://doi.org/10.1093/ije/dyl129

Enders, W., and Hoover, G.A. (2004). "Whose line is it? Plagiarism in economics." Journal of Economic Literature, 42(2), 487–493. https://doi.org/10.1257/0022205041409066

Epidemiology (2010). "The registration of observational studies—when metaphors go bad." Epidemiology, 21(5), 607–609. https://doi.org/10.1097/EDE.0b013e3181eafbcf

Erlingsson, Ú. (2014, October 30). "Learning statistics with privacy, aided by the flip of a coin." https://security.googleblog.com/2014/10/learning-statistics-with-privacy-aided.html

Fanelli, D. (2012). "Negative results are disappearing from most disciplines and countries." Scientometrics, 90(3), 891–904. https://doi.org/10.1007/s11192–011–0494–7

Feilden, T. (2017). "Most scientists 'can't replicate studies.'" BBC News, February 22. http://www.bbc.com/news/science-environment-39054778

Ferguson, C., Marcus, A., and Oransky, I. (2014). "Publishing: the peer-review scam." Nature, 515, 480–482. https://doi.org/10.1038/515480a

Fernández, C., Ley, E., and Steel, M.F.J. (2001). "Model uncertainty in cross-country growth regressions." Journal of Applied Econometrics, 16(5), 563–576. https://doi.org/10.1002/jae.623

Feynman, R.P. (1974). "Cargo cult science." Presented at the Caltech Commencement Address, Pasadena, CA. http://calteches.library.caltech.edu/51/2/CargoCult.htm

Findley, M., Jensen, N.M., Malesky, E.J., and Pepinsky, T.B. (2016). "Introduction: Special Issue on Research Transparency in the Social Science." Comparative Political Studies.

Fink, G., McConnell, M., and Vollmer, S. (2014). "Testing for heterogeneous treatment effects in experimental data: false discovery risks and correction procedures." Journal of Development Effectiveness, 6(1), 44–57. https://doi.org/10.1080/19439342.2013.875054

Finkelstein, A., Taubman, S., Wright, B., Bernstein, M., et al. (2012). "The Oregon health insurance experiment: evidence from the first year." The Quarterly Journal of Economics, 127(3), 1057–1106. https://doi.org/10.1093/qje/qjs020

Fisher, R.A. (1956a). "Mathematics of a lady tasting tea." In The World of Mathematics, vol. 3, part 8 (pp. 1514–1521). New York: Simon and Schuster.

———. (1956b). Statistical Methods and Scientific Inferences. Oxford, UK: Hafner.

———. (1992). "The arrangement of field experiments." In Kotz, S., and Johnson, N.L. (Eds.), Breakthroughs in Statistics (pp. 82–91). New York: Springer.

Food and Drug Administration (1998). E9 Statistical Principles for Clinical Trials (Guidance for Industry). http://www.fda.gov/downloads/drugs/guidancecomplianceregulatoryinformation/guidances/ucm073137.pdf

Foster, A., Karlan, D., and Miguel, E. (2018). "Registered reports: piloting a pre-results review process at the Journal of Development Economics." World Bank Development Impact Blog, March 9. https://blogs.worldbank.org/impactevaluations/registered-reports-piloting-pre-results-review-process-journal-development-economics

Franco, A., Malhotra, N., and Simonovits, G. (2014). "Publication bias in the social sciences: unlocking the file drawer." Science, 345, 1502–1505. https://doi.org/10.1126/science.1255484

Freese, J. (2007). "Replication standards for quantitative social science: why not sociology?" Sociological Methods & Research, 36(2), 153–172. https://doi.org/10.1177/0049124107306659

Freese, J., and Peterson, D. (2017). "Replication in social science." Annual Review of Sociology, 43(1), 147–165. https://doi.org/10.1146/annurev-soc-060116-053450

Freese, J., and Powell, B. (2001). "Commentary and debate: making love out of nothing at all? Null findings and the Trivers-Willard hypothesis." American Journal of Sociology, 106(6), 1776–1788. https://doi.org/10.1086/321304

Friedman, T. L. (2003). "Present at . . . what?" The New York Times, February 12. http://www.nytimes.com/2003/02/12/opinion/present-at-what.html

Galak, J., Leboeuf, R. A., Nelson, L. D., and Simmons, J. P. (2012). "Correcting the past: failures to replicate ψ." Journal of Personality and Social Psychology, 103(6), 933–948. https://doi.org/10.1037/a0029709

Gandrud, C. (2016). Reproducible Research with R and R Studio, 2nd ed. New York: CRC Press.

Gelman, A., and Carlin, J. (2014). "Beyond power calculations: assessing type S (sign) and type M (magnitude) errors." Perspectives on Psychological Science, 9(6), 641–651. https://doi.org/10.1177/1745691614551642

Gelman, A., Carlin, J., Stern, H., Dunson, D., Vehtari, A., and Rubin, D. (2013). Bayesian Data Analysis, 3rd ed. New York: CRC Press.

Gelman, A., and Fung, K. (2016). "The power of the 'power pose.'" Slate, January 19. http://www.slate.com/articles/health_and_science/science/2016/01/amy_cuddy_s_power_pose_research_is_the_latest_example_of_scientific_overreach.html

Gelman, A., and Hill, J. (2006). Data Analysis Using Regression and Multilevel/Hierarchical Models. Cambridge, UK: Cambridge University Press.

Gelman, A., and Loken, E. (2013). "The garden of forking paths: why multiple comparisons can be a problem, even when there is no 'fishing expedition'or 'p-hacking' and the research hypothesis was posited ahead of time." http://www.stat.columbia.edu/~gelman/research/unpublished/p_hacking.pdf

Gelman, A., and Tuerlinckx, F. (2000). "Type S error rates for classical and Bayesian single and multiple comparison procedures." Computational Statistics, 3(15), 373–390.

Gentzkow, M., and Shapiro, J. M. (2014). "Code and data for the social sciences: a practitioner's guide." University of Chicago mimeo. https://web.stanford.edu/~gentzkow/research/CodeAndData.pdf

Gerber, A., Arceneaux, K., Boudreau, C., Dowling, C., et al. (2014). "Reporting guidelines for experimental research: a report from the Experimental Research Section Standards Committee." Journal of Experimental Political Science, 1(1), 81–98. https://doi.org/10.1017/xps.2014.11

Gerber, A., Green, D., and Nickerson, D. (2001). "Testing for publication bias in political science." Political Analysis, 9(4), 385–392.

Gerber, A., and Malhotra, N. (2008a). "Do statistical reporting standards affect what is published? Publication bias in two leading political science journals." Quarterly Journal of Political Science, 3(3), 313–326. https://doi.org/10.1561/100.00008024

———. (2008b). "Publication bias in empirical sociological research: do arbitrary significance levels distort published results?" Sociological Methods & Research, 37(1), 3–30. https://doi.org/10.1177/0049124108318973

Gibson, J.L. (1995). "Cautious reflections on a data-archiving policy for political science." PS: Political Science & Politics, 28(3), 473–476. https://doi.org/10.2307/420310

Glennerster, R., and Takavarasha, K. (2013). Running Randomized Evaluations: A Practical Guide. Princeton, NJ: Princeton University Press.

Goldacre, B. (2016). "How did NEJM respond when we tried to correct 20 misreported trials?" http://compare-trials.org/blog/how-did-nejm-respond-when-we-tried-to-correct-20-misreported-trials/

Gorg, H., and Strobl, E. (2001). "Multinational companies and productivity spillovers: a meta-analysis." The Economic Journal, 111, 723–739.

Greenberg, B.G., Abul-Ela, A.-L.A., Simmons, W.R., and Horvitz, D.G. (1969). "The unrelated question randomized response model: theoretical framework." Journal of the American Statistical Association, 64(326), 520–539. https://doi.org/10.2307/2283636

Greenwald, A.G. (1976). "An editorial." Journal of Personality and Social Psychology, 33, 1–7.

Hacking, I. (1983). Representing and Intervening: Introductory Topics in the Philosophy of Natural Science. Cambridge, UK: Cambridge University Press.

Hagger, M. S., Chatzisarantis, N.L.D., Alberts, H., Anggono, C.O., et al. (2016). "A multilab preregistered replication of the ego-depletion effect." Perspectives on Psychological Science, 11(4), 546–573. https://doi.org/10.1177/1745691616652873

Hamermesh, D.S. (2013). "Six decades of top economics publishing: who and how?" Journal of Economic Literature, 51(1), 162–172. https://doi.org/10.1257/jel.51.1.162

Hansen, P.R. (2005). "A test for superior predictive ability." Journal of Business & Economic Statistics, 23(4), 365–380. https://doi.org/10.1198/073500105000000063

Hart, E.M., Barmby, P., LeBauer, D., Michonneau, F., et al. (2016). "Ten simple rules for digital data storage." PLoS Computational Biology, 12(10), e1005097. https://doi.org/10.1371/journal.pcbi.1005097

Hartung, D.M., Zarin, D.A., Guise, J.-M., McDonagh, M., Paynter, R., and Helfand, M. (2014). "Reporting discrepancies between the ClinicalTrials.gov results database and peer-reviewed publications." Annals of Internal Medicine, 160(7), 477–483. https://doi.org/10.7326/M13-0480

Harvey, C.R., Liu, Y., and Zhu, H. (2015). ". . . and the cross-section of expected returns." The Review of Financial Studies, 29(1), 5–68. https://doi.org/10.1093/rfs/hhv059

Havranek, T., and Irsova, Z. (2012). "Survey article: publication bias in the literature on foreign direct investment spillovers." Journal of Development Studies, 48(10), 1375–1396.

Hawkins, C.B., Fitzgerald, C.E., and Nosek, B.A. (2015). "In search of an association between conception risk and prejudice." Psychological Science, 26(2), 249–252. https://doi.org/10.1177/0956797614553121

Hayes, R.J., and Bennett, S. (1999). "Simple sample size calculation for cluster-randomized trials." International Journal of Epidemiology, 28(2), 319–326. https://doi.org/10.1093/ije/28.2.319

Head, M.L., Holman, L., Lanfear, R., Kahn, A.T., and Jennions, M.D. (2015). "The extent and consequences of p-hacking in science." PLoS Biology, 13(3), e1002106. https://doi.org/10.1371/journal.pbio.1002106

Heene, M. (2010). "A brief history of the fail safe number in applied research." ArXiv:1010.2326 [Stat]. http://arxiv.org/abs/1010.2326

Heffetz, O., and Ligett, K. (2014). "Privacy and data-based research." Journal of Economic Perspectives, 28(2), 75–98. https://doi.org/10.1257/jep.28.2.75

Henry, E. (2009). "Strategic disclosure of research results: the cost of proving your honesty*." The Economic Journal, 119(539), 1036–1064. https://doi.org/10.1111/j.1468–0297.2009.02265.x

Henry, E., and Ottaviani, M. (2014). "Research and the approval process." http://www.cepr.org/sites/default/files/Henry-submission%20CEPR.pdf

Herndon, T., Ash, M., and Pollin, R. (2014). "Does high public debt consistently stifle economic growth? A critique of Reinhart and Rogoff." Cambridge Journal of Economics, 38(2), 257–279. https://doi.org/10.1093/cje/bet075

Hewitt, J.K. (2012). "Editorial policy on candidate gene association and candidate gene-by-environment interaction studies of complex traits." Behavior Genetics, 42(1), 1–2. https://doi.org/10.1007/s10519–011–9504–z

Higgins, J.P.T., and Thompson, S.G. (2002). "Quantifying heterogeneity in a meta-analysis." Statistics in Medicine, 21(11), 1539–1558. https://doi.org/10.1002/sim.1186

Higgins, J.P.T., Thompson, S.G., Deeks, J.J., and Altman, D.G. (2003). "Measuring inconsistency in meta-analyses." BMJ, 327, 557–560. https://doi.org/10.1136/bmj.327.7414.557

Hines, W.C., Su, Y., Kuhn, I., Polyak, K., and Bissell, M.J. (2014). "Sorting out the FACS: a devil in the details." Cell Reports, 6(5), 779–781. https://doi.org/10.1016/j.celrep.2014.02.021

Hirshleifer, S., McKenzie, D., Almeida, R., and Ridao-Cano, C. (2015). "The impact of vocational training for the unemployed: experimental evidence from Turkey." The Economic Journal, 126, 2115–2146. https://doi.org/10.1111/ecoj.12211

Holm, S. (1979). "A simple sequentially rejective multiple test procedure." Scandinavian Journal of Statistics, 6(2), 65–70.

Horowitz, J.L. (2001). "The bootstrap." In Heckman, J.J., and Leamer, E. (Eds.), Handbook of Econometrics, vol. 5 (pp. 3159–3228). London: Elsevier. https://doi.org/10.1016/S1573–4412(01)05005-X

Hsiang, S.M., Burke, M., and Miguel, E. (2013). "Quantifying the influence of climate on human conflict." Science, 341, 1235367. https://doi.org/10.1126/science.1235367

———. (2014). "Reconciling climate-conflict meta-analyses: reply to Buhaug et al." Climatic Change, 127(3–4), 399–405. https://doi.org/10.1007/s10584–014–1276-z

Huff, C., and Kruszewska, D. (2016). "Banners, barricades, and bombs: the tactical choices of social movements and public opinion." Comparative Political Studies, 49(13), 1774–1808. https://doi.org/10.1177/0010414015621072

Humphreys, M., Sanchez de la Sierra, R.S., and van der Windt, P. (2013). "Fishing, commitment, and communication: a proposal for comprehensive

nonbinding research registration." Political Analysis, 21(1), 1–20. https://doi
.org/10.1093/pan/mpso21

Hung, H. M. J., O'Neill, R. T., Bauer, P., and Kohne, K. (1997). "The behavior
of the p-value when the alternative hypothesis is true." Biometrics, 53(1),
11–22. https://doi.org/10.2307/2533093

Husereau, D., Drummond, M., Petrou, S., Carswell, C., et al. (2013). "Consolidated Health Economic Evaluation Reporting Standards (CHEERS)
statement." Value in Health, 16(2), e1–e5. https://doi.org/10.1016/j.jval.2013
.02.010

Ioannidis, J. P. A. (2005). "Why most published research findings are false."
PLoS Medicine, 2(8), e124. https://doi.org/10.1371/journal.pmed.0020124

———. (2008). "Effectiveness of antidepressants: an evidence myth constructed
from a thousand randomized trials?" Philosophy, Ethics, and Humanities in
Medicine, 3(1), 14. https://doi.org/10.1186/1747-5341-3-14

Ioannidis, J. P. A., and Trikalinos, T. A. (2005). "Early extreme contradictory
estimates may appear in published research: the Proteus phenomenon in
molecular genetics research and randomized trials." Journal of Clinical Epidemiology, 58(6), 543–549. https://doi.org/10.1016/j.jclinepi.2004.10.019

Isis-2 (Second International Study Of Infarct Survival) Collaborative Group
(1988). "Randomised trial of intravenous streptokinase, oral aspirin, both,
or neither among 17 187 cases of suspected acute myocardial infarction:
Isis-2." The Lancet, 332, 349–360. https://doi.org/10.1016/S0140-6736(88)
92833-4

Jackson, M., and Cox, D. R. (2013). "The principles of experimental design and
their application in sociology." Annual Review of Sociology, 39(1), 27–49.
https://doi.org/10.1146/annurev-soc-071811-145443

Jacoby, W. G., and Lupton, R. N. (2016, February 22). "Guidelines for preparing replication files." https://ajpsblogging.files.wordpress.com/2016/04
/replic-guidelines-draft-4-1-16.pdf

Jain, A., Marshall, J., Buikema, A., Bancroft, T., Kelly, J. P., and Newschaffer,
C. J. (2015). "Autism occurrence by MMR vaccine status among US children
with older siblings with and without autism." JAMA, 313(15), 1534–1540.
https://doi.org/10.1001/jama.2015.3077

Jung, K., Shavitt, S., Viswanathan, M., and Hilbe, J. M. (2014). "Female hurricanes are deadlier than male hurricanes." Proceedings of the National
Academy of Sciences, 111(24), 8782–8787. https://doi.org/10.1073/pnas
.1402786111

Kahneman, D., Fredrickson, B. L., Schreiber, C. A., and Redelmeier, D. A.
(1993). "When more pain is preferred to less: adding a better end." Psychological Science, 4(6), 401–405.

Kilkenny, C., Browne, W. J., Cuthill, I. C., Emerson, M., and Altman, D. G.
(2010). "Improving bioscience research reporting: the ARRIVE guidelines
for reporting animal research." PLoS Biology, 8(6), e1000412. https://doi
.org/10.1371/journal.pbio.1000412

King, G., Honaker, J., Joseph, A., and Scheve, K. (2001). "Analyzing incomplete political science data: an alternative algorithm for multiple imputation." American Political Science Review, 95(1), 49–69.

Kinney, S. K., Reiter, J. P., Reznek, A. P., Miranda, J., Jarmin, R. S., and Abowd, J. M. (2011). "Towards unrestricted public use business microdata: the synthetic longitudinal business database" (CES 11–04). U.S. Census Bureau, Center for Economic Studies. https://www.census.gov/ces/pdf/CES-WP-11–04.pdf

Kirsch, I., Deacon, B. J., Huedo-Medina, T. B., Scoboria, A., Moore, T. J., and Johnson, B. T. (2008). "Initial severity and antidepressant benefits: a meta-analysis of data submitted to the Food and Drug Administration." PLoS Medicine, 5(2). https://doi.org/10.1371/journal.pmed.0050045

Kitzes, J., Turek, D., and Deniz, F. (2017). The Practice of Reproducible Research: Case Studies and Lessons from the Data-Intensive Sciences. Berkeley: University of California Press.

Klein, J. R., and Roodman, A. (2005). "Blind analysis in nuclear and particle physics." Annual Review of Nuclear and Particle Science, 55(1), 141–163. https://doi.org/10.1146/annurev.nucl.55.090704.151521

Klein, R. A., Ratliff, K. A., Vianello, M., Adams, R. B., et al. (2014). "Investigating variation in replicability." Social Psychology, 45(3), 142–152. https://doi.org/10.1027/1864-9335/a000178

Kling, J. R., Liebman, J. B., and Katz, L. F. (2007). "Experimental analysis of neighborhood effects." Econometrica, 75(1), 83–119. https://doi.org/10.1111/j.1468-0262.2007.00733.x

Knell, M., and Stix, H. (2005). "The income elasticity of money demand: a meta-analysis of empirical results*." Journal of Economic Surveys, 19(3), 513–533. https://doi.org/10.1111/j.0950-0804.2005.00257.x

Knittel, C. R., and Metaxoglou, K. (2011). "Challenges in merger simulation analysis." American Economic Review, 101(3), 56–59.

———. (2013). "Estimation of random-coefficient demand models: two empiricists' perspective." The Review of Economics and Statistics, 96(1), 34–59. https://doi.org/10.1162/REST_a_00394

Knuth, D. E. (1984). "Literate programming." The Computer Journal, 27(2), 97–111. https://doi.org/10.1093/comjnl/27.2.97

———. (1992). Literate Programming. Stanford, CA: Center for the Study of Language and Information.

Laine, C., Horton, R., DeAngelis, C. D., Drazen, J. M., et al. (2007). "Clinical trial registration—looking back and moving ahead." New England Journal of Medicine, 356(26), 2734–2736. https://doi.org/10.1056/NEJMe078110

Lakens, D., Adolfi, F. G., Albers, C., Anvari, F., et al. (2017). "Justify your alpha: a response to 'Redefine statistical significance.'" PsyArXiv. https://doi.org/10.17605/OSF.IO/9S3Y6

LaLonde, R. J. (1986). "Evaluating the econometric evaluations of training programs with experimental data." American Economic Review, 76(4), 604–620.

Lancet (2010). "Should protocols for observational research be registered?" The Lancet, 375, 348. https://doi.org/10.1016/S0140-6736(10)60148-1

Langan, D., Higgins, J. P. T., and Simmonds, M. (2017). "Comparative performance of heterogeneity variance estimators in meta-analysis: a review of simulation studies." Research Synthesis Methods, 8(2), 181–198. https://doi.org/10.1002/jrsm.1198

Leamer, E. E. (1983). "Let's take the con out of econometrics." American Economic Review, 73(1), 31–43.

———. (2010). "Tantalus on the road to Asymptopia." Journal of Economic Perspectives, 24(2), 31–46. https://doi.org/10.1257/jep.24.2.31

LeBel, E.P., Borsboom, D., Giner-Sorolla, R., Hasselman, F., Peters, K.R., Ratliff, K.A., and Smith, C.T. (2013). "PsychDisclosure.org: grassroots support for reforming reporting standards in psychology." Perspectives on Psychological Science, 8(4), 424–432. https://doi.org/10.1177/1745691613491437

Lee, S., and Shaikh, A.M. (2014). "Multiple testing and heterogeneous treatment effects: re-evaluating the effect of progresa on school enrollment." Journal of Applied Econometrics, 29(4), 612–626. https://doi.org/10.1002/jae.2327

Levine, D.I. (2001). Editor's introduction to "The Unemployment Effects of Minimum Wages: Evidence from a Prespecified Research Design." Industrial Relations, 40(2), 161–162. https://doi.org/10.1111/0019-8676.00204

Levine, R., and Renelt, D. (1992). "A sensitivity analysis of cross-country growth regressions." American Economic Review, 82(4), 942–963. https://doi.org/10.2307/2117352

Libgober, J. (2015). "False positives in scientific research" (SSRN Scholarly Paper No. ID 2617130). Rochester, NY: Social Science Research Network. http://papers.ssrn.com/abstract = 2617130

Lin, W., and Green, D.P. (2016). "Standard operating procedures: a safety net for pre-analysis plans." PS: Political Science & Politics, 49(3), 495–500. https://doi.org/10.1017/S1049096516000810

List, J.A., Shaikh, A.M., and Xu, Y. (2016). "Multiple hypothesis testing in experimental economics" (Working Paper No. 21875). National Bureau of Economic Research. http://www.nber.org/papers/w21875

Loder, E., Groves, T., and MacAuley, D. (2010). "Registration of observational studies: the next step towards research transparency." BMJ, 340, c950–c950. https://doi.org/10.1136/bmj.c950

Long, J.S. (2008). The Workflow of Data Analysis Using Stata. College Station, TX: Stata Press.

Longhi, S., Nijkamp, P., and Poot, J. (2005). "A meta-analytic assessment of the effect of immigration on wages." Journal of Economic Surveys, 19(3), 451–477. https://doi.org/10.1111/j.0950-0804.2005.00255.x

Longo, D.L., and Drazen, J.M. (2016). "Data sharing." New England Journal of Medicine, 374(3), 276–277. https://doi.org/10.1056/NEJMe1516564

Lovell, M.C. (1983). "Data mining." The Review of Economics and Statistics, 65(1), 1–12. https://doi.org/10.2307/1924403

MacCoun, R., and Perlmutter, S. (2015). "Blind analysis: hide results to seek the truth." Nature, 526, 187–189. https://doi.org/10.1038/526187a

Machanavajjhala, A., Kifer, D., Abowd, J., Gehrke, J., and Vilhuber, L. (2008). "Privacy: theory meets practice on the map." In IEEE 24th International Conference on Data Engineering (pp. 277–286). https://doi.org/10.1109/ICDE.2008.4497436

Maggioni, A.P., Darne, B., Atar, D., Abadie, E., Pitt, B., and Zannad, F. (2007). "FDA and CPMP rulings on subgroup analyses." Cardiology, 107(2), 97–102. https://doi.org/10.1159/000094508

Maglione, M. A., Das, L., Raaen, L., Smith, A., et al. (2014). "Safety of vaccines used for routine immunization of U.S. children: a systematic review." Pediatrics, 134(2), 325–337. https://doi.org/10.1542/peds.2014–1079

Maley, S. (2014). "Statistics show no evidence of gender bias in the public's hurricane preparedness." Proceedings of the National Academy of Sciences, 111(37), E3834. https://doi.org/10.1073/pnas.1413079111

Malter, D. (2014). "Female hurricanes are not deadlier than male hurricanes." Proceedings of the National Academy of Sciences, 111(34), E3496. https://doi.org/10.1073/pnas.1411428111

Manski, C. F. (2013). Public Policy in an Uncertain World: Analysis and Decisions. Cambridge, MA: Harvard University Press.

Masicampo, E. J., and Lalande, D. R. (2012). "A peculiar prevalence of p values just below .05." Quarterly Journal of Experimental Psychology, 65(11), 2271–2279. https://doi.org/10.1080/17470218.2012.711335

Mathieu, S., Boutron, I., Moher, D., Altman, D. G., and Ravaud, P. (2009). "Comparison of registered and published primary outcomes in randomized controlled trials." JAMA, 302(9), 977–984. https://doi.org/10.1001/jama.2009.1242

McAleer, M., Pagan, A. R., and Volker, P. A. (1985). "What will take the con out of econometrics?" American Economic Review, 75(3), 293–307.

McCloskey, D. N., and Ziliak, S. T. (1996). "The standard error of regressions." Journal of Economic Literature, 34(1), 97–114.

McCrary, J., Christensen, G., and Fanelli, D. (2015). "Conservative tests under satisficing models of publication bias." PLoS One, 11(2), e0149590.

McCullough, B. D., and Vinod, H. D. (2003). "Verifying the solution from a nonlinear solver: a case study." American Economic Review, 93(3), 873–892.

———. (2004a). "Verifying the solution from a nonlinear solver: a case study: reply." American Economic Review, 94(1), 391–396. https://doi.org/10.1257/000282804322970887

———. (2004b). "Verifying the solution from a nonlinear solver: a case study: reply." American Economic Review, 94(1), 400–406. https://doi.org/10.1257/000282804322970904

McDonald, M. M., Asher, B. D., Kerr, N. L., and Navarrete, C. D. (2011). "Fertility and intergroup bias in racial and minimal-group contexts evidence for shared architecture." Psychological Science, 22(7), 860–865. https://doi.org/10.1177/0956797611410985

McNutt, M. (2016). "Taking up TOP." Science, 352, 1147. https://doi.org/10.1126/science.aag2359

Merton, R. K. (1942). "A note on science and democracy." Journal of Legal and Political Sociology, 1, 115–126.

———. (1973). The Sociology of Science: Theoretical and Empirical Investigations. Chicago, IL: University of Chicago Press.

Mervis, J. (2014). "Why null results rarely see the light of day." Science, 345, 992. https://doi.org/10.1126/science.345.6200.992

Miguel, E., Camerer, C., Casey, K., Cohen, J., et al. (2014). "Promoting transparency in social science research." Science, 343, 30–31. https://doi.org/10.1126/science.1245317

Miguel, E., and Kremer, M. (2004). "Worms: identifying impacts on education and health in the presence of treatment externalities." Econometrica, 72(1), 159–217.

Mitroff, I. (1974). "Norms and counter-norms in a select group of the Apollo moon scientists: a case study of the ambivalence of scientists." American Sociological Review, 39(4), 579–595. https://doi.org/10.2307/2094423

Monogan, J. E. (2013). "A case for registering studies of political outcomes: an application in the 2010 House elections." Political Analysis, 21(1), 21–37. https://doi.org/10.1093/pan/mps022

Montgomery, P., Grant, S., Hopewell, S., Macdonald, G., et al. (2013). "Protocol for CONSORT-SPI: an extension for social and psychological interventions." Implementation Science, 8(1), 99. https://doi.org/10.1186/1748-5908-8-99

Mookerjee, R. (2006). "A meta-analysis of the export growth hypothesis." Economics Letters, 91(3), 395–401.

Murphy, K. R., Myors, B., and Wolach, A. (2014). Statistical Power Analysis: A Simple and General Model for Traditional and Modern Hypothesis Tests, 4th ed. New York: Routledge.

Narayanan, A., and Shmatikov, V. (2008). "Robust de-anonymization of large sparse datasets." In 2008 IEEE Symposium on Security and Privacy (pp. 111–125). https://www.ieee-security.org/TC/SP2008/oakland08.html

Navarrete, C. D., Fessler, D. M. T., Fleischman, D. S., and Geyer, J. (2009). "Race bias tracks conception risk across the menstrual cycle." Psychological Science, 20(6), 661–665. https://doi.org/10.1111/j.1467-9280.2009.02352.x

Neumark, D. (2001). "The employment effects of minimum wages: evidence from a prespecified research design." Industrial Relations, 40(1), 121–144. https://doi.org/10.1111/0019-8676.00199

Neumark, D., and Wascher, W. (1998). "Is the time-series evidence on minimum wage effects contaminated by publication bias?" Economic Inquiry, 36(3), 458–470.

Neuroskeptic (2012). "The nine circles of scientific hell." Perspectives on Psychological Science, 7(6), 643–644. https://doi.org/10.1177/1745691612459519

Nijkamp, P., and Poot, J. (2005). "The last word on the wage curve?" Journal of Economic Surveys, 19(3), 421–450.

Nosek, B. A., Alter, G., Banks, G. C., Borsboom, D., et al. (2015). "Promoting an open research culture." Science, 348, 1422–1425. https://doi.org/10.1126/science.aab2374

Nosek, B. A., and Lakens, D. (2014). "Registered reports." Social Psychology, 45(3), 137–141. https://doi.org/10.1027/1864-9335/a000192

Nosek, B. A., Spies, J. R., and Motyl, M. (2012). "Scientific Utopia II. Restructuring incentives and practices to promote truth over publishability." Perspectives on Psychological Science, 7(6), 615–631. https://doi.org/10.1177/1745691612459058

Nuijten, M. B., Hartgerink, C. H., van Assen, M. A., Epskamp, S., and Wicherts, J. M. (2016). "The prevalence of statistical reporting errors in psychology (1985–2013)." Behavior Research Methods, 48(4), 1205–1226.

O'Brien, P.C. (1984). "Procedures for comparing samples with multiple end-points." Biometrics, 40(4), 1079–1087. https://doi.org/10.2307/2531158

Ogrinc, G., Davies, L., Goodman, D., Batalden, P., Davidoff, F., and Stevens, D. (2016). "SQUIRE 2.0–Standards for Quality Improvement Reporting Excellence: revised publication guidelines from a detailed consensus process." Journal of the American College of Surgeons, 222(3), 317–323. https://doi.org/10.1016/j.jamcollsurg.2015.07.456

Olken, B.A. (2015). "Promises and perils of pre-analysis plans." Journal of Economic Perspectives, 29(3), 61–80. https://doi.org/10.1257/jep.29.3.61

Olken, B.A., Onishi, J., and Wong, S. (2012). "Should aid reward performance? Evidence from a field experiment on health and education in Indonesia" (Working Paper No. 17892). National Bureau of Economic Research. http://www.nber.org/papers/w17892

Open Science Collaboration (2015). "Estimating the reproducibility of psychological science." Science, 349, aac4716. https://doi.org/10.1126/science.aac4716

Patel, J. (2014, November 26). "Who reviews the reviewers?" http://blogs.biomedcentral.com/bmcblog/2014/11/26/who-reviews-the-reviewers/

Pedulla, D.S., and Thébaud, S. (2015). "Can we finish the revolution? Gender, work-family ideals, and institutional constraint." American Sociological Review, 80(1), 116–139. https://doi.org/10.1177/0003122414564008

Perkel, J. (2015). "The immortal challenge." BioTechniques, 58(4), 154–160.

Pitman, E.J.G. (1937). "Significance tests which may be applied to samples from any populations." Supplement to the Journal of the Royal Statistical Society, 4(1), 119–130. https://doi.org/10.2307/2984124

Piwowar, H.A., and Vision, T.J. (2013). "Data reuse and the open data citation advantage." PeerJ, 1, e175. https://doi.org/10.7717/peerj.175

Powers, J.J. (1988). "Mathematics of a lady tasting tea revisited." Journal of Sensory Studies, 3(2), 151–158. https://doi.org/10.1111/j.1745-459X.1988.tb00437.x

Prayle, A.P., Hurley, M.N., and Smyth, A.R. (2012). "Compliance with mandatory reporting of clinical trial results on ClinicalTrials.gov: cross sectional study." BMJ, 344, d7373. https://doi.org/10.1136/bmj.d7373

Ram, K. (2013). "Git can facilitate greater reproducibility and increased transparency in science." Source Code for Biology and Medicine, 8, 7. https://doi.org/10.1186/1751-0473-8-7

Ranehill, E., Dreber, A., Johannesson, M., Leiberg, S., Sul, S., and Weber, R.A. (2015). "Assessing the robustness of power posing: no effect on hormones and risk tolerance in a large sample of men and women." Psychological Science, 26(5), 653–656. https://doi.org/10.1177/0956797614553946

Redelmeier, D.A., Katz, J., and Kahneman, D. (2003). "Memories of colonoscopy: a randomized trial." Pain, 104(1–2), 187–194.

Ritchie, S.J., Wiseman, R., and French, C.C. (2012). "Failing the Future: three unsuccessful attempts to replicate Bem's 'retroactive facilitation of recall' effect." PLoS One, 7(3), e33423. https://doi.org/10.1371/journal.pone.0033423

Roberts, C.J. (2005). "Issues in meta-regression analysis: an overview." Journal of Economic Surveys, 19(3), 295–298. https://doi.org/10.1111/j.0950-0804.2005.00248.x

Romano, J.P., Shaikh, A.M., and Wolf, M. (2008). "Control of the false discovery rate under dependence using the bootstrap and subsampling." Test, 17(3), 417–442. https://doi.org/10.1007/s11749-008-0126-6

Romano, J.P., and Wolf, M. (2005). "Exact and approximate stepdown methods for multiple hypothesis testing." Journal of the American Statistical Association, 100(469), 94–108. https://doi.org/10.1198/016214504000000539

Romer, P.M. (2015). "Mathiness in the theory of economic growth." American Economic Review, 105(5), 89–93. https://doi.org/10.1257/aer.p20151066

Rose, A.K., and Stanley, T.D. (2005). "A meta-analysis of the effect of common currencies on international trade." Journal of Economic Surveys, 19(3), 347–365.

Rosenthal, R. (1966). Experimenter Effects in Behavioral Research, vol. 8. East Norwalk, CT: Appleton-Century-Crofts.

———. (1979). "The file drawer problem and tolerance for null results." Psychological Bulletin, 86(3), 638–641. https://doi.org/10.1037/0033-2909.86.3.638

Sala-i-Martin, X. (1997). "I just ran two million regressions." American Economic Review, 87(2), 178–183.

Sala-i-Martin, X., Doppelhofer, G., and Miller, R.I. (2004). "Determinants of long-term growth: a Bayesian averaging of classical estimates (BACE) approach." American Economic Review, 94(4), 813–835.

Saquib, N., Saquib, J., and Ioannidis, J.P.A. (2013). "Practices and impact of primary outcome adjustment in randomized controlled trials: meta-epidemiologic study." BMJ, 347, f4313. https://doi.org/10.1136/bmj.f4313

Scargle, J.D. (2000). "Publication bias: the 'file-drawer' problem in scientific inference." The Journal of Scientific Exploration, 14(1), 91–106.

Schulz, K.F., Altman, D.G., and Moher, D. (2010). "CONSORT 2010 statement: updated guidelines for reporting parallel group randomised trials." BMC Medicine, 8(1), 18.

Schulz, K.F., and Grimes, D.A. (2002). "Allocation concealment in randomised trials: defending against deciphering." The Lancet, 359, 614–618.

Schulz, K.F., and Grimes, D.A. (2005). "Multiplicity in randomised trials II: subgroup and interim analyses." The Lancet, 365, 1657–1661. https://doi.org/10.1016/S0140-6736(05)66516-6

Schwarz, G. (1978). "Estimating the dimension of a model." The Annals of Statistics, 6(2), 461–464. https://doi.org/10.1214/aos/1176344136

Shachar, R., and Nalebuff, B. (2004). "Verifying the solution from a nonlinear solver: a case study: comment." American Economic Review, 94(1), 382–390. https://doi.org/10.1257/000282804322970878

Shen, H. (2014). "Interactive notebooks: sharing the code." Nature, 515, 151–152. https://doi.org/10.1038/515151a

Silberzahn, R., and Uhlmann, E.L. (2015). "Crowdsourced research: many hands make tight work." Nature, 526, 189–191. https://doi.org/10.1038/526189a

Silberzahn, R., Uhlmann, E.L., Martin, D., Anselmi, P., et al. (2017). "Many analysts, one dataset: making transparent how variations in analytical choices affect results." PsyArXiv. https://doi.org/10.17605/OSF.IO/QKWST

Simmons, J.P., Nelson, L.D., and Simonsohn, U. (2011). "False-positive psychology undisclosed flexibility in data collection and analysis allows presenting anything as significant." Psychological Science, 22(11), 1359–1366. https://doi.org/10.1177/0956797611417632

———. (2012). "A 21 word solution." Dialogue, 26(2), 4–7.

———. (2017, December 6). "[66] Outliers: evaluating a new p-curve of power poses." http://datacolada.org/66

———. (2018). "False-positive citations." Perspectives on Psychological Science, 13(2), 255–259.

Simmons, J.P., and Simonsohn, U. (2015, May 8). "[37] Power posing: reassessing the evidence behind the most popular TED talk." http://datacolada.org/37

———. (2017). "Power posing: p-curving the evidence." Psychological Science, 28(5), 687–693. https://doi.org/10.1177/0956797616658563

Simons, D.J., Holcombe, A.O., and Spellman, B.A. (2014). "An introduction to registered replication reports at Perspectives on Psychological Science." Perspectives on Psychological Science, 9(5), 552–555. https://doi.org/10.1177/1745691614543974

Simonsohn, U. (2013). "Just post it: the lesson from two cases of fabricated data detected by statistics alone." Psychological Science, 24(10), 1875–1888. https://doi.org/10.1177/0956797613480366

———. (2017, March 21). "[58] The funnel plot is invalid because of this crazy assumption: r(n,d) = 0." http://datacolada.org/58

Simonsohn, U., Nelson, L.D., and Simmons, J.P. (2014a). "P-curve: a key to the file-drawer." Journal of Experimental Psychology: General, 143(2), 534–547. https://doi.org/10.1037/a0033242

———. (2014b). "p-curve and effect size correcting for publication bias using only significant results." Perspectives on Psychological Science, 9(6), 666–681. https://doi.org/10.1177/1745691614553988

Simonsohn, U., Simmons, J.P., and Nelson, L.D. (2015a). "Better p-curves: making p-curve analysis more robust to errors, fraud, and ambitious p-hacking, a reply to Ulrich and Miller (2015)." Journal of Experimental Psychology: General, 144(6), 1146–1152. https://doi.org/10.1037/xge0000104

———. (2015b). "Specification curve: descriptive and inferential statistics on all reasonable specifications" (SSRN Scholarly Paper No. ID 2694998). Rochester, NY: Social Science Research Network.

Sinisi, S.E., Polley, E.C., Petersen, M.L., Rhee, S.-Y., and van der Laan, M.J. (2007). "Super learning: an application to the prediction of HIV-1 drug resistance." Statistical Applications in Genetics and Molecular Biology, 6(1). https://doi.org/10.2202/1544-6115.1240

Sorge, R.E., Martin, L.J., Isbester, K.A., Sotocinal, S.G., et al. (2014). "Olfactory exposure to males, including men, causes stress and related analgesia in rodents." Nature Methods, 11(6), 629–632. https://doi.org/10.1038/nmeth.2935

Sripada, C., Kessler, D., and Jonides, J. (2014). "Methylphenidate blocks effort-induced depletion of regulatory control in healthy volunteers." Psychological Science, 25(6), 1227–1234. https://doi.org/10.1177/0956797614526415

Stanley, T.D. (2001). "Wheat from chaff: meta-analysis as quantitative literature review." Journal of Economic Perspectives, 15(3), 131–150. https://doi.org/10.1257/jep.15.3.131

———. (2005). "Beyond publication bias." Journal of Economic Surveys, 19(3), 309–345. https://doi.org/10.1111/j.0950-0804.2005.00250.x

———. (2008). "Meta-regression methods for detecting and estimating empirical effects in the presence of publication selection." Oxford Bulletin of Economics and Statistics, 70(1), 103–127. https://doi.org/10.1111/j.1468-0084.2007.00487.x

Stanley, T.D., and Doucouliagos, H. (2010). "Picture this: a simple graph that reveals much ado about research." Journal of Economic Surveys, 24(1), 170–191. https://doi.org/10.1111/j.1467-6419.2009.00593.x

———. (2012). Meta-regression Analysis in Economics and Business. New York: Routledge.

———. (2015). "Neither fixed nor random: weighted least squares meta-analysis." Statistics in Medicine, 34(13), 2116–2127. https://doi.org/10.1002/sim.6481

Steegen, S., Tuerlinckx, F., Gelman, A., and Vanpaemel, W. (2016). "Increasing transparency through a multiverse analysis." Perspectives on Psychological Science, 11(5), 702–712. https://doi.org/10.1177/1745691616658637

Sterling, T.D. (1959). "Publication decisions and their possible effects on inferences drawn from tests of significance—or vice versa." Journal of the American Statistical Association, 54(285), 30–34. https://doi.org/10.1080/01621459.1959.10501497

Sterling, T.D., Rosenbaum, W.L., and Weinkam, J.J. (1995). "Publication decisions revisited: the effect of the outcome of statistical tests on the decision to publish and vice versa." The American Statistician, 49(1), 108–112. https://doi.org/10.1080/00031305.1995.10476125

Stodden, V., Leisch, F., and Peng, R.D. (2014). Implementing Reproducible Research. New York: CRC Press.

Stojmenovska, D., Bol, T., and Leopold, T. (2017). "Does diversity pay? A replication of Herring (2009)." American Sociological Review, 82(4), 857–867. https://doi.org/10.1177/0003122417714422

Sullivan, R., Timmermann, A., and White, H. (1999). "Data-snooping, technical trading rule performance, and the bootstrap." Journal of Finance, 54(5), 1647–1691. https://doi.org/10.1111/0022-1082.00163

Tabery, J. (2014). Beyond Versus: The Struggle to Understand the Interaction of Nature and Nurture. Cambridge, MA: MIT Press.

Taubman, S.L., Allen, H.L., Wright, B.J., Baicker, K., and Finkelstein, A.N. (2014). "Medicaid increases emergency-department use: evidence from Oregon's health insurance experiment." Science, 343, 263–268. https://doi.org/10.1126/science.1246183

Terrin, N., Schmid, C.H., and Lau, J. (2005). "In an empirical evaluation of the funnel plot, researchers could not visually identify publication bias." Journal of Clinical Epidemiology, 58(9), 894–901. https://doi.org/10.1016/j.jclinepi.2005.01.006

Thomas, D., Frankenberg, E., Friedman, J., Habicht, J.-P., et al. (2003). "Iron deficiency and the well-being of older adults: early results from a randomized nutrition intervention." Minneapolis, MN: Population Association of America Annual Meetings. http://www.populationassociation.org/sidebar/annual-meeting/past-future/

Thomas, D., Frankenberg, E., Friedman, J., Habicht, J.-P., et al. (2006). "Causal effect of health on labor market outcomes: experimental evidence." Los Angeles: California Center for Population Research.

Tufte, E. (1983). The Visual Display of Quantitative Information. Cheshire, CT: Graphics Press.

Turner, E.H., Matthews, A.M., Linardatos, E., Tell, R.A., and Rosenthal, R. (2008). "Selective publication of antidepressant trials and its influence on apparent efficacy." New England Journal of Medicine, 358(3), 252–260. https://doi.org/10.1056/NEJMsa065779

Ulrich, R., and Miller, J. (2015). "p-hacking by post hoc selection with multiple opportunities: detectability by skewness test? Comment on Simonsohn, Nelson, and Simmons (2014)." Journal of Experimental Psychology: General, 144(6), 1137–1145. https://doi.org/10.1037/xge0000086

van der Laan, V., J.M., Polley, E.C., and Hubbard, A.E. (2007). "Super learner." Statistical Applications in Genetics and Molecular Biology, 6(1). http://www.degruyter.com/view/j/sagmb.2007.6.1/sagmb.2007.6.1.1309/sagmb.2007.6.1.1309.xml

Veroniki, A.A., Jackson, D., Viechtbauer, W., Bender, R., et al. (2016). "Methods to estimate the between-study variance and its uncertainty in meta-analysis." Research Synthesis Methods, 7(1), 55–79. https://doi.org/10.1002/jrsm.1164

Viscusi, W.K. (2015). "The role of publication selection bias in estimates of the value of a statistical life." American Journal of Health Economics, 1(1), 27–52. https://doi.org/10.1162/AJHE_a_00002

Vivalt, E. (2015). "Heterogeneous treatment effects in impact evaluation." American Economic Review: Papers and Proceedings, 105(5), 467–470.

von Elm, E., Altman, D.G., Egger, M., Pocock, S.J., Gøtzsche, P.C., and Vandenbroucke, J.P. (2007). "The Strengthening the Reporting of Observational Studies in Epidemiology (STROBE) statement: guidelines for reporting observational studies." Preventive Medicine, 45(4), 247–251. https://doi.org/10.1016/j.ypmed.2007.08.012

Wacholder, S., Chanock, S., Garcia-Closas, M., Ghormli, L.E., and Rothman, N. (2004). "Assessing the probability that a positive report is false: an approach for molecular epidemiology studies." Journal of the National Cancer Institute, 96(6), 434–442. https://doi.org/10.1093/jnci/djh075

Wakefield, A., Murch, S., Anthony, A., Linnell, J., et al. (1998). "RETRACTED: Ileal-lymphoid-nodular hyperplasia, non-specific colitis, and pervasive developmental disorder in children." The Lancet, 351, 637–641. https://doi.org/10.1016/S0140-6736(97)11096-0

Wasserstein, R.L., and Lazar, N.A. (2016). "The ASA's statement on p-values: context, process, and purpose." The American Statistician, 70(2), 129–133. https://doi.org/10.1080/00031305.2016.1154108

Wegner, D.M. (1992). "The premature demise of the solo experiment." Personality and Social Psychology Bulletin, 18(4), 504–508.

Westfall, P.H., and Young, S.S. (1993). Resampling-Based Multiple Testing: Examples and Methods for P-Value Adjustment. New York: Wiley.

White, H. (2000). "A reality check for data snooping." Econometrica, 68(5), 1097–1126. https://doi.org/10.1111/1468–0262.00152

Whitlock, M.C. (2005). "Combining probability from independent tests: the weighted Z-method is superior to Fisher's approach." Journal of Evolutionary Biology, 18(5), 1368–1373. https://doi.org/10.1111/j.1420–9101.2005.00917.x

Wicherts, J.M., Bakker, M., and Molenaar, D. (2011). "Willingness to share research data is related to the strength of the evidence and the quality of reporting of statistical results." PLoS One, 6(11), e26828.

Wicherts, J.M., Borsboom, D., Kats, J., and Molenaar, D. (2006). "The poor availability of psychological research data for reanalysis." American Psychologist, 61(7), 726.

Wilson, G., Aruliah, D.A., Brown, C.T., Hong, N.P.C., et al. (2014). "Best practices for scientific computing." PLoS Biology, 12(1), e1001745. https://doi.org/10.1371/journal.pbio.1001745

Wilson, G., Bryan, J., Cranston, K., Kitzes, J., Nederbragt, L., and Teal, T.K. (2017). "Good enough practices in scientific computing." PLoS Computational Biology, 13(6), e1005510. https://doi.org/10.1371/journal.pcbi.1005510

Wydick, B., Katz, E., and Janet, B. (2014). "Do in-kind transfers damage local markets? The case of TOMS shoe donations in El Salvador." Journal of Development Effectiveness, 6(3), 249–267. https://doi.org/10.1080/19439342.2014.919012

Xie, Y. (2013). Dynamic Documents with R and knitr. New York: CRC Press.

———. (2014). "knitr: a comprehensive tool for reproducible research in R." In Implementing Reproducible Research (pp. 3–32). New York: CRC Press.

Yong, E. (2012). "Replication studies: bad copy." Nature News, 485, 298. https://doi.org/10.1038/485298a

Young, C., and Holsteen, K. (2017). "Model uncertainty and robustness: a computational framework for multimodel analysis." Sociological Methods & Research, 46(1), 3–40. https://doi.org/10.1177/0049124115610347

Young, C., and Horvath, A. (2015, August 11). "Sociologists need to be better at replication." https://orgtheory.wordpress.com/2015/08/11/sociologists-need-to-be-better-at-replication-a-guest-post-by-cristobal-young/

Yu, L., Ke, W., Wang, Y., Ding, W., et al. (2016). "Retraction notice to 'Predictive and prognostic value of ER-α36 expression in breast cancer patients treated with chemotherapy' [Steroids 84 (2014) 11–16]." Steroids, 106, 94. https://doi.org/10.1016/j.steroids.2016.02.001

Ziliak, S.T., and McCloskey, D.N. (2004). "Size matters: the standard error of regressions in the American Economic Review." The Journal of Socio-Economics, 33(5), 527–546. https://doi.org/10.1016/j.socec.2004.09.024

———. (2008). The Cult of Statistical Significance: How the Standard Error Costs Us Jobs, Justice, and Lives. Ann Arbor: University of Michigan Press.

Index